Sustainable Energy Systems in Architectural Design

Sustainable Energy Systems in Architectural Design

A Blueprint for Green Building

Peter Gevorkian, Ph.D.

McGraw-Hill

New York   Chicago   San Francisco   Lisbon   London
Mexico City   Milan   New Delhi   San Juan   Seoul
Singapore   Sydney   Toronto

The McGraw·Hill Companies

Library of Congress Cataloging-in-Publication Data

Gevorkian, Peter.
  Sustainable energy systems in architectural design : a blueprint for green building / Peter Gevorkian.
    p. cm.
  Includes bibliographical references and index.
  ISBN 0-07-146982-6
    1. Electric power systems. 2. Photovoltaic power systems. 3. Sustainable buildings. 4. Solar buildings. 5. Wind power plants. I. Title.
  TK1005.G47 2006
  721′.04672—dc22

                                                                              2005054461

1 2 3 4 5 6 7 8 9 0   DOC/DOC   0 1 0 9 8 7 6 5

ISBN   0-07-146982-6

The sponsoring editor for this book was Cary Sullivan and the production supervisor was Richard Ruzycka. It was set in New Century Schoolbook by Matrix Publishing Services. The art director for the cover was Anthony Landi.

Printed and bound by RR Donnelley.

 This book was printed on recycled, acid-free paper containing a minimum of 50% recycled, de-inked fiber.

McGraw-Hill books are available at special quantity discounts to use as premiums and sales promotions, or for use in corporate training programs. For more information, please write to the Director of Special Sales, McGraw-Hill Professional, Two Penn Plaza, New York, NY 10121-2298. Or contact your local bookstore.

This book examines solar power generation and renewable energy sources, with sole intent to familiarize the reader with the existing technologies in order to encourage policy makers, architects and engineers to promote available energy conservation options in their designs (LEED).

Contents

Introduction

Since the dawn of agriculture and civilization, human beings have hastened deforestation, impacting climatic and ecological conditions. Deforestation and the use of fossil fuel energy diminish the natural recycling of carbon dioxide gases. This accelerates and increases the inversion layer that traps the reflected energy of the sun. The augmented inversion layer has an elevated atmospheric temperature, giving rise to global warming, which in turn has caused melting of the polar ice, substantial changes to climatic conditions, and depletion of the ozone layer.

Within a couple of centuries, the unchecked effects of global warming will not only change the make up of the global land mass but will affect human life style on the planet.

Continued melting of the polar ice capswill increase sea water levels and will gradually cover some habitable areas of global shorelines. It will also result in unpredictable climatic changes, such as unusual precipitation, floods, hurricanes, and tornados.

In view of the rapid expansion of the world's economies, particularly those of developing countries with large population, such as China and India, demand for fossil fuel and construction materials will become severe. Within the next few decades, if continued at present projected pace, the excessive demand for fossil fuel energy resources, such as crude oil, natural gas, and coal, will result in the demise of the ecology of our planet and, if not mitigated, may be irreversible.

Today, China's enormous demand for energy and construction materials has resulted in considerable cost escalations of crude oil, construction steel, and lumber, all of which require the expenditure of fossil fuel energy.

Developing countries are the most efficient consumers of energy, since every scrap of material, paper, plastic, metal cans, rubber, and even common trash, is recycled and reused. However, when the 2.3 billion combined populations of China and India attain a higher margin of families with middle class incomes, new demand for electricity, manufacturing, and millions of automobiles will undoubtedly change the balance of ecological and social stability to a level beyond imagination.

The United States is the richest country in the world. With five percent of the world's population, the country consumes twenty-five percent of the global aggregate energy. As a result of its economic power, the United States enjoys one of the highest standards of life with the best medical care and human longevity. Relative affluence of the country as a whole has resulted in cheapest cost of energy and its wastage.

Most consumption of fossil fuel energy is a result of inefficient and wasteful transportation and electric power generation technologies. Due to lack of comprehensive energy control policies and lobbying efforts of special interest groups, research and development funds to accelerate sustainable and renewable energy technologies has been neglected.

In order to curb the waste of fossil fuel energy, it is imperative that our nation, as a whole, from politicians and educators to the general public, be made aware of the dire consequences of our nation's energy policies and make every effort to promote use of all available renewable energy technologies so that we can reduce the demand for nonrenewable energy and safeguard the environment for future generations.

As scientists, engineers, and architects, we have throughout the last few centuries been responsible for elevation of human living standards and contributed to the advancement technology. We have succeeded in putting a man on the moon, while ignoring the devastating side effects to the global ecology. In the process of creating betterment and comforts of life, we have tapped into the most precious nonrenewable energy resources, miraculously created over the life span of our planet, and have been misusing them in a wasteful manner to satisfy our most rudimentary energy needs.

The deterioration of our planet's ecosystem and atmosphere cannot be ignored or considered a matter that is not of immediate concern. Our planet's ozone layer according to scientists has been depleted by about forty percent over the past century and green house gases have altered meteorological conditions. Unfortunately, the collective social consciousness of educated masses of our society has not concerned itself with the disaster awaiting our future generations and continues to ignore the seriousness of the situation.

Press Clippings

As principal agents of human welfare, we scientists, engineers, and architects must individually and collectively assume responsibility for correcting the course of future technological development. To accentuate the seriousness of the misuse of the nonrenewable energy resources, I would like the reader to take notice of the following news articles published in various periodicals.

Detroit Free Press, Michigan—04-23-2005

Emissions of "greenhouse gasses," believed to cause global warming, have risen in Michigan. University of Michigan researchers released findings from the first statewide inventory of such emissions. The report said that nine percent more emissions were released in 2002 than in 1990.

Reuters South Africa, Minnesota—02-20-2005

Global warming cloud stifle cleansing summer winds across parts of northern United States over the next 50 years and worsen air pollution. Further warming of the atmosphere, as is happening now, would block cold fronts bringing cooler, cleaner air from Canada and allow stagnant air and ozone pollution to build up over the cities in the Northeast and Midwest. "The air just cooks" said Loretta Mickley of Harvard University's Division of Engineering and Applied Sciences.

Vallejo Times-Herald, California—03-01-2005

The geologists, who believe in global warming, said the Carquinez Strait's future would depend on how much the trend plays out. "If the sea level continues to rise, it would continue to flood the San Francisco Bay and the back into Delta. There would be several tens of meters of rise in world's oceans, then it would be Venice, then it would be under water."

Environment News Service, New Zealand—03-03-2005

A major study of Arctic lake sediments provides new evidence of human-induced climate change and concludes it may soon be impossible to find pristine Arctic environment untouched by climate warming. Arctic lakes have undergone dramatic ecological change in the past 150 years, and the timing of these changes mirrors the warming trends that commenced when humans began the widespread burning of fossil fuels. The findings were published in the Proceedings of the National Academy of Sciences.

ABS CBN News, Philippines—12-01-2004

Singapore—The weather predictions for Asia in 2050 read like a script from a doomsday movie. Except many climatologists and green groups fear they will come true unless there is a concerted global effort to rein in greenhouse gas emissions. In the decades to come, Asia, home to more than 6.3 billion people, will lurch from one climate extreme to another, with impoverished farmers battering droughts, floods, diseases, food shortages, and rising sea levels.

CTV, Canada—03-12-2005

Acid rain is causing forest decline in much of Eastern Canada, with losses to the forest industry estimated at hundreds of millions of dollars annually in the Atlantic region alone, says an Environmental Canada report. Even though acid pollution in Canada has been cut in half over the past 20 years, an additional 75% cut is needed says the Canadian Acid Deposition Sciences Assessment.

My reason for writing this book

During years of practice as a research and design engineer, I have come to realize that the best way to promote use of sustainable energy design can be achieved by the proper education of key professionals, such as architects and engineers, whose opinions direct project development.

I have found that even though solar power at present is a relatively mature technology, its use and application in the building industry is hampered due to lack of exposure and education. Regardless of present federal and state incentive programs, sustainable design by use of renewable energy will not be possible without a fundamental change in the way we educate our architects, engineers, and decision makers.

As engineers, scientists, architects, and public policy makers, we are collectively and individually responsible to weigh in on every aspect of the renewable energy design and make maximum use of resources and technologies available to us today. Development of renewable energy technologies requires substantial national investment and commitment to our research and development effort, which inevitably will define the future economic well-being of our nation, which is as significant as the national defense and social health and welfare.

Peter Gevorkian, Ph.D.

Acknowledgments

I would like to thank my colleagues and individuals who have encouraged and assisted and me to write this book. I am especially grateful to all agencies and organizations that provided photographs and allowed use of some textual material and my colleagues who read the manuscript and provided valuable insight.

Joe DesMeres, PhD., Kamyar Motamedi, MS, PE, Lida Gharibian, IDA, G. Hovakimian PE, Mark Gangi, AIA Michael Lehrer, FAIA, Mary Olson Khanian, Environmentalist, Patrick Crawley, AIA, Annett Malekandrasian EE, A. Markarian PE, Steve Dyer, AIA, H. Vartanian AIA, Razmik Matevosian PE, Neil Hagigat, AIA, Sam Avanessians.

Special thanks to the following organizations for providing photographs and technical support materials.

American Wind Energy Manufacturers
  Association
And U.S. Department of Energy
National Renewable Energy Laboratories
Airplus Engineering Consultants, LLC
10850 Riverside Dr, Suite 509
Toluca Lake, CA 91602

Ballard Power Systems
4343 North Fraser Way
Burnaby, BC
Canada V5J 5J9

California Energy Commission
1516, 9th St, MS-45
Sacramento, CA 95814-5512

Capstone Turbine Corporation
21211 Nordhoff St
Chatsworth Street, CA 91311

California Green Design, Inc.
18025 Rancho Street, Suite 200
Encino, CA 91316

Danish Wind Turbine Manufacturers
  Association
Vester Voldgade 106
Copenhagen, Denmark

Ms. Marilyn Nemzer, Executive Director
Geothermal Education Office
664 Hilary Dr
Tiburon, CA 94920

Sylvie Head
Marine Current Turbines Ltd.
The Court, The Green
Stoke Gifford, Bristol, BS 34 8PD, UK

Southwest Technology Development
    Institute
New Mexico State University
1505 Payne St
Las Cruces, NM 88003

J.A. Consulting
Tidal stream Turbine Specialists
26 Dukes Avenue
London, England

Sandia National Laboratories
U.S. Department of Energy
Office of scientific and Technical
    Information
P.O. Box 62
Oakridge, TN 37831

Solargenix Energy
3501 Jamboree Road, Suite 606
Newport Beach, CA 92660

Solar Electric Company
2500 Townsgate Rd., Suite J
Westlake Village, CA 91361

Office of Industrial Technologies
Energy Efficiency and Renewable
    Energy
U.S. Department of Energy
Washington, DC 20585

UMA/Heliocol
13620, 49th St
Clearwater, FL 33762

Sustainable Energy Systems in Architectural Design

Solar Power Technology

Solar or photovoltaic solar cells (PV) are electronic devices that essentially convert solar energy (fuel) of sunlight into electric energy or electricity. The basic physics of solar cells are the same semiconductor principles as diodes and transistors that form the building blocks of the entire world of electronics.

Solar cells convert energy as long as the there is sunlight. In the evenings and cloudy conditions, the conversion process diminishes. It stops completely at dusk and resumes at dawn. Solar cells do not store electricity, but batteries can be used to store energy.

One of the most fascinating aspects of the solar cells is the ability to convert the most abundant and free form of energy into electricity, without moving parts or components and without producing any adverse forms of pollution that affect the ecology, as is associated with most known forms of nonrenewable energy production methods, such as fossil fuel, hydroelectric, or nuclear energy generating plants.

In part one, we will review the overall solar energy conversion process, system configurations, and the economics associated with the technology. We will also briefly look into the mechanism of hydrogen fuel cells.

In the second part of this book, we will review the fundamentals of solar power cogeneration design and explore a number of applications including an actual design of a 500 kW solar power installation project, which includes detail analysis of all system design parameters.

A Brief History of the Photoelectric Phenomenon

In later part of the 19th century, physicists discovered a phenomenon, when light was incident on liquids and metal cell surfaces, electrons were released. However, no one had an explanation for the bizarre occurrences. At the turn of the 20th century, Albert Einstein provided a theory on the PHOTOELECTRIC EFFECT, for which he won the Nobel Prize in physics and laid the groundwork for the theory of the PHOTOVOLTAIC EFFECT. The following diagram shows the photoelectric effect. When light is shone on a metal, electrons are released that are attracted toward a positive charged plate, thereby giving rise to photoelectric current.

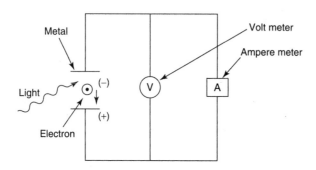

Photoelectric effect experiment

Einstein explained the observed phenomenon by a contemporary theory of QUANTIZED ENERGY LEVELS, which was previously developed by Max Plank. The theory described light as being made out of miniscule bundles of energy called PHOTONS. Photons impinging on metals or semiconductors knock electrons from atoms.

In the 1930s, these theorems led to new discipline in physics called QUANTUM MECHANICS, which consequently led to the discovery of transistors in 1950s and the development of semiconductor electronics.

Solar Cell Physics

Most solar cells are constructed from semiconductor material, such as silicon (14th element in Mendeleyev Table of Elements). Silicon is a semiconductor, which has the combined properties of a conductor and an insulator.

Metals such as gold, copper, iron, have loosely bound electrons in the outer shell or orbit of the atomic configuration. Those electrons can be detached when subjected to electrical voltage or current. On the contrary, atoms of insulators, such as glass, have extremely strong-bonded electrons in the atomic configuration and do not allow the flow of electrons even under the severest application of voltage or current.

Semiconductor materials, on the other hand, bind electrons midway between that of metals and insulators.

Semiconducting elements used in electronics are constructed from fusing two adjacent doped silicon wafer elements. Doping implies impregnation of silicon by positive and negative agents, such as phosphor and boron. Phosphor creates a free electron that produces, so called, "n-type" material. Boron creates a hole or a shortage of an electron that produces, so called, "p-type" material. Impregnation is accomplished by depositing the above referenced "dopants" on the surface of silicon under a certain heating or chemical process. The n-type material has a propensity to lose electrons and gain holes, so it acquires a positive charge. The p-type material has a propensity to lose holes and gain electrons, so it acquires a negative charge.

When n-type and p-type doped silicon wafers are fused together they form a "p-n junction," usually designated as PN junction. The negative charge on p-type material prevents electrons from crossing the junction and positive charge on the n-type material prevents holes crossing the junction. A space created by the "p and n or PN" wafers creates a potential barrier across the junction.

This PN junction that forms the basic block of most electronic components, such as diodes and transistors, has the following specific operational uses when applied in electronics:

In DIODES, a PN device allows for the flow of electrons and, therefore, current in one direction. For example a battery (DC, direct current) connected across a diode allows the flow of current from positive to negative leads. When an alternating sinusoidal current (AC) is connected across the device, only the positive portion of the waveform is allowed to pass through. The negative portion of the waveform is blocked.

In TRANSISTORS, a wire secured in a sandwich of a PNP junction device (formed by three doped junctions), when properly polarized or biased, controls the amount of DC from positive lead to negative, thus forming the basis for current control, switching, and amplification.

In LIGHT EMITTING DIODES (LEDs), a controlled amount and type of doping material in a PN type device connected across a DC voltage source converts the electrical energy to visible light with differing frequencies and colors, such as white, red, blue, amber, and green.

In SOLAR CELLS, when a PN junction is exposed to sunshine, the device converts the stream of photons (packets of quanta) that form the visible light into electrons (reverse of the LED function), making the device behave like a minute battery with a unique characteristic voltage and current, which is dependant on the material dopants and PN junction physics. This is shown in Figure 1.1.

The bundles of photons that penetrate the PN junction randomly strike silicon atoms and give energy to the outer electrons. The acquired energy allows the outer electrons to break free from the atom. Thus the photons in the process are converted to electron movement or electric energy.

It should be noted that the photovoltaic energy conversion efficiency is dependant on the wavelength of the impinging light; red light with lower frequency produces insufficient energy, whereas blue light has more energy than needed to break the electrons, which gets wasted and dissipated as heat. This is shown in Figure 1.2.

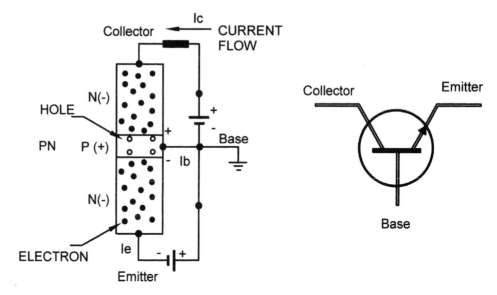

Figure 1.1 NPN Junction showing holes and electron flow

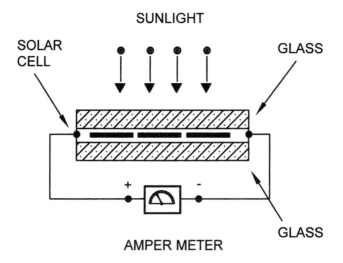

SOLAR CELL OPERATION

Figure 1.2 Solar cell operation

Solar Cell Electronics

An electrostatic field is produced at a PN junction of a solar cell by impinging photons that create a half (.5) volt of potential energy, which is characteristic of most PN junctions and all solar cells. This miniscule potential resembles, in function, to a small battery with positive and negative leads. These are then connected front to back in series to achieve higher voltages.

For example, 48 solar cell modules connected in series will result in 24 volts of output. An increase in the number of solar cells within the solar cell bank will result in higher voltage. This voltage is employed to operate inverters (discussed below), which convert the DC power into a more suitable AC form of electricity.

In addition to the above-discussed PN junction device, solar cells contain construction components, for mechanical assembly purposes, that are laid over a rigid or flexible holding platform or a substrate, such as a glass or a flexible film, and are interconnected by micron thin, highly conductive metals.A typical solar panel used in photovoltaic power generation, is constructed from a glass supportive plate that houses solar PV modules each formed from several hundreds of interconnected PN devices.Depending on the requirement of specific application, most solar panels manufactured today produce 6, 12, 24, or 48-volt DC outputs. The amount of power produced by a solar panel, expressed in watts, represents an aggregate power output of all solar PN devices. For example, a manufacturer will express various panel characteristics by voltage, wattage, and surface area.

Types of Solar Cells

Solar cell technologies at present fall into the three main categories MONOCRYSTALLINE (single crystal construction), POLYCRYSTALLINE (semi-crystalline) and AMORPHOUS SILICONE.

Monocrystalline Photovoltaic Solar Cells

Monocrystalline cells have highest conversion efficiency. They have currently a well-established semiconductor manufacturing process that dates over several decades. The cells are manufactured from extremely pure silicon by processes known as CZOCHRALSKY or FLOATING ZONE TECHNIQUE.

In the above referenced processes, monocrystalline silicone grows on a seed, which is pulled slowly out of the silicon melt. Silicone rods produced from the process are sliced into 0.2 mm to 0.4 mm thick wafer disks by carbide thread saws. The wafers produced undergo several production steps that consist of the following:

Grinding, Polishing and Cleaning, Doping, and Anti-reflective Coating. The manufacturing process for monocrystalline silicon solar cell is highly intensive and expensive.

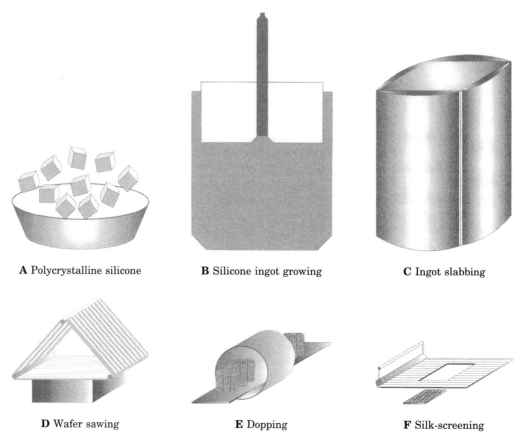

A Polycrystalline silicone   **B** Silicone ingot growing   **C** Ingot slabbing

D Wafer sawing   **E** Dopping   **F** Silk-screening

Figure 1.3 Monocrystalline solar panel manufacturing process (Courtesy of Shell Solar)

Polycrystalline Photovoltaic Solar Cells

In the polycrystalline process, the silicon melt is cooled very slowly, under controlled condition. The silicon ingot produced in this process has crystalline regions, which are separated by grain boundaries. After solar cell production, the gaps in the grain boundaries cause lower efficiency compared to the monocrystalline described process above.Despite the efficiency disadvantage, a number of manufacturers favor polycrystalline PV cell production because of the lower manufacturing cost.

Amorphous Photovoltaic Solar Cells

In this process, a thin wafer of silicon is deposited on a carrier material and doped in several process steps an amorphous silicon film produced, similar to

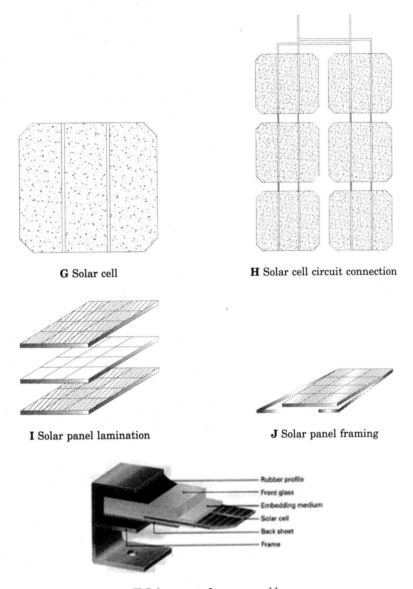

G Solar cell

H Solar cell circuit connection

I Solar panel lamination

J Solar panel framing

- Rubber profile
- Front glass
- Embedding medium
- Solar cell
- Back sheet
- Frame

K Solar power frame assembly

Figure 1.3 (Continued)

monocrystalline manufacturing process, is sandwiched between glass plates, which form the basic PV solar panel module.

Even though the process yields relatively inexpensive solar panel technology, it has the following disadvantages:

- Requires larger installation surface
- Lower conversion efficiency
- An inherent degradation during the initial months of operation that continues over the lifespan of the PV panels

The main advantages of this technology are:

- Relative simple manufacturing process
- Lower manufacturing cost
- Lower production energy consumption

Other Technologies

Other prevalent production processes that are currently being researched and will be serious contenders in the future of solar power production technology include:

Thin Film Cells.   In this process, thin crystalline layers of cadmium-telluride (CdTe of about 15% efficiency) or copper-indium-diselenide (CuInSe2, of about 19% efficiency) are deposited on the surface of a carrier base. This process uses very little energy and is very economical. It has simple manufacturing processes and has relatively high conversion efficiencies.

Gallium Arsenide Cells.   This manufacturing process yields a highly efficient PV cell. But as result of rarity of gallium deposits and poisonous qualities of arsenic, the process is very expensive. The main feature of gallium arsenide (GaAs) cells in addition to high efficiency is that their output is relatively independent of the operating temperature and is primarily used in space programs.

Tandem or Multi-junction-cells.   This process employs two layers of solar cell such as Si and GaAs components one on top of another that convert solar power with higher efficiency.

Concentrators

Concentrators are lenses or reflectors that focus sunlight onto the solar cell modules. Fresnel lenses, which have concentration ratios of ten to 500 times, are mostly made of inexpensive plastic materials engineered with refracting features that direct the sunlight onto small narrow PN junction area of the cells. Module efficiencies of GaAs single crystalline PV cells, which normally range from 10% to 14%, can be augmented in excess of 30%.

Reflectors are used to increase power output, increase intensity of light on the module or extend the time that sunlight falls on the modules. The main disadvantage of concentrators is their inability to focus scattered light, which limits their use to areas, such as deserts.

Solar Panel Arrays

Serial or parallel interconnections in solar panels are called SOLAR PANEL ARRAYS (SPA). Generally a series of solar panel arrays are configured to produce a specific voltage potential and collective power production capacity to meet the demand requirements of a project.

Depending on the size of the mounting surface, solar panels are secured on tilted structures called STANCHIONS. Solar panels installed in the Northern Hemisphere are mounted facing south with stanchions tilted to a specific degree angle. In the Southern Hemisphere solar panels are installed facing north.

Solar panel arrays feature a series of interconnected positive (+) and negative (−) outputs of solar panels in a serial or parallel arrangement that provides a required DC voltage to an inverter (described below). Figure 1.4 shows the internal wiring of a solar power cell. Figure 1.5 shows an entire panel.

The average daily output of solar power systems is entirely dependent on the amount of exposure to sunlight. This exposure is dependent on the following factors. Accurate north-south orientation of solar panels (facing the sun) as referenced above has a significant effect on the efficiency of power output. Even a slight shadowing will affect a module's daily output. Other natural phenomena that affect solar production include diurnal variations (due to the rotation of the Earth about its axis), seasonal variation (due to the tilt of the Earth's axis), annual variation (due to elliptical orbit of the Earth around the Sun), solar flares, solar sunspots, atmospheric pollution, dust, and haze.

Photovoltaic solar array installation in the vicinity of trees and elevated structures, which may cast a shadow on the panels, should be avoided. Geographic location of the project site and seasonal changes are also significant factors that must be taken into consideration.

In order to account for average daily solar exposure time, design engineers refer to world sunlight exposure maps, shown in Figure 1.6. Each area is assigned an "Area Exposure Time Factor" which depending on location may vary from two (2) to six (6) hours.

A typical example for calculating daily watt-hours for a solar panel array consisting of 10 modules with a power rating of 75 watts in an area located with a multiplier of 5 will be $(10 \times 75W) \times 5h = 3750$ watt-hours of average daily power.

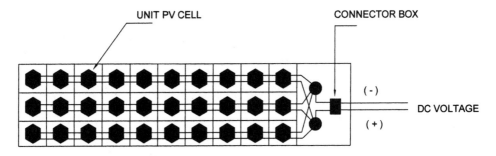

Figure 1.4 Solar power cell internal wiring configuration

Figure 1.5 Photovoltaic panel (Courtesy of Sharp Electronics)

Solar Power System Configurations

Photovoltaic modules only represent the basic element of a solar power system. They work only in conjunction with complementary components, such as batteries, inverters, and transformers. Power distribution panels and metering complete the energy conversion process.

The following represent essential components of a solar power system used in a wide variety of applications.

Storage Batteries

As mentioned above, solar cells are devices that merely convert solar energy into a DC voltage. Solar cells do not store energy. To store energy beyond daylight, the DC voltage is used to charge an appropriate set of batteries.

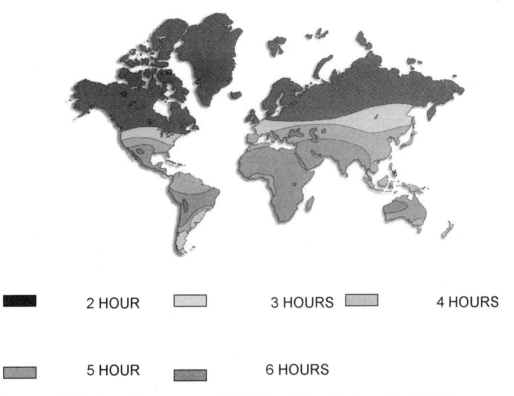

2 HOUR   3 HOURS   4 HOURS

5 HOUR   6 HOURS

Figure 1.6 Global solar performance map and daylight multipliers (Courtesy of Shell Solar)

The reserve capacity of batteries is referred to as SYSTEM AUTONOMY. This varies according to the requirements of specific application. Batteries in applications, which require autonomy, form a critical component of a solar power system. Battery banks in photovoltaic application are designed to operate at deep-cycle discharge rates and are generally maintenance free.

The amount of the required autonomy time depends on the specific application. Circuit loads, such as telecommunication and remote telemetry stations, may require two weeks of autonomy, whereas a residential unit may require no more than 12 hours. Batteries must be properly selected to store sufficient energy for the daily demand. When calculating battery ampere-hours and storage capacity, additional de-rating factors, such as cloudy conditions and sunless conditions, must be taken into consideration.

Charge Regulators

Charge regulators are electronic devices designed to protect batteries from overcharging. Charge regulators are installed between the solar array termination boxes and the batteries.

Inverters

As described, photovoltaic panels generate direct current, which can only be used by a limited number of devices. Most residential, commercial, and industrial devices and appliances are designed to work with AC. Inverters are devices that convert DC to AC. Although inverters are usually designed for specific application requirements, the basic conversion principles remain the same. Essentially, the inversion process consists of the following.

Wave Chopping Process.   Direct current, characterized by continuous potential of positive and negative references (bias), is essentially chopped into equidistant segments, which then are processed through circuitry that alternately eliminate positive and negative portions of the chopped pattern, resulting into a waveform pattern called a SQUARE WAVE.

Wave Shaping or Filtration Process.   A square wave, when analyzed mathematically (Fourier Series Analysis), consists of a combination of a very large number of sinusoidal (alternating) wave patterns called harmonics. Each wave harmonic has a distinct number of cycles (rise and fall pattern within a time period).

An electronic device referred to as a choke (magnetic coils) or filter discriminate or pass through 60 cycle harmonics, which form the basis of sinusoidal current. Solid-state inverters use a highly efficient conversion technique known as envelope construction. Direct current is sliced into fine sections, which are then converted into a progressive rising (positive) and falling (negative) sinusoidal 60 cycle waveform pattern. This chopped sinusoidal wave is passed through a series of electronic filters that produce an output current, which has a smooth curvature.

Protective Relaying Systems.   In general, most inverters used in photovoltaic application are built from sensitive solid-state electronic devices that are very susceptible to external stray spikes, load short circuits, and overload voltage and currents. To protect the equipment from harm, inverters incorporate a number of electronic protective circuitry known as PROTECTIVE RELAYING, which consists of the following.

- Synchronization relay
- Under voltage relay
- Over current relay
- Ground trip or over-current relay
- Over voltage relay
- Over frequency relay
- Under frequency relay

Most inverters designed for photovoltaic application, are designed in to allow simultaneous paralleling of multiple units. For instance, to support a

60 kW load, outputs of three 20 kW inverters may be connected in parallel. Depending on power system requirements, inverters can produce single or three phase power at any required voltage or current capacity. Standard outputs available are single-phase 120 VAC and three-phase120/208 VAC. Step-up transformers are used to convert the output of 120/208 VAC inverters to higher voltages.

Input and Output Power Distribution Systems.   To protect inverters from stray spikes resulting from lightning or high-energy spikes, DC inputs from PV arrays are protected by set fuses, housed at a junction box located in close proximity to the inverters. Additionally, inverter DC input ports are protected by various types of semiconducting devices that clip excessively high voltage spikes.

To prevent damages resulting from voltage reversal, each positive (+) output lead within a PV cell is connected to a rectifier, a unidirectional (forward biased) element. Alternating current output power from inverters is connected to the loads by means of electronic or magnetic type circuit breakers. These serve to protect the unit from external over-current and short circuits.

Solar Power System Applications

The simplest solar power applications require output from a PV cell or an array, to supply power to direct current motors or circuit devices requiring DC power. An example of a rudimentary application is a pump driven by a DC motor that provides a continuous stream of water from a well. This application is quite prevalent in remotely located cattle ranches. Other examples of simple PV cell applications include remotely located communications transmitters, repeater stations, highway signs, roadside emergency telephones, telephone booths, landscape fixtures, surveillance cameras, and large variety commercial equipment and appliances.

To prevent damage from power surges resulting from strong magnetic field interference and lightening, most of this equipment incorporates appropriate power input surge protection, lightning arresters, and ground fault protection devices. Equipment that requires a specific autonomy time is provided with battery back-up systems that provide adequate power sustenance. In applications requiring AC power, DC output of a solar array is connected to an inverter system. Likewise, depending on the application, PV systems can be equipped with battery back up and a wide variety of distribution and voltage transformation equipment.

Power Demand Calculations

To properly size and specify solar power system components, which consist of PV cells, batteries, and inverters, transformer and power distribution systems, are determined by the following DC and AC power calculation steps.

Daily Direct Current Power Requirements

1. List each DC load in watts.
2. Multiply the loads by daily hours used.
3. Sum the loads to establish average daily DC load.
4. Add 20% to 30% compensation for losses resulting from voltage drops, batteries, and inverters.

Daily Alternating Current Power Requirements

1. List each AC load.
2. Multiply each load by average daily hours used.
3. Sum the loads to find the average daily AC load.
4. Add 40% compensation for losses resulting from voltage drops, batteries, and inverters.

Battery Storage Capacity Sizing

1. Use daily power requirements calculated per above (sum AC and DC power if applicable).
2. Multiply (1) by number of days that the batteries must sustain the load without solar charge (autonomy time) Add a safety factor of 30%, for reserve capacity.

Solar Module Requirements

1. Establish total solar power requirements from above.
2. Divide load wattage (including compensation losses) by PV panel wattage to arrive at number of solar panels required.
3. Multiply surface area of the PV cell by number of modules.
4. Form fit the PV cell arrays and stanchion configuration within the available space.

Commercial Projects Best Suited for Solar Power Installation

When planning for photovoltaic power systems, special consideration such as physical space requirements, geographic location, seasonal weather conditions, and initial investment costs must be taken into consideration. As discussed below, at present, the initial investment for PV systems constitutes the most significant decision making parameter.

In remote telemetry or communication system installations, where there are no conventional means of power generation, solar power, regardless of economics, becomes the only viable alternative.

In some industrial and commercial applications, where peak power penalties represent a significant cost of energy, solar power systems could provide significant peak power shaving, which could result into considerable expenditure reduction.

In view of the fact that office building operational hours coincide with the peak power production time of solar power systems, installation of a PV system could, under suitable conditions, result in a significant increase in peak power shaving.

Some important factors when deciding to install solar power systems are the longevity of the PV cells, the absolute minimal maintenance of the equipment, and, unlike FUEL CELLS and MICRO TURBINES, PV cells are fuel free.

Most manufacturers warrantee PV cells for a period of 25 years. As discussed below, system financing, when considering an average of 8 years to 10 years of investment amortization pay-off period, will provide the owner a substantial amount of cost savings for, at least, 15 years.

Another significant factor favoring photovoltaic system power production is that, most local municipalities and gas and electric utilities within Southern California have power BUY-BACK METERING systems, as shown in Chart 1.1. Excess power is fed back into the utility grid and results in an energy credit that can be quite significant for reducing overhead costs.

Grid-Connected PV Capacity Installed in California by Year

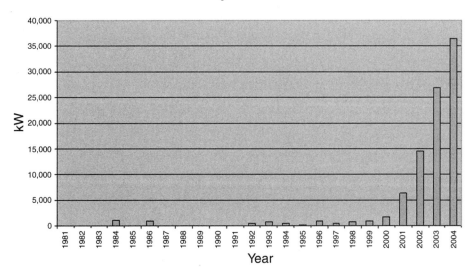

Chart 1.1 Grid connected PV capacity installation in California by year

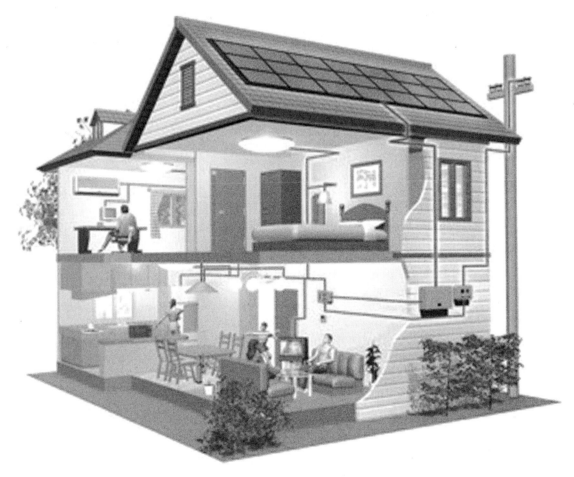

Figure 1.7 Residential solar power installation diagram (Courtesy of Sharp Solar)

Solar Power Application in Residential Installations

Photovoltaic panels installed atop roofs facing southward have been gaining significant popularity among homeowners and developers throughout Europe and the United States. In addition to added architectural aesthetics, as shown in Figure 1.7, residential solar energy systems can provide a significant reduction of up to 20 kW to 25 kW per hour of power per day. See daily residential power usage in Chart 1.2.

If each of the 150,000 new homes built in California had a modest 2 kW PV system installed, it would eliminate 300 MW per hour and 1650 MW of energy per day. Building solar panels into new homes has an intrinsic advantage over form fitting panels on existing roofs. In a newly constructed single residential unit, the solar panel system can be designed into the house, as shown being installed in Figure 1.8, and significantly reduce the installation cost.

DAILY RESIDENTIAL POWER USAGE

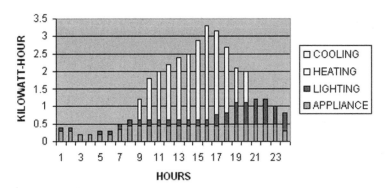

Chart 1.2 Daily residential power usage

Figure 1.8 Example of a transparent solar power panel installation (Courtesy of Atlantis Energy)

Figure 1.9 Example of a transparent solar power panel application in a solarium (Courtesy of Atlantis Energy)

Even though the installation cost of a typical 2 kW residential solar power system may be as high as $15,000 to $20,000, with buy-back programs offered by state government, municipalities, and gas and power utilities, the actual cost to the owner can be reduced to around $6,000.

Most significantly, cost rollover into a long-term mortgage (15 to 30 years) will nearly pencil out the extra cost burden. The most significant aspect of PV solar power in residential installations is the added sale and resale value of the home.

A 2 kW solar power system can readily provide about one-half of the power used by daylight illumination (300 W), TV (100 W), stereo (60 W), microwave oven (450-750 W), refrigerator (90-150 W), evaporating cooler (200-300 W), and about 400 watts for general receptacles. Figures 1.9 and 1.10 show other applications of solar power systems. See Chart 1.3 for daily and peak power use information.

Design Considerations for Commercial and Residential Projects

When conceptualizing the overall design of a project intended to include a solar power system as part of the integral design, the architect, as prime coor-

Figure 1.10   Example of a solar carport design (Courtesy of Atlantis Energy)

dinator, must review the overall details of PV system structure and space requirements with the electrical design engineer.When PV cells are to be located on roofs, stanchion locations, stanchion spacing, air conditioning platforms, solar power system conduit installation, conduit shafts, additional roof load-

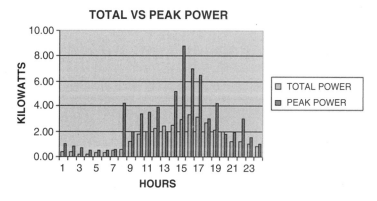

Chart 1.3   Total daily power use versus peak power demand

ing, wind gust conditions, downspout positions, and roof pitches and slopes must given a serious consideration. In addition to architectural and structural specifics, the mechanical engineer must take into account resulting solar panel shade contribution to roof insulation when calculating air conditioning, Title 24, energy calculations. This may amount to as much as a 10% increases to insulation value.

Design Guidelines for Residential Solar Projects

When planning single or multiple residential units, the following design guideline will result into substantial economical energy use savings if applied properly. Now that the utilization has become practical component of an ENERGY EFFICIENT HOME DESIGN, dismissal of solar power system as superfluous and unnecessary requirement is shortsighted. Even though PV power systems are at the start of the economic bell curve; within a very short time their application will be as prevalent and basic as microwave ovens, computers, and cellular phones.

To dismiss PV system requirements at conceptual or planning stages of design, will be proven to be a costly error, since undoubtedly, solar power energy contribution in most future residences will be considered as a mandatory requirement. Moreover, residential housing units with PV systems will unquestionably have far better resale value than regular ones.

The following design guidelines outlined below are based on practical construction practices and numerous published research articles.

Orientation

The basic architectural design principle dictates that the longest wall of the home should face south, since the winter sun rises from Southeast and sets at Southwest. Therefore, placing large glass windows on the South wall will ensure that the home will receive the optimal solar energy.

Declination of magnetic south varies across the country. In the Northern Hemespheric Photovoltaic cells work best when facing TRUE SOUTH.

Photovoltaic Pane Tilt Angle

Stanchion or roof tilts for best efficiency must be tilted at an angle to provide maximum insolation.

Solar Exposure

To ensure complete solar exposure to the suns, PV cells should be installed in locations that avoid building or tree shades.

Windows

The amount of window surface on the south wall is optimally about 7% of the homes total square footage. For example, a 3000 square foot house, excluding the window trims, should have about 210 square feet of glass. The above design criteria apply to conventional home constructions, which use wall-to-wall carpeting.

To avoid overheating, the amount of window surface should not exceed 7% since it will create unnecessary overheating. To increase window surface beyond the above-suggested design limit, an additional increase must be made in thermal mass (concrete, floor tiles, etc.).

East wall and north wall window surfaces should be limited to a maximum of 4% of the total square footage. West window glass surface areas must be limited to 2% of the total square footage.

Additional design consideration should include structural slab insulation (Sole Plate), wall insulation, and attic insulation (R-30 blown insulation for moderate climates, R-40 and 50 for colder).

Use of fluorescent lamps, ceiling fans, and natural ventilation from windows can also drastically reduce running time of air conditioners.

Electrical Engineering System Design

To incorporate a solar power generation system as integral part of an existing or a new project, the electrical engineer must have required expertise and qualification to evaluate the entire project from both a technical and a costing point of view.

One of the most important steps, when considering a solar system design, is an initial feasibility study, where the electrical engineer or designer undertakes a detailed study of all aspects of the design. These include, site evaluation, systems engineering configuration, equipment integration, service demand transfer switching requirements, and all issues that concern system installation and integration. The feasibility study should, in addition to technical issues, include economics of engineering, material, and installation cost. A typical cost evaluation matrix that outlines cost and equipment performance parameters from various competitors must be included as part of the report.

Thorough understanding of all technical issues concerning particular performance characteristics of existing PV cell technologies and specific system integration requirements are essential for designing an efficient solar power system. The electrical engineer or designer should assume primary responsibility to coordinate all technical aspects of the project with all design disciplines.

Due to specific performance characteristics of PV cells and conversion equipment, the designer should exercise diligence to minimize power losses. Equipment selected should be reliable, efficient, and durable, requiring minimal amount of maintenance and care.

Advances in Design and Development of Photovoltaic Technology

In view of increasing shortage of non-renewable energy resources and the increasing cost of conventional energy production in recent years, there has been an accelerated international research and product development effort to produce efficient and inexpensive photovoltaic power production technology.

A large portion of research and development funds are subsidized by national funds. Subsides in the United States exceed $100 million annually. Sandia National Laboratories in Albuquerque, NM, is a major recipient of research funds from U.S. Department of Energy, and, in addition to technology research, evaluation, and product development, has a Photovoltaic System Assistance Center, which assures technology transfer to the private industry. Similar entities in Canada, Japan, Germany, and the Untied Kingdom promote research and development assistance to private enterprises.

The impact of photovoltaic technology in view of depleted non-renewable energy resources is enormous and will represent a significant upward impact on the global economies.

Some of the recent research and development noteworthy of reference are as follow:

Japan Energy Corporation

The company has developed and fabricated a photovoltaic module named RECORD ONE-SUN CELL. The unit has 30.28% efficiency and is made of InGa/GaAs, a two-junction device. Marketing and mass-fabrication dates are currently unknown.

NREL USA

The lab has recently announced the successfully development of a module called RECORD CIGS DEVICE, the experimental PV cell has a surface area of 1 cm^2 and has an efficiency of 17.7%. The device is made from Cu, (InGa) Se2 (CIGS) junctions. The date for production model is currently unknown.

Georgia Institute of Technology

The institute has developed a multicrystalline silicon PV cell that has an efficiency of 18.6%. The PV module is named HEM RECORD CELL. The date for production model is currently unknown.

University of New South Wales, Australia

The university has reported successful test completion of a PV cell module named RECORD MODULE that has 22.3% efficiency. The date for the production module is currently unknown.

Texas Instruments

Other interesting PV technologies include a spherical solar cell is a very thin photovoltaic films that are recently being used as curtain walls in high-rise buildings.

Figure 1.11 Flexible spheral solar panel system (Courtesy of ATS Automation Tooling Systems, Inc., Canada)

University of Waterloo, Ontario, Canada

The university has successfully developed a spheral solar power cell, shown in Figure 1.11, that makes use of imbedded aluminum spheres in silicone wafers and has achieved a basis of an inexpensive solar production technology, which will produce affordable solar power products within the next few years. Present efficiency of the spherical power cells is about 7% to 11%; however, the research team is aiming to extend it to 30%. Currently flexible spheral solar cell products are marketed by ATS Automation Tooling Systems, Inc., Cambridge, Ontario, Canada.

U.S. Government Annual Research Expenditure

In recent past, the U.S. Federal Government had allocated about $90 million for solar energy research, as shown in Chart 1.4. Unfortunately, the solar power fund, at the expense of coal, oil, and fusion energy research, has been reducing by 50%.

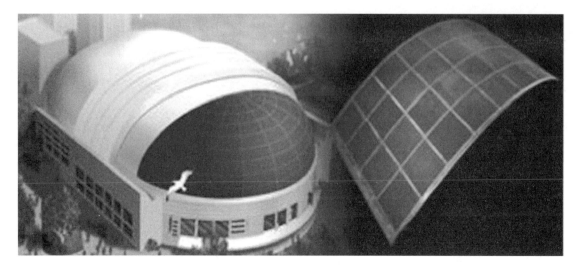

Figure 1.12 Possible design of spherical power cells with greater efficiency (Courtesy of ATS Automation Tooling Systems, Inc., Canada)

Evaluation of Photovoltaic Systems

When evaluating PV cells or panels, system performance and installation cost must be the principal guiding factors, which are different for each project. For instance, requirements of a project located in a desert area, which poses no installation space limitations, could tilt the designers choice to select less expensive low efficiency solar panels. In applications, such as rooftop installations, design constraints will dictate use of costlier but highly efficient PV panels, which occupy the least amount of space. Social problems in implementing solar power systems are shown in Chart 1.5, and US energy consumption for 1996 is shown in Chart 1.6.

TABLE 1.1 Typical Solar Module and Cell Conversion Efficiencies Under Standard Test Conditions.

Type	Typical module efficiency (%)	Maximum efficiency (%)	Laboratory efficiency (%)
Single Crystal Silicone	12–15	22.7	24.7
Multicrystalline Silicone	11–14	15.3	19.8
Amorphous Silicone	5–7	—	12.7
Cadmium Telluride	—	10.5	16.0
Copper Idium	—	—	—
Gallium Diselenide	—	12.1	18.2

RESEARCH SPENDING

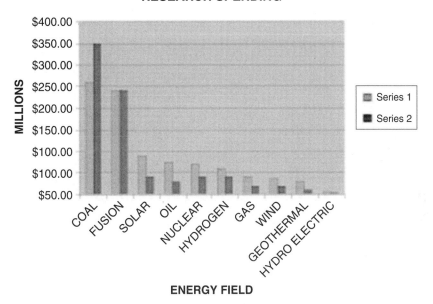

Chart 1.4 The U.S. Energy research fund distribution chart

EXPANSION AND USE BARRIER

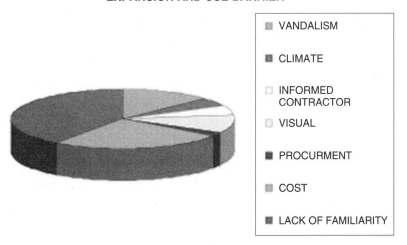

Chart 1.5 Solar power system expansion and use barrier

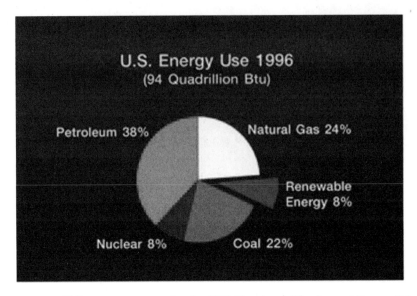

Chart 1.6 U.S. energy consumption for 1996 (Courtesy of Geothermal Energy Education Office)

Photovoltaic Design

In general PV module design parameters to be taken into consideration should be as follows.

- Panel rated power (185 W, 175 W, 750 W, etc.)
- Unit voltage (6 V, 12 V, 24 V, 48 V, etc.)
- Rated amps
- Rated voltage
- Short circuit amps
- Short circuit current
- Open circuit volts
- Panel width, length, and thickness
- Panel weight
- Ease of cell interconnection and wiring
- Unit protection for polarity reversal
- Years of warrant by the manufacturer
- Reliability of technology
- Efficiency of the cell per unit surface
- Degradation rate during expected lifespan (warranty period) of operation

- Longevity of the product
- Number of installations
- Project references and contacts
- Product manufacturers financial viability

Inverter and Automatic Transfer System

Inverter and automatic transfer system evaluation parameters to be taken into consideration should be as follows.

- Unit conversion efficiency
- Waveform harmonic distortion
- Protective relaying features (as referenced above)
- Input and output protection features
- Service and maintenance availability and cost
- Output waveform and percent harmonic content
- Unit synchronization feature with utility power
- Longevity of the product
- Number of installations in similar type of application
- Project references and contacts
- Product manufacturers financial viability

It should be noted that solar power installation PV cells and inverters that are subject to California Energy Commission's rebate must be listed in the commission's ELIGIBLE MODULES OF EMERGING RENEWABLE PROGRAM.

Installation Contractor Qualification

- Contractors experience and technical qualification
- Years of experience in solar panel installation and maintenance
- Familiarity with system components
- Number of experience with the particular system product
- Labor pool and number of full time employees
- Trouble shooting experience
- Financial viability
- Shop location
- Union affiliation

- Performance bond and liability insurance amount
- Previous litigation history
- Material, manpower, overhead and profit markups
- Payment schedule
- Installation warrantee for labor and material

Financial Analysis

The financial analysis of a solar power projects involve standard techniques applied in commercial and industrial capital equipment acquisition. At present, the State of California, due to recent energy shortages, has taken a number of measures to encourage use of solar power systems in residential, commercial, and industrial installations. Specific financial aids available include buy-back programs by municipalities and most major power utility companies, such as Southern California Edison (SCE), Santiago Gas and Electric (SGE) and Pacific Gas and Electric (PG&E). In addition, there are a number of lending institutions that under sponsorship of federal and state governments offer low interest rate capital equipment loans at 5% over a period of 5 years.

Buy Back Procedures and Documentation Requirements

To apply for state, municipal, or utility sponsored buy-back programs referenced above, the applicant must complete the following requirements.

- The project must be located in one of the sponsoring agencies locations.
- The solar power systems design must be completed.
- A licensed installation contractor must be selected.
- Hardware installed must have a minimum of 5 years of warrantee.
- Hardware must be certified by national standards (IEC 1648).
- The applicant must acquire a municipal permit for the project.
- A complete set of design documentation, which must include site location, PV cell installation, power demand calculation, electrical riser diagram, and so forth, must be submitted to the sponsoring agency for evaluation.
- The applicant should obtain the sponsoring agency's FUND RESERVATION application forms from that agency's web site.
- Submit equipment purchase order from the retailer or contractor, a copy of the letter of intent, if an existing project; submit a copy of one year of electric bills (not applicable to new projects) to the CALIFORNIA ENERGY COMMISION.

Upon California Energy Commission's review, the applicant will receive a Fund Reservation Confirmation and Claim. Fund reservation will be valid for a period of 18 months for systems larger than a 10 kW rating. For smaller power systems, the reservation period is 9 months.

Please refer to Chapter 5 for California incentive program application forms. When starting the solar power system installation, the applicant must submit these claim forms to the California Energy Commission for rebate. The rebate is made available within 30 days. It is a common notion that State of California sponsored rebate programs, which are intended to reduce the energy crisis, will most likely last for a limited period of time.

Global Warming and Climate Change

Ever since the industrial revolution, human activities have constantly changed the natural composition of Earth's atmosphere. Concentrations of trace atmospheric gases, nowadays termed "greenhouse gases," are increasing in an alarming rate. There is conclusive evidence that consumption of fossil fuels, conversion of forests to agricultural land, and the emission of industrial chemicals are principal contributing factors to air pollution.

According to the National Academy of Sciences, the earth's surface temperature has risen by about one degree Fahrenheit in the past century, with accelerated warming occurring in the past three decades. According to statistical review of the atmospheric and climatic records there is substantial evidence that global warming over the past 50 years is directly attributable to human activities.

Under normal atmospheric conditions, energy from the sun controls the earth's weather and climate patterns. Heating of the earth's surface resulting from the sun radiates energy back into space. Atmospheric greenhouse gases, including carbon dioxide (CO_2), methane (CH_4), nitrous oxide (N_2O), tropospheric ozone (O_3) and water vapor (H_2O) trap some of this outgoing energy, retaining it in the form of heat, somewhat like a glass dome. This is referred to as GREENHOUSE EFFECT.

Without greenhouse effect, surface temperatures on earth would be roughly 30 degrees Celsius (54 degrees Fahrenheit) colder than they are today - too cold to support life. Reducing greenhouse gas emissions depends on reducing the amount of fossil fuel fired energy that we produce and consume.

Fossil fuels include coal, petroleum, and natural gas, all of which are used to fuel electric power generation and transportation. Substantial increases in use of nonrenewable fuels have been principal factors in the rapid increase in global greenhouse gas emissions. Use of renewable fuels can be extended to power industrial, commercial, residential, and transportation applications to substantially reduce air pollution.

Examples of zero-emission, renewable fuels include solar, wind, geothermal, and renewably powered fuel cells. These fuel types, in combination with advances in energy efficient equipment design and sophisticated energy management techniques, can reduce the risk of climate change and the resulting harmful effects on the ecology. It should be kept in mind that natural greenhouse gases are a necessary part of sustaining life on earth. It is the anthropogenic or human caused increase in greenhouse gases that is of concern to the international scientific community and governments around the world.

Since the beginning of the modern industrial revolution, atmospheric concentrations of carbon dioxide have increased nearly 30%, methane concentrations have more than doubled, and nitrous oxide concentrations have also risen by about 15%. These increases in greenhouse gas emissions have enhanced the heat-trapping capability of Earth's atmosphere.

Fossil fuels burned to operate electric power plants, run cars and trucks, and heat homes and businesses are responsible for about 98% of U.S. carbon dioxide emissions, 24% of U.S. methane emissions, and 18% of U.S. nitrous oxide emissions. Increased deforestation, landfills, large agricultural production, industrial production, and mining also contribute a significant share of emissions. In 2000, the United States produced about 25% of total global greenhouse gas emissions, the largest contributing country in the world.

Estimating future emissions depends on demographic, economic, technological policy and institutional developments. Several emissions scenarios have been developed based on differing projections of these underlying factors. It is estimated that by year 2100, in the absence of emission control policies, carbon dioxide concentrations will be about 30% to150% higher than today's levels.

Increasing concentrations of greenhouse gases are expected to accelerate global climate change. Scientists expect that the average global surface temperatures could raise an additional 1 degree to 4.5 degrees Fahrenheit within the next fifty years and 2.2 degrees to 10 degrees Fahrenheit over the next century, with significant regional variation. Records show that the 10 warmest years of the 20th century all occurred in the last 15 years of that century.

The expected impacts of weather warming trend include the following.

Water Resources

Warming-induced decrease in mountain snowpack storage will increase winter stream flows (and flooding) and decrease summer flows. This along with an increased evapotranspiration rate is likely to cause a decrease in water deliveries.

Agriculture

The agricultural industry will be adversely affected by lower water supplies and increased weather variability, including extreme heat and drought.

Forestry

Increase in summer heat and dryness is likely to result in forest fires, insect population increase, and disease.

Electrical Energy

Increased summer heat is likely to cause an increase in the demand for electricity due to increased reliance on air conditioning. Reduced snow pack is likely to decrease the availability of hydroelectric supplies.

Regional Air Quality and Human Health

Higher temperatures may worsen existing air quality problems, particularly if there is a greater reliance on fossil fuel generated electricity. Higher heat would also increase health risks for segments of the population.

Rising Ocean Levels

Thermal expansion of the ocean and glacial melting are likely to cause a 0.5 m to 1.5 m (2 to 4 ft) rise in the ocean level by 2100.

Natural Habitat

Rising ocean levels and reduced summer river flow are likely to reduce coastal and wetland habitats. These changes could also adversely affect spawning fish populations. General increase in temperatures and accompanying increase in summer dryness could also adversely affect wild land plant and animal species.

Scientists calculate that without considering feedback mechanisms a doubling of carbon dioxide would lead to a global temperature increase of 1.2 degrees Celsius (2.2 degrees Fahrenheit). But, the net effect of positive and negative feedback patterns appear to cause substantially more warming than would the change in greenhouse gases alone.

Pollution Abetment Consideration

According to a 1999 study report by the U.S. Department of Energy (DOE), one kilowatt of energy produced by a coal fired electrical power generating plant requires about 5 lb of coal. Likewise generation of 1.5 kW hour of electrical energy per year requires about 7,400 lb of coal that in turn produces 10,000 lb of carbon dioxide (CO_2). Commercial energy pollution is further illustrated in Chart 1.7.

Roughly speaking the calculated projection of the power demand for the project totals to about 2,500 kW hours to −3,000 kW hours. This will require between 12 million pounds– 15 million pounds of coal, thereby producing about 16 million pounds to 200 million pounds of carbon dioxide.

Solar power, if implemented as previously discussed, will substantially minimize the air pollution index. The Environmental Protection Agency (EPA) will soon be instituting an air pollution indexing system that will be factored into all future construction permits. All major industrial projects will be required to meet and adhere to the air pollution standards and offset excess energy consumption by means of solar or renewable energy resources.

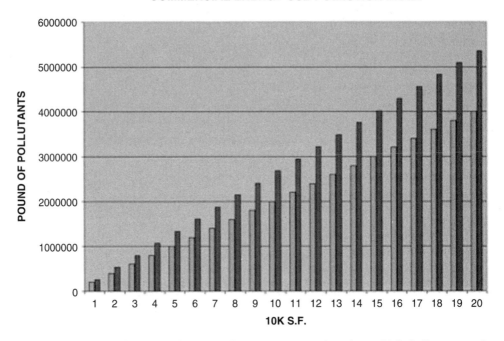

Chart 1.7 Commercial energy pollution graph per 1,000 square feet of area: Light indicates pounds of coal, and dark indicates pounds of CO_2.

Energy Escalation Cost Projection

According to Energy Information Administration data source published in 1999, California consumes just as much energy as Brazil or United Kingdom. The entire global crude oil reserves are estimated to last about 30 years to 80 years, and over 50% of the nation's energy is imported from abroad. It is inevitable that energy costs will surpass historical cost escalation averaging projections. Growth of fossil fuel consumption is illustrated in Chart 1.8. It is estimated that cost of nonrenewable energy will, within the next decade, increase by approximately 4% to 5% by producers. When compounded with a general inflation rate of 3%, the average energy cost increase, over the next decade, could be expected to rise at a rate of about 7% per year. This cost increase does not take into account other inflation factors, such as regional conflicts, embargos, and natural catastrophes.

Solar power cogeneration systems require nearly zero maintenance and are more reliable than any man made power generation devices. The systems have an actual life span of 35 years to 40 years and are guaranteed by the manufacturers for a period of 25 years. It is my opinion that in a near perfect geographic setting, the integration of the systems into the mainstream of ar-

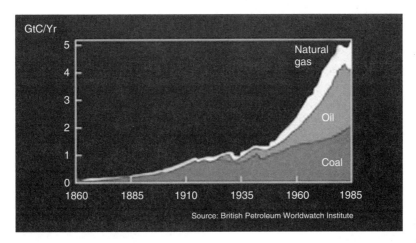

Chart 1.8 Growth in fossil fuel consumption (Courtesy of Geothermal Education Office)

chitectural design will not only enhance the design aesthetics but also will generate considerable savings and mitigate adverse effects on the ecology and global warming.

Social and Environmental Concerns

Nowadays, we do not think twice about leaving lights on or turning off the television or computers, which run for hours. Most people believe that energy seems infinite, but in fact, that is not the case. World consumption of fossil fuels, which supply us with most of our energy, is steadily rising. In 1999, it was found that out of 97 quads of energy used (a quad is 3x1011 kWh) 80 quads came from coal, oil, and natural gas. As we know, sources of fossil fuels will undoubtedly run out within a few generations and the world has to be ready with alternative and new sources of energy.

In reality, as early as 2020, we could be having some serious energy deficiencies. Therefore, interest in renewable fuels such as wind, solar, hydropower, and others is a hot topic among many people.

Renewable fuels are not a new phenomenon; although, they may seem so. In fact, the industrial revolution was launched with renewable fuels. The United States and the world has, for a long time, been using energy without serious concern, until 1973 and 1974 energy conferences, when the energy conservation issues were brought to the attention of the industrialized world. Ever since, we were forced to realize that the supply of fossil fuels would one day run out, and we had to find alternate sources of energy.

In 1999, the U.S. Department of Energy (DOE) published a large report in which it was disclosed that by the year 2020 there will be a 60% increase in

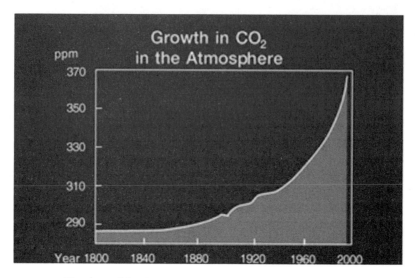

Chart 1.9 (Courtesy of Geothermal Education Office)

carbon dioxide emissions, which will create a serious strain on the environment, as it will further aggravate the dilemma with greenhouse gasses. Chart
1.9 shows the growth of carbon dioxide in the atmosphere.

A simple solution may seem to reduce energy consumption; however, it
would not be feasible. It has been found that there is a correlation between
high electricity consumption (4,000 kWh per capita) and a high Human Development Index (HDI), which measures quality of life. In other words there
is a direct correlation between quality of life and amount of energy used.

This is one of the reasons that our standard of living in the industrialized
countries is better than in third world countries, where there is very little access to electricity. In 1999, the United States had 5% of the world's population and produced 30% of the gross world product. We also consumed 25% of
the world's energy and emitted 25% of the carbon dioxide.

It is not hard to imagine that countries, such as China and India, with increasing population and economic growth, can do to state of the global ecology.

Solar energy is an excellent type of renewable fuel, as shown being collected
in Figure 1.13. The most significant feature of solar energy is that it does not
harm the environment. It is clean energy. Using solar power does not emit
any of the extremely harmful greenhouse gasses that contribute to global
warming. There is a small amount of pollution when the solar panels are produced, but it is miniscule in comparison to fossil fuels. The sun is also a free
source of energy. As technology advances, solar energy will become increas-
ingly economically feasible because the price of the photovoltaic modules will
go down.

Figure 1.13 The collection of renewable fuel (Courtesy of Shell Solar)

The only concern with solar power is that it is not energy on demand and that it only works during the day and when it is very sunny. The only way to overcome this problem is to build storage facilities to save up some of the energy in batteries; however, that adds more to the cost of solar energy.

Project Cost Analysis

As indicated in the preliminary solar power cogeneration study, the average installed cost per watt of electrical energy is approximately $9.00. The unit cost encompasses all turnkey cost components, such as engineering design documentation, solar power components, PV support structures, electrical hardware, inverters, integration labor, and manpower training.

Structures in the above cost include roof mount support frames and simple carport canopies, only. Special architectural monuments if required may necessitate some incremental cost adjustment.

As per State of California Energy Commission (CEC), all solar power cogeneration program rebate applications applied for before December of 2002 were subject to a 50% subsidy. At present, rebate allotments are strictly dependent on the amount of funding available at the time of application and are granted on first come first serve basis.

Leadership in Energy and Environmental Design

Under sponsorship of U.S. Department of Energy, Office of Building Technology, the U.S. Green Building Council was authorized to develop design standards that provides improve environmental and economic performance for commercial buildings by use of established or advance industry standards, principles, practices, and materials.

It should be noted that the United States with 5% of the world population, presently consumes 25% of the global energy resources. The energy consumptions of other countries are shown in Chart 1.10.

As a result of the above study, the Leadership in Energy and Environmental Design (LEED) rating system and checklist was introduced. The system establishes qualification and rating standards that categorize the construction project in various standing designations, such as the silver, gold, and platinum categories. Depending on adherence to the maximum number of points specified in the project checklist, the project is bestowed recognition and a set amount of financial contribution by state and federal agencies.

Categories of the LEED project checklist are as follows:

- Sustainable Sites, with a weight of 5 points

- Water Efficiency, with a weight of 17 points

- Energy & Atmosphere, with a weight of 13 points

- Material & Resources, with a weight of 15 points

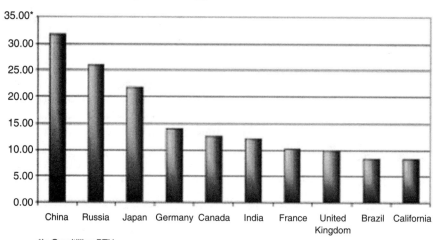

1999 Top Ten Energy Consumers in the World

*In Quadtillion BTU.
Data Source Energy Information Administration

Chart 1.10 Top ten energy consumers in the world excluding the United States (Courtesy of U.S. Department of Energy)

- Indoor Environment Quality, with a weight of 5 points
- Innovation & Design Process, with a weight of 5 points

The total project weight is of a possible 69 points. Under the Energy & Atmosphere category, renewable energy resources are assigned the following points, which are directly proportional to the overall percent of the overall energy contribution required by the building.

- Renewable energy supplying 5% of the building energy – 1 point
- Renewable energy supplying 10% of the building energy – 2 points
- Renewable energy supplying 20% of the building energy – 3 points

System Maintenance and Operational Costs

As mentioned above, solar power systems have a near zero maintenance requirement. This is due to solid-state technology, lamination techniques, and total absence of mechanical or moving parts. However to prevent marginal degradation in output performance from dust accumulation, solar arrays require a bi-yearly rinsing with a water hose.

Since solar power arrays are completely modular, system expansion, module replacement, or troubleshooting is simple and requires no special maintenance skills. All electronic DC to AC inverters are modular and can be replaced with a minimum of down time.

An optional (and relatively inexpensive) computerized system-monitoring console can provide a real time performance status of the entire solar power cogeneration system. A software based supervisory program featured in the monitoring system can also provide instantaneous indication of solar array performance and malfunction.

Conclusion

Even though a solar power cogeneration system requires an initial investment, the long term financial and ecological advantages are so significant that deployment in the existing project should be given special consideration.

A solar power co-generation system, if applied as per above recommendations, will provide a unique significance to the program that will undoubtedly attract national and international attention.

Special Note

In view of depletion of existing CEC rebate funds, it is recommended that application for the rebate program be initiated at the earliest possible time. Furthermore, due to design integration of solar power systems with the service grid, decision to proceed with the program must be taken at the commencement of the construction design document stage.

Solar Power Generation Design

This section is intended to acquaint the reader with basic design concepts of solar power applications. Typical solar power application reviewed include stand alone systems with battery back up, commonly used in remote telemetry, vehicle charging stations, communication repeater stations, and numerous installations where installation cost of regular electrical service become prohibitive. An extended design application of stand-alone systems also includes integration of emergency power generator system.

Grid connected solar power systems, which form a large majority of residential and industrial applications, are reviewed in detail. To familiarize the reader with prevailing state and federal assistance rebate programs, a special section is devoted to the subject, which reviews salient aspects of existing rebates.

Solar power design essentially consists of electronics and power systems engineering, which requires thorough understanding of the electrical engineering disciplines and prevailing standards outlined in Article 690 of the National Electrical Code.

Solar power design presented, in addition to reviewing various electrical design methodologies, provides detailed insight into photovoltaic modules, inverters, charge controllers, lighting protection, power storage, battery sizing, and critical wiring requirements. To assist the reader with the economic issues of solar power cogeneration, detailed analysis of a typical project, including system planning, photovoltaic power system cogeneration estimates, economic cost projection, and payback analysis are covered in part three.

Solar Power System Components and Materials

As described in part one of this text, solar power photovoltaic (PV) modules are constructed from series of cross welded solar cells, each typically producing a specific wattage with an output of 0.5 V.

Effectively, each solar cell could be considered as a 0.5 V battery that produces current under adequate solar ray conditions. To obtain a desired voltage output from a PV panel assembly, the cells, similar to batteries, are connected in series to obtain a required output.

For instance, to obtain a 12 V output, an assembly of 24 cell modules is connected in tandem. Likewise, for a 24 V output, an assembly of 48 modules is connected in series. To obtain a desired wattage, a group of several series connected solar cells are connected in parallel.

Output power of a unit solar cell or its efficiency is dependant on a number of factors such as crystalline silicon, polycrystalline silicon, and amorphous silicon materials, which have specific physical and chemical properties, details of which have been explored in Chapter 1.

Solar panel assemblies commercially available mostly employ proprietary cell manufacturing technologies and lamination techniques, which include cell soldering. Soldered group of solar cells are in general sandwiched between two tempered glass panels, which are offered in framed or frameless assemblies.

Solar Power System Configuration and Classifications

- Directly connected direct current (DC) solar power system
- Stand-alone DC solar power system with battery backup
- Stand-alone hybrid solar power system with generator and battery backup
- Grid connected solar power system

Directly Connected Direct Current Solar Power System

As shown in Figure 2.1, the solar system configuration consists of a required number of solar photovoltaic cells, commonly referred to as PV modules are connected in series or parallel to attain required voltage output. Shown in Figure 2.2, four PV modules have been connected in parallel.

Positive output of each module is protected by an appropriate over current device, such as fuse. Paralleled output of the solar array is in turn connected to a DC motor via a two-pole single throw switch.

In some instances, each individual PV module is also protected with a forward biased diode, connected to the positive output of individual solar panels (not shown in the diagram).

An appropriate surge protector connected between the positive and negative supply provides protection against lighting surges, which could damage the solar array system components.

In order to provide equipment-grounding bias, chassis or enclosures of all PV modules and the DC motor pump are tied together by means of grounding clamps. The system ground is in turn connected to an appropriated grounding rod.

Figure 2.1 Photovoltaic module (PV) interconnection

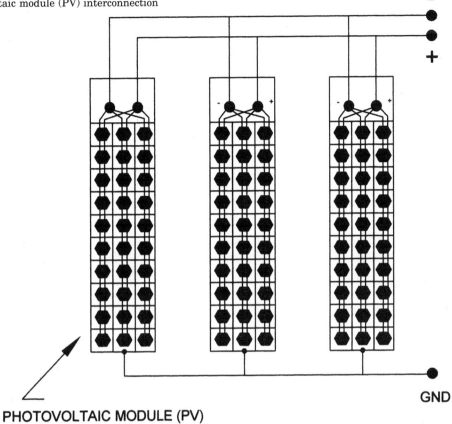

PHOTOVOLTAIC MODULE (PV)

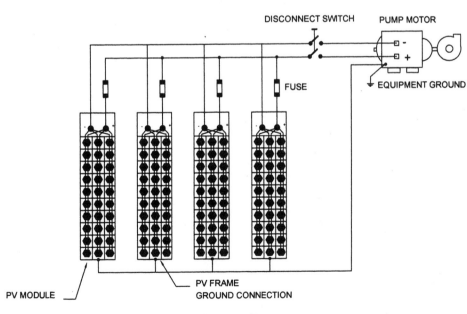

Figure 2.2 Direct connected solar power direct current (DC) pump diagram

All PV interconnecting wires are sized and type selected to prevent power losses caused by a number of factors, such as exposure to sun, excessive wire resistance, and additional requirements that are mandated by the National Electrical Code (NEC).

The photovoltaic solar system described is typically used as an agricultural application, where regular electric service is either unavailable or cost is prohibitive. A floating or submersible DC pump connected to a DC PV array can provide a constant stream of well water that can be accumulated in a reservoir for farm or agricultural use. In subsequent sections we will discuss specification and use of all system components used in solar power cogeneration applications.

Stand-Alone Direct Current Solar Power System with Battery Backup

Solar power photovoltaic array configuration shown in Figure 2.3, a direct current (DC) system with battery backup, is essentially the same as the one without the battery except there are a few additional components that are required to provide battery charge stability.

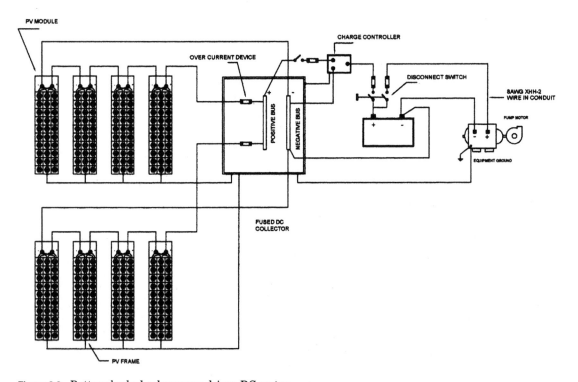

Figure 2.3 Battery backed solar power driven DC motor

In stand alone PV system arrays are connected in series to obtain the desired DC voltage, such as 12 V, 24 V or 48 V, outputs of which are in turn connected to a DC collector pane equipped with specially rated over current devices, such as ceramic type fuses.

The positive lead of each PV array conductor is connected to a dedicated fuse and the negative lead is connected to a common neutral bus. All fuses as well are connected to a common positive bus. Output of the DC collector bus, which represents the collective amps and voltages of the overall array group, are connected to a DC charge controller, which regulates the current output and prevents the voltage level from exceeding the maximum level needed for charging the batteries.

Output of the charge controller, is connected to the battery bank by means of a dual DC cut-off disconnect. As depicted in the diagram, the cut-off switch, when turned off for safety measures, disconnects the load and the PV arrays simultaneously.

Under normal operation, during daytime when there is adequate solar insolation, the load is supplied with DC power while charging the battery, simultaneously. When sizing the solar power system, the DC power output from the PV arrays should be adequate enough to sustain the connected load and the battery trickle charge requirements.

Battery storage sizing depends on a number of factors, such as duration of uninterrupted power supply to the load when the solar power system is inoperative, such as nighttime or cloudy days. It should be noted that battery banks inherently, when in operation, produce a 20% to30% power loss due to heat, which also must be taken into consideration.

When designing a solar power system with a battery back up, the designer must take into consideration appropriate location for the battery racks and room ventilation, to purge the hydrogen gas generated during the charging process. Sealed type batteries do not require special ventilation.

All DC wiring calculations discussed take into consideration losses resulting from solar exposure, battery cable current de-rating, and equipment current resistance requirements, as stipulated in NEC Code 690 articles.

Stand-Alone Hybrid Alternating Current Solar System with Stand-by Generator

A stand-alone hybrid solar power configuration is essentially identical to the DC solar power system discussed, except that it incorporates two additional components, as shown in Figure 2.4. The first component is an inverter. Inverters is a power electronic equipment that is designed to convert DC into AC. The second component is a stand-by emergency DC generator that will be discussed later.

Alternating Current Inverters. The principle mechanisms of DC to AC conversion consist of chopping or segmenting the DC current into specific portions,

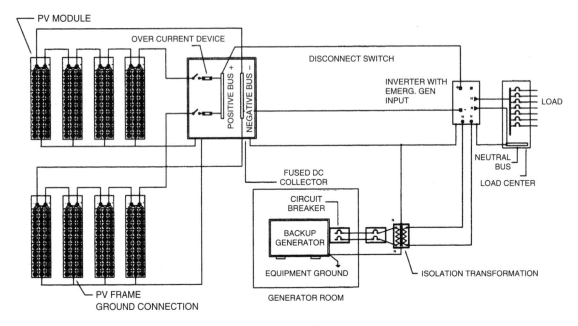

Figure 2.4 Stand alone hybrid solar power system with stand-by generator.

which are referred to as square waves, then filtering the square waves in such a fashion as to transform them into sinusoidal waveforms.

Any power waveform, when analyzed from mathematical point view, essentially consists of superimposition of many sinusoidal waveforms, referred to as harmonics. The first harmonic represents a pure sinusoidal waveform, which has a unit base wavelength, amplitude, and frequency of repetition over a unit of time called a cycle. Additional waveforms with higher cycles when superimposed on the base waveform add or subtract from the amplitude of the base sinusoidal waveform.

The resulting combined base waveform and higher harmonics produce a distorted wave shape that resembles distorted sinusoidal. The higher the harmonic content, the squarer the wave shape becomes.

Chopped DC output, derived from the solar power, is considered as a numerous superimposition of odd and even numbers of harmonics. To obtain a relatively clean sinusoidal output, most inverters employ electronic circuitry to filter a large number of harmonics.

Filter circuits consist of specially designed inductive and capacitor circuits that trap or block certain unwanted harmonics, the energy of which is dissipated as heat. Some types of inverters, mainly of earlier design technology, makes use of inductor coils to produce sinusoidal wave shapes.

In general DC to AC inverters are intricate electronic power conversion equipment, which are designed to convert DC to single or three phase currents that replicate the regular electrical services provided by utilities.

Special electronics within inverters, in addition to converting DC to AC current, are designed to regulate the output voltage, frequency, and current under specified load conditions. As discussed in the following sections, inverters also incorporate special electronics that allow them to automatically synchronize with other inverters when connected in parallel.

Most inverters, in addition to PV input power, accept auxiliary input power to form a stand-by DC generator, used to provide power when the battery voltage is dropped to a minimum level.

A special type of inverter, referred to as the GRID CONNECTED type, incorporates synchronization circuitry that allows the production of sinusoidal waveforms in unison with the electrical service grid. When the inverter is connected to the electrical service grid, it can effectively act as an AC power generation source.

Grid type inverters used in grid connected solar power systems are strictly regulated by utility agencies that provide net metering.

Some inverters incorporate an internal AC transfer switch that is capable of accepting an output from an AC type stand-by generator. In such designs, the inverters include special electronics that transform power from the generator.

Stand-by Generators.   A stand-by generators consist of an engine driven generator that is used to provide auxiliary power during solar blackouts or when the battery power discharge is reached to a minimum level. The output of the generator is connected to the auxiliary input of the inverter.

Engines that drive the motors operate with gasoline, diesel, natural gas, propane, or any type of fuel. Fuel tank sizes vary with the operational requirements. Most emergency generators incorporate under-chassis fuel tanks with sufficient fuel storage capacity to operate the generator up to 48 hours. Detached tanks could also be designed to hold much larger fuel reserves, which are usually located outside the engine room. In general, large fuel tanks include special fuel level monitoring and filtration systems.

As an option, the generators can be equipped with remote monitoring and annunciation panels that indicate power generation data, logging, and monitoring of engine functional and dynamic parameters, such as coolant temperature, oil pressure, and malfunction.

Engines also incorporate special electronic circuitry to regulate the generator output frequency, voltage, and power under specified load conditions.

All of the above design parameters also apply to AC type emergency generators.

Hybrid System Operation.   As discussed above, the DC output generated from the PV arrays and output of the DC generator can be simultaneously connected to a DC to AC inverter. The AC output of the inverter is in turn connected to an AC load distribution panel, which provides power to various loads by means of AC type over-current protection devices.

In all instances, solar power design engineers must ensure that all chassis of equipment and PV arrays, including stanchions and pedestals, are connected together via appropriate grounding conductors that are connected to a single point service ground bus bar, usually located within the vicinity of the main electrical service switchgear.

Grid Connected Solar Power Cogeneration System

With reference to Figure 2.5, a connected solar power diagram, the power cogeneration system configuration is similar to the hybrid system described above.

The essence of a grid-connected system is NET METERING. Standard service meters are odometer type counting wheels that record power consumption at a service point by means of a rotating disc, which is connected to the counting mechanism. The rotating discs operate by an electro-physical principal called Eddy Current, which consists of voltage and current measurement sensing coils that generate a proportional power measurement.

New electrical meters make use of digital electronic technology that register power measurement by solid state current and voltage sensing devices that convert analog measured values into binary values that are displayed on the meter bezels by LCD (liquid crystal) readouts.

In general, conventional meters only display power consumption that is the meter counting mechanism is unidirectional.

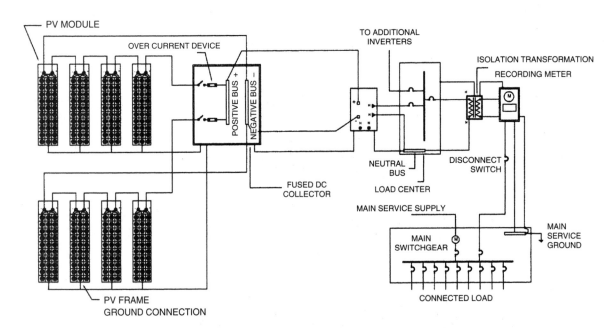

Figure 2.5 Grid connected solar power system.

Net Metering. The essential difference between a grid connected system and a stand-alone system is that inverters, which are connect to the main electrical service, must have an inherent line frequency synchronization capability to deliver the excess power to the grid.

Net meters, unlike conventional meters, have a capability to record consumed or generated power in an exclusive summation format, that is the recorded power registration is the net amount of power consumed—the total power used minus the amount of power that is produced by the solar power cogeneration system.

Net meters are supplied and installed by utility companies that provide grid connection service systems. Net-metered solar power cogenerators are subject to specific contractual agreements and are subsidized by state and municipal governmental agencies, such as the California Energy Commission (CEC).

Southern California Edison, Southern California Gas (Sempra Power), and San Diego Gas and Electric (SG&E), as well as principal municipalities, such as Los Angeles Department of Water and Power, are the major agencies that undertake distribution of State of California renewable energy rebate funds for various projects. When designing net metering solar power cogeneration systems, the solar power designers and their clients must familiarize themselves with the CEC rebate fund requirements.

Essential to any solar power implementation is the preliminary design and economic feasibility study that is essential for project cost justification and return on investment analysis. The first step of the study usually entails a close coordination with the architect in charge and the electrical engineer engineering consultant. A preliminary PV array layout and a computer aided shading study are essential for providing the required foundation for the design.

Based on the above study, the solar power engineer must undertake an econometrics study to verify the validity and justification of the investment. Upon completion of the study, the solar engineer must assist the client to complete the required CEC rebate application forms and submit it to the service agency responsible for the energy cogeneration program.

Grid Connection Isolation Transformer. In order to prevent spurious noise transfer from grid to the solar power system electronics, a delta-y isolation transformer is placed between the main service switchgear disconnects switch and the inverters.

The delta winding of the isolation transformer, which is connected to the service bus, circulates noise harmonics in the winding and dissipates the energy as heat.

The isolation transformers are also used to convert or match the inverter output voltages to the grid. Most often, in commercial installations, inverter output voltages range from 208 V to 230 V (three phase), which must be connected to an electric service grid that supplies 277/480 V power.

Central Monitoring and Logging System Requirements

In large commercial solar power cogeneration systems, power production from the PV arrays is monitored by a central monitoring system that provides a log of operation performance parameters. The central monitoring station consists of a PC type computer that retrieves operational parameters from group of solar power inverters by means of an RS-232 interface, a power line carrier, or wireless communication systems. Upon reception of performance parameters, a supervisory software program processes the information and provides data in display or print format. Supervisory data obtained from the filed can also be accessed from distant locations through web networking. Some examples of monitored data include the following.

- Weather monitoring data
- Temperature
- Wind velocity and direction
- Sun intensity
- Solar power output
- Inverter output
- Total system performance and malfunction
- Direct current power production
- Alternating current power production
- Accumulated, daily, monthly, and yearly power production

Monitoring System General Description

The following central monitoring system reflects the actual configuration of the Water and Life Museum project, located in Hemet California and designed by the author. This state of the art monitoring system provides a real-time interactive display for education and understanding of photovoltaic and the solar electric installation as well as monitoring the solar electric system for maintenance and troubleshooting purposes.

The system is assembled from wireless inverter data transmitters, weather station, data storage computer, and data display computer with a 26" LCD-kiosk. In the above configuration, the inverters, which are connected in parallel, output data to wireless transmitters located in their close proximity. Wireless transmitters throughout the site transmit data to a single central receiver located in a central data gathering and monitoring center, as shown in Figure 2.6.

The received data is stored and analyzed using the sophisticated software in a supervisory computer that also serves as a data-maintenance interface

Figure 2.6 Sun tracker solar monitoring system (Courtesy of Schott Solar)

for the overall solar power system. A weather station also transmits weather related information to the central computer.

The stored data is analyzed and forwarded to a display computer that is used for data presentation and also stores information, such as video, sound, pictures, and text file data.

Displayed Information

A standard display will usually incorporate a looping background of pictures, from the site, graphical overlays of the power generation in watts and watt-hours for each building and the environmental impact from the solar system. The display also shows current meteorological conditions.

Displayed data in general should include the following combination of items, described below.

1. Project location (On globe coordinates-zoom in-out)
2. Current and historic weather conditions
3. Current positions of Sun / Moon; Date / Time (Local and Global)
4. Power generation – total system and/or individual buildings/inverters
5. Historic power generation

6. Solar system environmental Impact
7. Looping background solar system photos and videos, from drawing board to operation.
8. Educational power point presentations:
   a. About solar electric power.
   b. Promoting renewable energy and its impact.
   c. Any other display information supplied by the customer.

The display should also be programmed periodically to show additional information related to building energy management or schedule of maintenance relevant to the project.

Component Specifications

Weather Station Transmitted Data.

- Air Temperature
- Solar cell temperature
- Wind Speed
- Wind Direction
- Sun intensity pyrometer

Inverter Monitoring Transmitted Data.
Each inverter incorporates a watt-hour transducer with signal output. Each system measures the following.

- Voltage (DC and AC)
- Current (DC and AC)
- Power (DC and AC)
- AC Frequency
- Watt-hour accumulation
- Inverter error code and operation

Central Monitoring Computer

- Min. 1.6 GHz Computer
- 256 Ram
- 20 GB hard drive
- Windows XP operating system and required software

Wireless Transmission System Specification

- Switch selectable RS-232/422/485
- Software selectable 1200 bps to 57,600 bps

- Seven hop sequences share 25 frequencies
- Frequency hopping, 902 MHz to 928 MHz, direct FM
- Point-to-multipoint, point-to-point multi-drop transparent

Data Logging System and Software – Sunny Boy Control

- Sunny data control hardware and software
- Sun viewer display software

Animated Video and Interactive Programming

- Graphical program builder
- Animated video and interactive programming is an interactive animated character that is programmed to display and explain the measurements.
- Customizable chart attributes, such as labels, trace color and thickness, and axis scale, limits, and ticks

Interactive Display System

- 26" Flat Panel LCD
- 17" Touch screen display
- Minimum of a 1.6 GHz Computer, 256 Ram, 20 GB hard drive
- Windows XP operating system with required software

Ground Mount Photovoltaic Module Installation and Support Structures

Ground mount outdoor photovoltaic array installations can be configured in a wide variety of ways. The most important factor when installing solar power modules is PV orientation and panel incline. A ground mount solar power instillation is shown in Figure 2.7.

In general maximum power from a PV modules is obtained when the angle of the solar rays are impinged directly on to the surface of the panels in perpendicular (90 degrees). Since sunray angles vary seasonally throughout the year, the optimum average tilt angle for obtaining the maximum output power is approximately local latitude minus nine or ten degrees (see Appendix – B for typical tilt angle installations for Los Angeles, Daggett, Santa Monica, Fresno, and San Diego, California).

In the Northern Hemisphere, PV modules are mounted in north-south tilt (high end north) and in a south-north tilt in the southern hemisphere.

To attain the required angle, solar panels are generally secured on tilted prefabricated or field constructed frames that use rust proof railings, such as

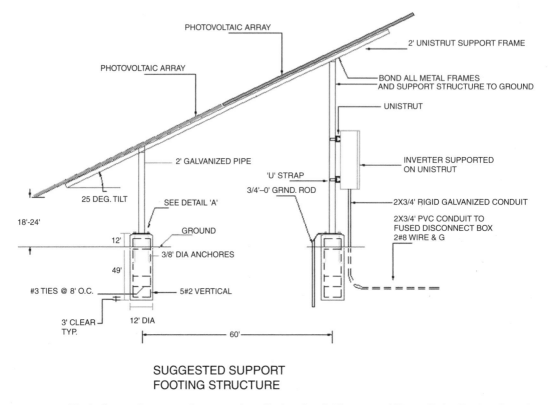

Figure 2.7 Typical ground-mount solar power installation detail (Courtesy of Vector Delta Design Group)

galvanized UNISTRUT or commercially available aluminum or stainless steel angle channels, and fastening hardware, such as nuts, bolts, and washers.

When installing solar support pedestals, also known as stanchions, attention must be paid to structural design requirements. Solar power stanchions and pedestals must be designed by a qualified registered professional engineer. Solar support structures must take into consideration prevailing geographic and atmospheric conditions, such as maximum wind gusts, flood conditions, and soil erosion.

Typical ground mount solar power installation includes agricultural grounds, parks and outdoor recreational facilities, car ports, sanitariums, and large commercial solar power generating facilities, also known as solar farms and shown in Figure 2.8, mostly owned and operated by electric energy generating entities such as Edison. Prior to installing a solar power system, structural and electrical plans must be reviewed by local electrical service authorities, such as building and safety departments. Solar power installation must be undertaken by a qualified licensed electrical contractor with special expertise in solar power installations.

Solar mounting support system profile, shown in Figure 2.8, consists of galvanized Unistrut railing frame that is field assembled with standard commercially available manufactured components used in the construction industry. Basic frame components include, 2-inch galvanized Unistrut channel, 90-degree and "T" type connectors, spring type channel nuts and bolts, and panel hold down "T" type or fender washer.

The main frame that supports the PV modules, are welded or bolted to a set of galvanized rigid metal round pipes or square channels. Foundation support is built from 12-inch to 18-inch diameter re-enforced concrete cast in a sauna tube. Metal support structure is secured to the concrete footing by means of expansion bolts. Depth of the footing and dimensions of channel hardware and method of PV frame attachment are designed by a qualified structural engineer.

A typical solar power support structural design should withstand wind gusts from 80 mph to 120 mph. Prefabricated structures that are specifically design for solar power applications are available from a number of manufacturers. Prefabricated solar power support structures, although somewhat more expensive, are usually designed to withstand 120 mph wind gusts and are manufactured from stainless steel, aluminum, or galvanized steel materials.

Figure 2.8 A typical solar power farm (Courtesy of Shell Solar)

Roof Mount Installations

Roof mount solar power installations comprise of either tilted or flat type roof support structures or a combination of both. Installation hardware and methodologies also differ depending weather the building already exists or is a new construction. Roof attachment hardware material also varies for wood base and concrete constructions.

Wood Constructed Roofing

In new construction, PV support system installation is relatively simple since locations of solar array frame pods, which are usually secured on roof rafters, can be readily identified.

Prefabricated roof-mount stands that support railings and associated hardware, such as fasteners, are commercially available from a number of manufacturers. Solar power support platforms are specifically designed to meet physical configuration requirements for various types of PV manufacturers.

Some PV installation, such as in Figure 2.9, have been designed for direct mounting on roof framing rafters without use of specialty railing or support hardware. As mentioned earlier, when installing roof mount solar panels, care must be taken to ensure proper directional tilt requirement.

An important factor, also to be considered, is that solar power installations, whether ground or roof mounted, should be located in areas free of shades that may be cast by adjacent buildings, trees, or air conditioning equipment. In the event of un-avoidable shading situations, solar power PV location, tilt angle, and stanchion separations should be analyzed to prevent cross shading.

Lightweight Construction Concrete Type Roofing

Solar power installation PV support systems for concrete roofs are configured from prefabricated support stands and railing systems, similar to the ones used in wooden roof structures. Stanchions are anchored to the roof by means of rust resistant expansion anchors and fasteners.

In order to prevent water leakage resulting from roof penetration, both wood and concrete standoff support pipe anchors are thoroughly sealed with water proofing compounds. Each standoff support is fitted with thermoplastic boots that are in turn thermally welded to roof cover material, such as single ply PVC.

Photovoltaic Stanchion and Support Structure
Tilt Angle

As discussed above, in order to obtain maximum output from the solar power systems, PV modules or arrays must have an optimum tilt angle that will ensure a perpendicular exposure to sunrays.

When installing rows or solar arrays, spacing between stanchions must be such that there should not be any cross shading. When designing solar power

Figure 2.9 Solar power slate system (Courtesy of Atlantis Energy)

array layout, the available roof area is divided into a template format that compartmentalizes rows or columns of PV arrays.

Electric Shock Hazard and Safety Considerations

Power arrays, while exposed to the sun, can produce several hundreds of volts of DC power. Any contact with an exposed or uninsulated component of the PV array can produce serious burns and fatal electric shock. As such, the electrical wiring design and installation methodology are subject to rigorous guidelines, which are outlined in NEC Code Article 690 discussed below.

System components, such as over current devices, breaker, disconnect switches and enclosures, are specifically rated for the application. All equipment that is subject to maintenance and repair is marked with special caution and safety warning tags to prevent inadvertent exposure to hazard (see Appendix – B for typical sign details).

Shock Hazard to Firefighters

An important safety provision, which has been overlooked in the past, has been collaboration with local fire departments when designing roof mount solar power systems on wood structure. In the event of fire emergency possibility of serious shock hazard to firefighters will exist in instances when roof penetration becomes necessary.

Under operational conditions, when solar power systems actively generate power, a line carrying current at several hundred volts could pose serious burn or bodily injury and electric shock, if exposed to during roof demolition process. To prevent injury under fire hazard conditions, all roof mount equipment that can be accessed must be clearly identified with large RED on WHITE labels. Additionally, the input to the inverter from the PV collector boxes must be equipped with a crowbar disconnect switch that will short the output of all solar arrays simultaneously.

Another design consideration, whenever economically feasible, solar array groups should incorporate shorting contacts (normally closed) that could be activated from a multi-contact relay that could by engaged during emergency conditions. Crowbar circuitry is not needed.

Designing a Typical Residential Solar Power System

A typical residential solar power system configuration will consist of system components, as shown in Figures 2.10 through 2.13. Principal components of the system consist of the following.

- Solar photovoltaic panels (PV)
- Collector boxes, which may include fuses, disconnect switches, and lightning protection devices
- Charge controller battery pack PV support structure and hardware
- Miscellaneous components, such as electrical conduits or wires and grounding hardware

Additional expenses associated with the solar power system will include installation labor and associated electrical installation permits.

To proceed with the design, first the residential power consumption component schedule must be compiled to represent exact daily power requirements of a residence. Electrical power consuming items in the above referenced schedule should include but not limited to the following.

- Lighting load—3 W per square foot
- Laundry load—about 1500 W

Figure 2.10 Residential solar power installation (Photo courtesy of Grant Electric, engineered by Vector Delta Design Group, Inc.)

- Refrigerator load—800 W
- General receptacle load, including small appliances—1500 W
- Cooling or heating load—6 W per square foot

Multiply total of the above load by 25% to 30%. A simpler method is to account for one watt of power per square foot of the building, excluding the basement or the garage. This is an approximate project of load components, total sums of which must be multiplied by 25% to 30% to increase the security margin figure.

In general, an average residential house with 2,000 square foot of living area may require a 2 kW solar power system. When using a battery backup, a 30% derating must be applied, which augments the solar power system to 2,500 W.

In order to size the battery bank, one must decide how many hours the overall power demand must be sustained during the absence of sun or insulation.

To figure out the ampere-hour capacity of the battery storage system, the aggregate wattage worked out above must be divided by the voltage and then

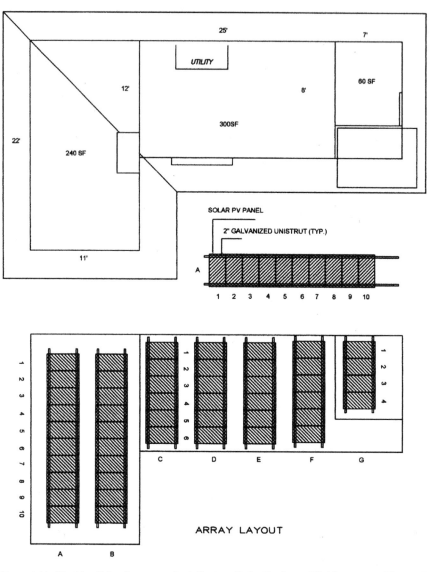

Figure 2.11 Residential solar power installation, Palm Springs, CA (Courtesy of Vector Delta Design Group, Inc)

multiplied by the back up supply hours. For example at 120 V AC, the amperes produced by the solar power system, which is stored in the battery bank, will be approximately 20 A, to maintain power backup for 6 hours, the battery system must be sized at about 160 Ah. The sizing rule of thumb is essentially appropriate for an average residential unit. Larger residential units

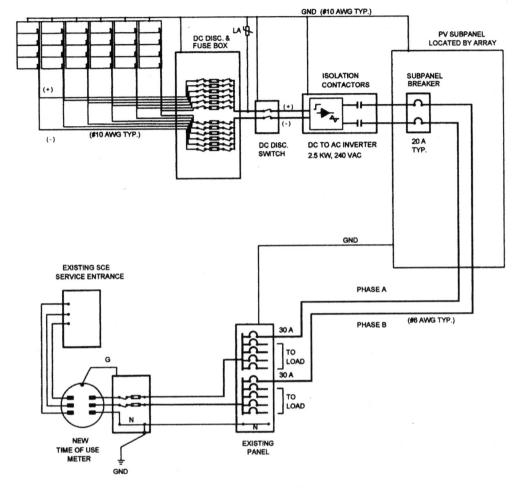

Figure 2.12 Wiring diagram for a Palm Springs residential project

may qualify for up to 10,000 W of solar power rebate; however, battery backup systems are not subject to the California Energy Commission rebate program.

Example of Typical Solar Power System Design and Installations Plans for a Single Residential Unit

The following project represents a complete design and estimating procedure for a small single-family residential solar power system. In order to establish requirements of a solar power system, the design engineer must establish the residential power demand calculations based on National Electrical Code design guideline as shown below.

Figure 2.13 Xantrex Inverter System from a Palm Springs residential project

Project location: Palm Springs, California
Electrical Engineer Consultant
Vector Delta Design Group, Inc.
2325 Bonita Dr
Glendale, CA 91208
Phone: (818) 241-7479

Solar Power Contractor
Grant Electric
16461 Sherman Way
Van Nuys, CA 91406
Phone: 818-375-1977

Project Design Criteria.   Residential power demand for a single-family dwelling involves specific limits of energy use allocations for area lighting, kitchen appliances, laundry, and air conditioning systems. For example, the allowed maximum lighting power consumption is 3 watts per square foot of habitable area. The laundry load allowed is 1,500 watts for the washer and dryer

The first 3,000 watts of the total combined lighting and laundry loads are accounted at 100% and the remaining balance is applied at 35%. The total appliance loads when exceeding quantity of 5 are also derated by 25%. Air conditioning and other loads such as pool, sauna, and Jacuzzi are applied at their 100% value.

The demand load calculation of a 1,400 square foot residential dwelling shown below indicates a continuous demand load of about 3,000 watts per hour. If it is assumed that the residence is fully occupied and is in use for 12 hours a day, the total daily demand load translates into 36,000 watt/hours per day.

Since the average daily insolation in Southern California is about 5.5 hours, the approximate solar power system required to satisfy the daily demand load will be about 6,000 watts. Occupancies which are not fully inhabited throughout the day may require somewhat smaller system.

In general, an average 8 hours of habitation time should be used for sizing the solar power system, which in this example would yield a total daily power demand of 24,000 watt hours, that in turn translates into a 4,000 watt solar power system.

Commercial Application

The following plans are provided for illustration purposes only. Actual design criteria and calculations may vary depending on the geographic location of the project, cost of labor, and materials, which can significantly vary from one project to another. The following projects were collaborations among the identified organizations.

TCA Arshag DICKranian Armenian School

Project Location: Hollywood, California

Architect
Garo Minassian and Associates
140 Acari Dr
Los Angeles, CA 90049
Phone: (310) 472-8683

Electrical Engineer Consultant
Vector Delta Design Group, Inc.
2325 Bonita Dr
Glendale, CA 91208
Phone: (818) 241-7479

Solar Power Contractor
Grant Electric
16461 Sherman Way
Van Nuys, CA 91406
Phone: (818) 375-1977

Project Design Criteria.   The project described below is a 70 kW roof mount solar power cogeneration system, which was completed in 2004. Design and estimating procedures of this project are similar to the residence in Palm Springs. Diagrams and pictures of this project are shown in Figures 2.14 through 2.20.

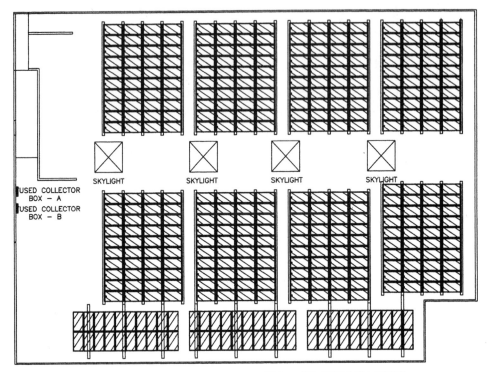

ROOF MOUNT PV ARRAY LAYOUT – TCA DICKRANIAN SCHOOL

Figure 2.14 Roof-mount solar power system for the TCA A. Dickranian Armenian School, Hollywood, CA

In order to establish requirements of a solar power system, the design engineer must establish the commercial power demand calculations based on National Electrical Code design guidelines. The power demand estimate for this project is shown in the solar power estimate that appears in Chart 2.1. Power demand calculations for commercial systems depend on the project use, which are unique to each application. Power demand calculations for this project were calculated to be about 280 kWh. The solar power installed represents about 25% of the total demand load. Since the school is closed during summer, energy credited cumulated for three months is expected to augment the overall solar power cogeneration contribution to about 35% of the overall demand.

This project was commissioned in March 2005 and has been operating at optimum capacity, providing a substantial amount of the lighting and power requirements of the school. Fifty percent of the overall installed cost of the

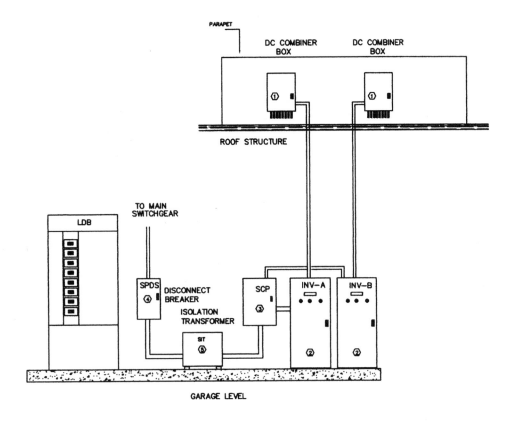

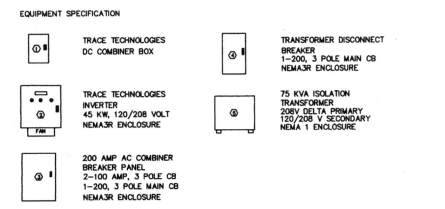

EQUIPMENT SPECIFICATION

TRACE TECHNOLOGIES
DC COMBINER BOX

TRANSFORMER DISCONNECT
BREAKER
1-200, 3 POLE MAIN CB
NEMA3R ENCLOSURE

TRACE TECHNOLOGIES
INVERTER
45 KW, 120/208 VOLT
NEMA3R ENCLOSURE
FAN

75 KVA ISOLATION
TRANSFORMER
208V DELTA PRIMARY
120/208 V SECONDARY
NEMA 1 ENCLOSURE

200 AMP AC COMBINER
BREAKER PANEL
2-100 AMP, 3 POLE CB
1-200, 3 POLE MAIN CB
NEMA3R ENCLOSURE

Figure 2.15 Solar power cogeneration system diagram for TCA A. Dickranian Armenian School

Figure 2.16 Inverter equipment for TCA A. Dickranian Armenian School's solar power cogeneration system diagram

Figure 2.17   TCA A. Dickranian Armenian School's emergency generator equipment

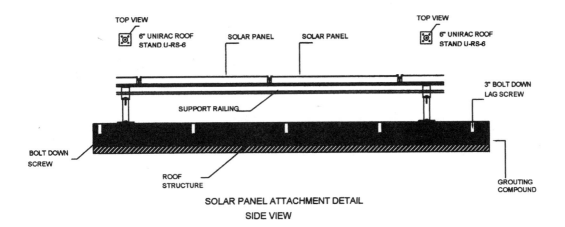

TOP VIEW
6" UNIRAC ROOF STAND U-RS-6

SOLAR PANEL   SOLAR PANEL

TOP VIEW
6" UNIRAC ROOF STAND U-RS-6

3" BOLT DOWN
LAG SCREW

SUPPORT RAILING

BOLT DOWN
SCREW

ROOF
STRUCTURE

GROUTING
COMPOUND

SOLAR PANEL ATTACHMENT DETAIL
SIDE VIEW

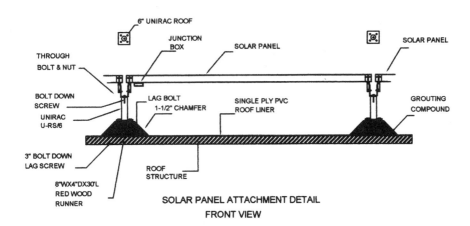

6" UNIRAC ROOF

JUNCTION
BOX

SOLAR PANEL

SOLAR PANEL

THROUGH
BOLT & NUT

BOLT DOWN
SCREW

UNIRAC
U-RS/6

3" BOLT DOWN
LAG SCREW

8"WX4"DX30'L
RED WOOD
RUNNER

LAG BOLT
1-1/2" CHAMFER

SINGLE PLY PVC
ROOF LINER

GROUTING
COMPOUND

ROOF
STRUCTURE

SOLAR PANEL ATTACHMENT DETAIL
FRONT VIEW

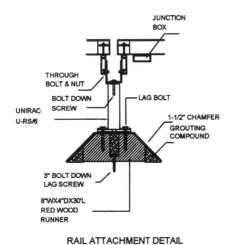

JUNCTION
BOX

THROUGH
BOLT & NUT

BOLT DOWN
SCREW

UNIRAC
U-RS/6

LAG BOLT

1-1/2" CHAMFER
GROUTING
COMPOUND

3" BOLT DOWN
LAG SCREW

8"WX4"DX30'L
RED WOOD
RUNNER

RAIL ATTACHMENT DETAIL

Figure 2.18 Solar panel support platform installation detail (Courtesy of Vector Delta Design Group, Inc.)

Figure 2.19 Roof mount support stems

Figure 2.20 Roof mounted solar cogeneration system at TCA A. Dickranian School, Hollywood, CA (Courtesy of Vector Delta Design Group, Inc.)

project was paid for by the CEC rebate, which was redeemed in a few weeks, upon completion inspection. The costs of and credits for this project are shown in the second part of Chart 2.1.

Solar Power Farm Cogeneration System

Project Location: Boron, California
Electrical Engineer Consultant
Vector Delta Design Group, Inc.
2325 Bonita Dr
Glendale, CA 91208
Phone: (818) 241-7479

Solar Power Contractor
Grant Electric
16461 Sherman Way
Van Nuys, CA 91406
Phone: (818) 375-1977

Project Design Criteria.   The project described below is a 200 kW solar power farm cogeneration system, which was completed in 2003. Design and estimating procedures of this project are similar to the two projects already described.

In view of vast project terrain, this project was constructed by use of relatively inexpensive lower efficiency film technology PV cells that have an estimated efficiency of about 8%. Frameless PV panels were secured on 2-inch Unistrut channels, which were mounted on telephone poles that penetrated deep within the desert sand. Power produced from the solar farm is being used by the local Indian reservation. The project is shown in Figures 2.21 and 2.22.

Water + Life Museum

Project Location: Hemet, California

Architects	Electrical Engineer Consultant	Solar Power Contractor
Lehrer Gangi, Architect	Vector Delta Design Group, Inc.	Morrow Meadows
Michael Lehrer, AIA	2325 Bonita Dr	231 Benton Ct
Mark Gangi, AIA	Glendale, CA 91208	City of Industry, CA 91789
239 East Palm Ave	Phone: (818) 241-7479	Phone: (909) 598-7700
Burbank, CA 91502		
Phone: (818) 845-3170		

Project Description.   This project is located in Hemet, CA, an hour-and-a-half driving distance from downtown Los Angeles (Figures 2-23 through 2-29). It consists of a 150-acre campus with a Water Education Museum, sponsored by Metropolitan Water District, Water Education Board; Archaeology and Pale-

SOLAR POWER ESTIMATE - TCA A DICKRANIAN ARMENIAN SCHOOL

TOTAL AREA	10000
67% USE	6310
PV VOLTAGE PV WATTS	24
MAX PV WATTS ARRAY	134.9 PTC
VOLTS ARRAY AMPS	240
LATITUDE	−116.52
LONGITUDE	33.77
TILT ANGLE SINE	5.62
COSINE	63%
% AREA USAGE	62.75
PANEL LENGTH-INCHES	32
PANEL WIDTH-INCHES	15
TILT ANGLE-DEGREES	32.0
TILT BASE-INCHES	15
TILT HEIGHT	8
STANCHION SPACING-INCHES	180
AREA WIDTH-FEET	360
AREA LENGTH-FEET	6310
AREA SQUARE FEET	32.5
PANEL WIDTH-INCHES SPACING	10
PANELS IN ARRAY	27
ARRAY LENGTH IN FEET	6
ARRAY WIDTH	155
ARRAY IN SQUARE FOOT	41
NUMBER OF ARRAYS	407
NUMBER OF PV UNITS	54873 PTC
DC WATTS PER ARRAY	6%
TOTAL DC WATTS (PTC)	12%
DC-AC INVERTER LOSS MISCELLANEOUS POWER	18%
LOSSES TOTAL LOSS	82%
CONVERSION EFFICIENCY	44996
SPECIFIC YIELD CAPACITY-AC WATTS INVERTER	135%
CAPACITY MULTIPLIER INVERTER CALCULATED SIZE	61
Kw INVERTER NOMINAL SIZE-kW	70

INITIAL COSTS AND CREDITS

	Hrs	Rate	Total
Engineering rate	8	$150.00	$ 1,200
Site investigation	4	$150.00	$ 600
Preliminary design coordination	24	$150.00	$ 3,600
Report preparation	8	$150.00	$ 1,200
Travel and accommodation	1	$ 500	$ 500
Other		$	
Subtotal			$ 5,900

Development

	Hrs	Rate	Total
Permits and rebate applications	16	$150.00	$ 2,400
Project management and coordination	24	$150.00	$ 3,600
Travel expenses		$ -	$
MATERIAL	1	$500.00	$ 500
Subtotal			$ 6,500

Chart 2.1 Engineering estimate for the TCA A. Dickranian Armenian School

Engineering

	Hrs	Rate	Total
PV systems design	72	$ 150	$ 10,800
Architectural design	10	$ 150	$ 1,500
Structural design	12	$ 150	$ 1,800
Electrical design	160	$ 150	$ 24,000
Tenders and contracting	8	$ 150	$ 1,200
Construction supervision	12	$ 150	$ 1,800
Training manuals	8	$ 150	$ 1,200
Subtotal			$ 42,300

Renewable energy equipment	A kW-DC	Cost	Total
PV modules - per kWh-DC	55	$ 3,000	$ 164,619
Transportation-per project	1	$ 500	$ 500.00
Other			
Tax		8.25%	$ 13,581
Subtotal			$ 178,700

Installation equipment

	kW-DC	Cost	Total
PV module support structure- per kWh	55	$ 1,000	$ 54,873
Transformation kWh	0		$
Inverter-per kWh	70	$ 500	$ 35,000
Electrical materials-per kW	70	$ 500	$ 35,000
System installation labor-per kWh	70	$ 828	$ 57,960
Transportation-per project	1	$ 1,000	$ 1,000.00
Other			
Tax		8.25%	$ 10,302
Subtotal			$ 194,135

Total cost $428,736.00

Cost per PTC watts $7.81

Chart 2.1 *Continued*

ontology Museum, sponsored by City of Hemet; several lecture halls; a book store; cafeteria; and two auditoriums.

In this installation photovoltaic panels are assembled on specially pre-fabricated sled type support structures which do not require roof penetration. Roof mount PV arrays are strapped together with connective ties which for large island platforms which can withstand 120 mile per hour winds.

A group of three PV assemblies with an output power capacity of about 6 kW are connected to a dedicated inverter. Each inverter assembly on the

Figure 2.21 Boron solar project (Courtesy of Grant Electric)

Figure 2.22 Boron inverter system (Courtesy of Grant Electric)

Figure 2.23 Water and Life Museum photovoltaic panel support assemble (Courtesy of Lehrer Gangi Architects and engineered by Vector Delta Design Group, Inc.)

Figure 2.24 Water and Life Museum photovoltaic panel support assembly (Courtesy of Vector Delta Design Group, Inc.)

Figure 2.25 Water and Life Museum partial photovoltaic panel array (Courtesy of Vector Delta Design Group, Inc.)

Figure 2.26 Water and Life Museum photovoltaic panel module inter-wiring (Courtesy of Vector Delta Design Group, Inc.)

Figure 2.27 Water and Life Museum Sunny Boy inverter assembly (Courtesy of Vector Delta Design Group, Inc.)

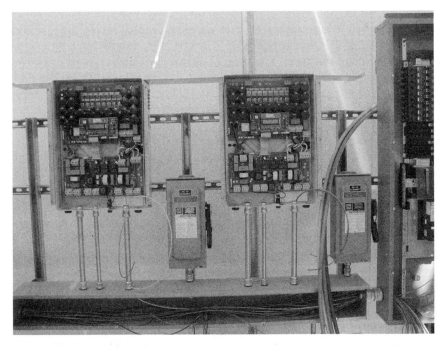

Figure 2.28 Water and Life Museum inverter electronics (Courtesy of Vector Delta Design Group, Inc.)

Figure 2.29 Water and Life Museum emergency generator system (Courtesy of Vector Delta Design Group, Inc.)

support sled incorporates over current protective circuitry, fusing, and power collection bussing terminals. The inverter chosen for this project includes all technology features, such as islanding, AC power isolation, voltage, and frequency synchronization required for grid connectivity. In addition, the inverters are also equipped with wireless monitoring transmitter, which can relay various performance and fault monitoring parameters to a centrally located data acquisition system.

Strategically located AC subpanels installed on rooftops cumulate the aggregated AC power outputs from inverters. Outputs of subpanels are in turn cumulated by a main AC collector panel, output of which are connected to a central collector distribution panel located within the vicinity of the main service switchgear. Grid connection of the central AC collector panel to the main service bus is accomplished by means of a fused disconnect switch and a net meter.

The central supervisory system gathers and displays the following data.

- Project location (on globe coordinates, zoom in and out)
- Current and historic weather conditions
- Current positions of Sun and Moon; date and time (local and global)
- Power generation – total system or individual buildings and inverters
- Historic power generation

- Solar system environmental impact
- System graphic configuration data.
- Educational power point presentations
- Temperature
- Wind velocity and direction
- Sun intensity
- Solar power output
- Inverter output
- Total system performance and malfunction
- Direct current power production
- Alternating current power production
- Accumulated daily, monthly, and yearly power production

Economics of Solar Power Systems

Perhaps the most important task of a solar power engineer is to conduct preliminary engineering and financial feasibility studies, necessary for establishing the actual design. The essence of the feasibility study is to project estimated power generation and cost of installation for the life span of the project. The feasibility study is conducted as a first step in determining the limitations of the solar project's power production and return on investment, without expending a substantial amount of engineering and manpower effort. The steps needed to conduct the preliminary engineering and financial study is as follows.

Preliminary Engineering Design

Conduct a field survey of the existing roof or mounting area. For new projects, review the available roof-mount area and mounting landscape. Care must be taken to ensure that there are no mechanical, construction, or natural structures that could cast a shadow on the solar panels. Shades from trees and sap drops could create unwanted loss of energy production. One of the solar photovoltaic modules in a chain, when shaded, could act as resistive element that will alter the current and voltage output of the whole array.

Always consult with the architect to ensure that installation of solar panels will not interfere with the roof mount solar window, vents, and air conditioning unit duct works. The architect must also take into consideration roof penetrations, installed weight, anchoring, and seismic requirements.

Upon establishment of solar power area clearances, the solar power designer must prepare a set of electronic templates representing standard array configuration assemblies. Solar array templates then could be used to establish a desirable output of direct current (DC) power. It should be noted that, when laying blocks of PV arrays, consideration must be given to desirable tilt inclination to avoid cross shadowing. In some instances, the designer must also consider trading solar power output efficiency to maximize the power output production. As mentioned in a previous chapter, the most desirable mounting position for a PV module that must be exposed to a maximum solar insolation is about latitude minus 10 degrees. For example, the optimum tilt angle in New York will be 39 degrees; whereas, in Los Angeles, it will be about 25 degrees to 27 degrees. The sun exposure caused by various insolation tilts over the course of the year in Los Angeles is shown in Figures 3.1 through 3.5. To avoid cross shading, the adjacent profiles of two solar rows of arrays could be determined by simple trigonometry that could determine the geometry of the tilt by the angle of the associated sine (shading height) and cosine (tandem array separation space) of the support structure incline. It should be noted that flatly laid solar photovoltaic arrays may incur about a 9% to 11% of power loss, but the number of installed panels could exceed 30% to 40% on the same mounting space.

An important design criteria when laying out solar arrays is grouping and aggregate number of PV modules that could provide adequate series connected

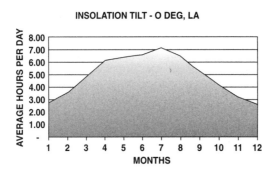

Figure 3.1   Insolation graph for Los Angeles photovoltaic panels mounted at 0 degree tile angle

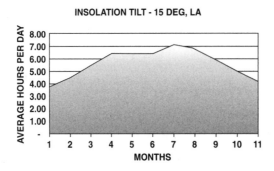

Figure 3.2   Insolation graph for Los Angeles photovoltaic panels mounted at −5 degree tile angle

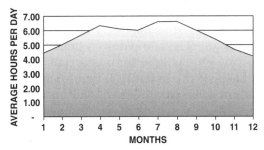

Figure 3.3 Insolation graph for Los Angeles photovoltaic panels mounted at 33.9 degree tile angle

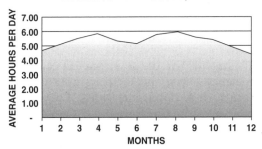

Figure 3.4 Insolation graph for Los Angeles photovoltaic panels mounted at +15 degree tile angle

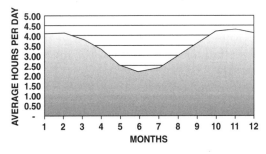

Figure 3.5 Insolation graph for Los Angeles photovoltaic panels mounted at −90 degree tile angle

voltages and current required by inverter specifications. Most inverters allow certain margins for DC inputs that are specific to make and model of a manufactured unit. Inverter power capacities may vary from few hundred to many thousands of watts. When designing a solar power system, the designer should decide about the use of specific PV and inverter makes and models in advance, thereby establishing the basis of the overall configuration. It is not uncommon to have different sizes of solar power arrays and matching inverters on the same installation. In fact, in some instances, the designer may for unavoidable occurrences of shading, decide to limit the size of the array to be as minimal as possible, thus limiting the number of PV units in the array, which may require a small size power capacity inverter. The most essential factor that must be taken into consideration is to ensure that all inverters used in the solar power system are completely compatible and are of the same make and manufacture.

When laying out the PV arrays, care should be taken to allow sufficient access to array clusters for maintenance and cleaning purposes. In order to avoid deterioration of power output, solar arrays must be washed and rinsed periodically. Adequately spaced hose bibs should be installed on rooftops to facilitate flushing the PV units in the evening time only when power output is below margin of shock hazard.

Upon completing the PV layout, the designer should count the total number of solar power system components, and by using a rule of thumb must arrive at a unity cost estimate such as dollars per watt of power, that will make it possible to approximate cost of the total project. In general net power output from power PV arrays, when converted to AC power, must be subjected to a number of factors that can degrade the output efficiency of the system. The California Energy Commission (CEC) rates each manufacturer approved PV units by a special power output performance factor referred to as PTC (Power Test Condition). This figure of merit is derived for each make and model of PV from extensive performance testing under various climatic conditions, which takes place in a specially certified laboratory environment.

Design parameters that contribute towards reduced system efficiency are as follows.

- Geographic location, latitude, longitude, associated yearly average insolation, and temperature variations—PV units work more efficiently under sunny but cool temperatures.
- Building orientation (North, South)
- Roof or support structure tilt
- Inverter efficiency
- Isolation transformer efficiency
- Direct current (DC) and alternating current (AC) wiring losses resulted from density of wires in conduits, solar power exposure, long runs, poor or loose

or corroded connectivity of wires, and AC power transmission to the isolation transformers

■ Poor maintenance and dust and grime collection on the PV modules

Meteorological Data

When designing floor mount solar power systems, the designer must investigate natural calamities such as extreme wind gusts, periodic or seasonal flooding, and snow precipitation. For meteorological data contact NASA Surface Meteorology and Solar Energy Data Set web site. To search for meteorological information from the above web site, for each geographic location, the inquirer must provide area latitude and longitude. For example to obtain data for Los Angeles, California, at latitude 34.09 and longitude – 118.4, the statistical data provided will include the following recorded information for each month of the year for the past 10 years.

■ Average daily radiation on horizontal surface ($kWh/m^2/day$)

■ Average temperature (Celsius)

■ Average wind speed (m/sec)

To obtain longitude and latitude information for a geographic area refer to the following web site, http://www.census.gov/cgi-bin/gazetter. Typical examples of latitudes for metropolitan areas are as follows.

■ Los Angeles, California – 34.09 N/ 118.40 W

■ Toronto, Canada – 43.67 / -79.38

■ Palm Springs, California – 33.7 N/ 116.52 W

■ San Diego, California – 32.82N/117.10 W

To obtain Ground surface Site Surface Insolation Measurements refer to http://eosweb.lac.nasa.gov/sse.

A certified registered structural engineer must design all solar power installation platforms and footings. Upon completing and integrating the above preliminary design parameters, the design engineer must conduct feasibility analysis of the subject solar power cogeneration project. Some of the essential cost components of a solar power system required for final analysis are as follows.

■ Solar PV module cost (dollars per DC watts)

■ Support structure hardware

■ Electrical devices and hardware, such as inverters, isolation transformers, and lightning protection devices

- Electrical wiring conduits, cables, and grounding wires.
- Material transport and storage
- Federal and state taxes
- Labor wages (prevailing or non-prevailing) and site supervision
- Engineering design, which includes electrical, architectural, and structural disciplines
- Permit fees
- Maintenance training manuals and instructor time
- Maintenance and warrantee
- Spare parts and components
- Testing and commissioning
- Overhead and profit
- Construction bond and liability insurance
- Mobilization cost, site office, and utility expenses
- Liquidated damages

Energy Cost Factor

Upon completion of the preliminary engineering study and solar power generation potential, the designer must evaluate present and project future cost of the electric energy for the entire life span of the solar power system.

To determine the present value of the electric energy cost for an existing building, it is required to evaluate the actual electric bills for past two years. It should be noted that general cost per kilowatt hour of energy provided by service providers consists of an average of numerous charges such as commissioning, decommissioning, bulk purchase, and other miscellaneous cost items that generally appear on the electric bills (that vary seasonally) but go unnoticed by consumers.

Most significant of the charges, which are in fact penalties, are classified as PEAK HOUR ENERGY. These charges occur when the consumer's power demand exceeds the established boundaries of energy consumption as stipulated in tariff agreements. In order to maintain a stable power supply and cost for a unit of energy (kWh), service distributors, such as Southern California Electric (SCE) and other power generating entities, generally negotiate a long term agreement whereby the providers guarantee distributors a set bulk of energy for a fixed sum. Since energy providers have a limited power generation capacity, limits are set as to the amount of power that is to be distributed for the duration of the contract. A service provider such as SCE uses statistics and demographics of the territories served to project power consumption demands, which form the base line for the energy purchase agreement. Energy consumption, when it exceeds the projected demand becomes subject to much costlier tariffs, which are generally referred to as the peak bulk energy rate.

A Few Hints About Energy Saving Design Measures Recommended by the California Energy Commission

Energy efficiency is an issue that affects all projects. Whether you are considering a renewable energy system for supplying electricity to your home or business or just want to save money with your current electrical service supplier, the following suggestions will help you reduce the amount of energy that you use.

If electricity is currently supplied from a local utility, increasing the energy efficiency of a project will help to conserve valuable nonrenewable resources. Invest in a renewable energy system, such as solar or wind, and increasing the energy efficiency of a project will reduce the size and cost of the solar or wind energy system needed.

There are many ways to incorporate energy efficiency into a design. Most aspects of energy consumption, within a building, have a more efficient option than traditional methods. The following are some suggestions based on different aspects of energy usage within buildings, which have been sponsored by CEC and SCE.

Lighting

Providing lighting within a building can account for up to 30% of the energy used. There are several options for reducing this energy usage. The easiest method for reducing the energy used to provide lighting is to invest in compact fluorescent lights, as opposed to traditional incandescent lights. Compact fluorescent lights use approximately 75% less energy than typical incandescent lights. A 15 watt compact fluorescent light will supply the same amount of light as a 60 watt incandescent, while using only 25% of the energy that a 60 watt incandescent light would require. Compact fluorescent lights also last significantly longer than incandescent lights, with an expected lifetime of 10,000 hours on most models. Most compact fluorescent lights also come with a one-year warranty.

Another option for saving money and energy related to lighting is to use torchieres. In recent years halogen torchieres have become relatively popular. However, halogen torchieres create extremely high levels of heat, approximately 90% of the energy used by a halogen lamp is transferred to heat, not light. Some halogen lamps generate enough heat to fry an egg on the top of the lamp. These lamps create a fire hazard due to the possibility of curtains touching the lamp and igniting or a lamp falling over and igniting carpet. Great alternatives to these types of lamps are compact fluorescent torchieres. Whereas a halogen torchieres used 4 hours per day will use approximately

438 kilowatt-hours throughout the year, a compact fluorescent torchieres used 4 hours per day will only use 80 kilowatt hours throughout the year. If you currently pay $0.11 per kilowatt-hour this would save you over $30 per year, just for changing one lamp.

Appliances

There are many appliances used in buildings that require a significant amount of energy to operate. However, most of these appliances are available in highly efficient models.

Refrigeration.   Conventional refrigerators are a major consumer of the energy. It is possible to make refrigerators more effective and efficient by keeping them full. In the event a refrigerator is not fully stocked with food, one must consider keeping jugs of water in them. By keeping the refrigerators full, the contents will retain the cold. If refrigerators are old then consideration should be given to investing in new, highly efficient, star-rated models. There are refrigerators in the market that use less than 20 kilowatt-hours per month. When you compare this to the 110 kilowatt-hours used per month by a conventional refrigerator, you can save over $90 per year (based on $0.11/kWh).

Clothes Washers.   Washing machines are a large consumer of not only electricity but water as well. By using a horizontal-axis washing machine, also known as a front loader because the door is on the front of the machine, it is possible to save money from using less electricity, water, and detergent.

Front loaders have a more efficient spin cycle than top loaders, which will further increase savings due to less time required in the dryer. These are the types of machines are typically found in Laundromats. The machines are more cost effective than conventional top loaders. Another option is to use a natural gas or propane washer and dryer, which is currently more cost effective than using electric models. If you are on a solar or wind energy system, gas or propane are options that will reduce the overall electric usage of your home.

Water Heaters.   Water heaters can be an overwhelming load for any renewable energy system, as well as a drain on the pocketbook for those using electricity from a local utility. The following are some suggestions to increase the electric heater efficiency.

- Lower the thermostat to 120-130 degrees Fahrenheit
- Fix any leaky faucets immediately
- Wrap your water heater with insulation
- Turn off the electricity to your indoor water heater if you will be out of town for three or more days.
- Use a timer to water heater during the hours of the day when no one is at home.

If you are looking for a higher efficiency water heater, you may want to consider using a "flash" or "tankless" water heater, which heats water on demand. This method of heating water is very effective and does not require excessive electricity to keep a tank of water hot. It also saves water because you do not have to leave the water running out of the tap while you wait for it to get hot. Propane or natural gas water heaters are another option for those who want to minimize their electricity demand as much as possible.

Insulation and Weatherization

Inadequate insulation and air leakage are leading causes of energy waste in many homes. By providing adequate insulation in your home, walls, ceilings, and floors will be warmer in the winter and cooler in the summer. Insulation can also help act as a sound absorber or barrier, keeping noise levels low within the home. The first step to improving the insulation of a building is to know the type of existing insulation.

To check the exterior insulation, simply switch off the circuit breaker to an outlet on the inside of an exterior wall. Then remove the electrical outlet cover and check to see if there is insulation within the wall. If there is no insulation, insulation can be added by an insulation contractor who can blow cellulose into the wall through small holes, which are then plugged. The geometry of attics will also determine the ease with which additional insulation can be added. Insulating an attic will significantly add ability to keep the heat in during the winter and out during the summer.

One of the easiest ways to reduce energy bills and contribute to the comfort of your home or office space is by sealing air leaks around windows and doors. Temporary or permanent weather stripping can be used around windows and doors. Use caulk to seal other gaps that are less than one-quarter-inch wide and expanding foam for larger gaps. Storm windows and insulating drapes or curtains will also help improve the energy performance of existing windows.

Heating and Cooling

Every indoor space requires an adequate climate control system to maintain comfortable environment. Most people live or work in areas where the outdoor temperature fluctuates beyond ideal living conditions. A traditional air conditioning or heating system can be a tremendous load on a solar or wind energy system, as well as a drain on the pocketbook for those connected to the utility grid. However, with use of some of the insulation and weatherization tips previously mentioned above, it is possible to significantly reduce heating losses and reduce the size of the heating system.

The following heating and cooling tips will help further reduce heating and cooling losses and help your system work as efficiently as possible. These tips are designed to increase the efficiency of heating and or cooling system without making drastic remodeling efforts.

Heating.   When considering use of renewable energy systems, an electric space and water heaters are not considered viable options. Electric space and water heaters require a significant quantity of electricity to operate at a time of the year when the least amount of solar radiation is available.

Forced air heating systems also use inefficient fans to blow heated air into rooms that may not even be used during the day. They also allow for considerable leakage through poorly sealed ductwork. Ideally, an energy independent home or office space will not require heating or cooling due to passive solar design and quality insulation. However, if the space requires a heating source, one should consider a heater that burns fuel to provide heat and does not require electricity. Some options to consider are woodstoves and gas or propane heaters.

Cooling.   A conventional air conditioning unit is an enormous electrical load on a renewable energy system and a costly appliance to use. As with heating, the ideal energy independent home should be designed to not require an air conditioning unit. However, since most homeowners considering renewable energy systems are not going to redesign their home or office space, an air conditioning unit may be necessary.

By adequately insulating a home or office space and plugging any drafts or air leaks, air conditioning units will have to run less and reduce energy expenditure. Air conditioning units must be used only when it is absolutely necessary.

Another option is to use an evaporative cooling system. Evaporative cooling is an energy efficient alternative to traditional air conditioning units. Evaporative cooling works by evaporating water into the air stream. An example of evaporative cooling is the chill you feel when stepping out of a swimming pool and feeling a breeze. The chill you feel is caused by the evaporation of the water from your body. Evaporative cooling is the use of this evaporation process to cool the air passing through a wetted medium.

Early civilizations used this method with something as simple as hanging wet cloth in a window to cool the incoming air. Evaporative cooling is an economical and energy efficient solution for your cooling needs. With an evaporative cooling unit there is no compressor, condenser, chiller coils, or cooling towers. Therefore, the cost of acquiring and operating an evaporative cooling unit is considerable less than a conventional air conditioning unit and maintenance costs are lower due to the units requiring simpler procedures and lower skilled maintenance workers. Also, unlike conventional air conditioning units, evaporative cooling does not release chlorofluorocarbons (CFCs) into the atmosphere.

By following these recommendations, it is possible to turn a home or office space into an energy efficient environment.

Energy Rate and Tariffs

In order to regulate the stability of the energy cost, energy distributors establish energy consumption service agreements with their clients. To ensure stability in power demand, service providers offer several different types of tariffs that suit best the needs of the end user.

Most tariffs are intended to maintain consumption limitation both in times of use and amount of power consumed. Each tariff stipulated boundaries of energy use and specifies the limits of maximum energy consumption.

When energy consumption exceeds the established limits, a peak energy charge is applied to the basic rate. In some instances if peak power demand exceed by 15 minutes a month, the entire kWh consumption for the entire month will reflect peak energy charges. Peak energy charges could in some instances be orders of magnitude higher than the normal prevailing rates. One of the significant features of using solar power cogeneration is to counteract and offset the cost of peak energy penalties, which is conventionally referred to as a "peak shaving generator."

Peak energy penalties mostly occur in summer time between 11 am and 3 pm, when electric grids are over burdened by air conditioning and cooling systems, which almost coincides with peak performance for solar cogeneration, hence offsetting or shaving off the power demand peaks that will otherwise result in excessive energy tariff rates.

Economic Analysis

It should be noted that economic cost analysis discussed below should not over shadow, ignore, or dismiss immense intangible cost benefits of solar power systems as a renewable and sustainable source of energy. When considering air quality degradation by nonrenewable energy sources, such as coal and fossil fuels, which generate over 1,000 pounds of carbon dioxide for every megawatt hour of electric power, solar or any sustainable type of renewable energy must be given a significant tangible value.

Upon completion of the overall hardware and manpower installation costs outlined above, the solar power engineer must evaluate the prevailing and projected costs associated with the electric energy for the life span of the solar power system, which may range from 10 years to 25 years, depending on the employed choice of PV technology. To establish an economic analysis framework, the solar power engineer assesses the cost benefit and financial merits of the solar power system investment. The designer should be familiar with engineering econometrics.

Solar Power Estimating Considerations

The following example includes fundamental design and accounting steps required for solar power economic analysis.

Site Parameters

- Solar power installation area dimensions
- Percent useable, unobstructed available space

- Shade clearance and walkway area dimensions.
- Net surface area

Photovoltaic (PV) Module and Array Data

- PV panel assembly dimensions (length and width)
- Rated Voltage
- PTC rated watts per PV
- Inverter input voltage bandwidth
- PV strings are required to match the inverter DC input requirement.
- PV array aggregate voltage
- PV array aggregate power
- PV array current

Geographic Surface Barometric Parameters

- Latitude
- Longitude
- Optimal tilt angle
- Sine and cosine of the tilt
- Optimum array length and width in tilt position
- Required array footprint separation to avoid cross shading

Solar Cogeneration System Losses

- Tilt angle loss
- Wiring and heat exposure losses
- Inverter losses
- Isolation transformer losses
- DC and AC feeder losses
- Maintenance and degradation losses

Solar Cogeneration System Power Contribution

- Project calculated operational power demand watts
- Net power contribution watts (after losses)
- Percent of solar power contribution

Cost Parameters

Preliminary Engineering

- Site investigation
- Preliminary design
- Feasibility report preparation
- Travel and accommodation

Project Development

- Permits and rebate applications
- Project management
- Travel expenses

Engineering Design Tasks

- Solar system electrical engineering design
- Architectural design
- Structural engineering design
- Tender evaluation
- Construction supervision
- Shop drawing check

Renewable Energy System Equipment

- PV module cost
- Transportation and storage
- Taxes

Equipment Installation

- PV module support structure
- Inverter system
- Isolation transformer, collector boxes, and disconnects
- Recorders and tantalizers
- Monitoring system
- Installation labor
- Site mobilization and utilities
- Transportation and storage
- Taxes

Training and Commissioning

- Instruction manuals
- Instruction courses
- Site acceptances test and reports

Contingencies

- Project delays
- Material escalation cost
- Material loss or vandalism

Bond and Insurances

- Bid bond
- Performance bond and liquidated damages
- Legal fees
- Insurance

Cost of Energy Production and Return on Investment

- Present energy cost per kWh.
- Projected energy cost escalation for the expected life span of the solar power system
- Net energy contribution during life expectancy of the solar power system
- Cost savings during the life span of the solar power system
- Initial capital investment
- State rebate contribution
- Federal and state tax deduction
- Accelerated capital equipment depreciation
- Finance charges
- Return on investment and pay-back period analysis

Chapter

4

Alternative Renewable
Energy Technologies

Passive Solar Heating

Another use of solar technology to form energy is by concentrating the sun's heat into electricity through mirrors. One way this is done is through parabolic trough systems. These systems use curved mirrors to concentrate the sun's heat onto a tube. The tube contains a fluid that has a high boiling point, such as oil. Once this fluid is hot enough, it can be used to produce steam and then electricity is produced. Similarly, mirrors in the shape of a dish are also used to concentrate the sun's heat onto a receiver. Then, the heat is transferred to a heat engine that converts the heat into energy that drives a generator, which produces electricity. Another method uses hot air that enters into a gas turbine, which drives the generator.

A passive solar water heater is shown in Figure 4.1.

Another form of concentrating the sun's heat uses power towers. These systems use a large field of mirrors that are able to track the sun, called heliostats. These heliostats then concentrate the heat onto a receiver on top of the towers. The receiver contains a fluid that once heated can be used to produce steam that then drives a turbine to produce electricity.

Pool Heating

Over the years, a wide variety of pool-heating panel types have been introduced. Each has its intrinsic advantages and disadvantages. Four primary types of solar pool collector design classifications are as follow.

- Rigid black plastic panels (polypropylene)
- EPDE rubber mat or other plastic or rubber formulations
- Tube and fin metal panels with a copper or aluminum fin attached to copper tubing
- Plastic type systems

Figure 4.1 Passive solar power water heater (Courtesy of Department of Energy)

Plastic Panels

This technology makes use of modular panels with panel dimensions ranging about 4 ft wide and 8 ft, 10 ft, or 12 ft in length. Individual panels are coupled together to achieve the desired surface area.

Principal advantages of this type of technology are lightness of product, chemical inertness, and high efficiency. The panels are also durable and can be mounted on racks. The products are available in a glazed version to accommodate for windy areas and colder climates.

The disadvantage of the technology is its numerous system surface attachments, which can limit mounting locations.

Rubber Mat

These systems are made up of parallel pipes, called headers, which are manufactured from extruded lengths of tubing that have stretching mats between the tubes. The length and the width of the mat are adjustable and are typically custom fit for each application, as seen in Figure 4.2.

The advantage of this technology is that due to flexibility of the product, it can be installed and adaptable to roof obstructions, like vent pipes. Installations require few, if any roof penetrations, and are considered highly efficient. Due to the expandability of the product, the headers are less subject to freeze expansion damage.

The main disadvantage the system is that the mats are glued to the roof and can be difficult to remove without damaging either the roof or the solar panel. The installation also cannot be applied in rack type installations.

Figure 4.2 Solar pool heater (Courtesy of UMA/HELICOL)

Metal Panels

These classes of products are constructed from copper waterways that are attached to either copper or aluminum fins. The fins collect the solar radiation and conduct it into the waterways.

Advantages of these classes of product include their rigidity and durability of construction. Like rubber mats, glazed versions of these panels are also available for application in windy areas and cold climates.

A significant disadvantage of this type of technology is that they require significantly more surface area, have low efficiency, and have no manufacturer's warranty.

Plastic Pipe Systems

In this technology, plastic pipes are connected in parallel or are configured in a circular pattern. The main advantage of the system is that installation can be done inexpensively and could easily be used as an overhead "trellis" for above deck installations, as shown in Figure 4.3.

Main disadvantage of this type of installation is that they require significantly larger surface area than other systems, and, like metal panel, they do not carry a manufacturer's warrantee.

Panel Selection

One of the most important considerations when selecting a pool heating system is the amount of panel surface area that is required to heat the pool. The

Figure 4.3 Solar pool heater (Courtesy of UMA/HELICOL)

relationship of the solar collector area to swimming pool surface area must be adequate in order to ensure that your pool achieves the temperatures you expect, generally in the high 70s to the low 80s at a minimum, during the swimming season. The percentage of solar panel surface area to pool surface area varies with geographic location, and is affected by factors, such as local "micro-climates", solar collector orientation, pool shading, and desired heating season.

Generally, it is desirable to mount the panels on a southerly exposure; however, an orientation within 45 degrees of south will not significantly decrease performance as long as shading is avoided. A due west exposure will work well if the square footage of solar collector is increased to compensate. However, a due east exposure is generally to be avoided, unless significantly more solar collectors are used.

It is very important to keep in mind that solar energy is a very dilute energy source. Only a limited amount of useful heat falls on each square foot of panel. Consequently, whatever type of solar system is used, a large panel area is needed to collect adequate amounts of energy.

In Southern California, Texas, and Arizona, where there is abundant sunshine and warm temperatures, the swimming season stretches from April or May to September or October. To heat a pool during this period, it is necessary to install enough solar collectors to equal a minimum of 70% of surface area of the swimming pool, when the solar panels are facing south.

As the orientation moves away from ideal, sizing should increase to 80%, to 100%, or more for west or southeast orientations. If climatic conditions are less favorable, such as near the ocean, even more coverage may be required. In general, it is always recommended to exceed the minimums to offset chang-

TABLE 4.1 A Typical Pool Heating Installation Economics

Pool Size:	7,500 square feet
Pool depth:	5 feet
Total Purchase Price:	$180,000
First Year Energy Savings:	$ 30,575 (fuel cost per therm $ 1.00)
Ten Year Energy Savings:	$ 38,505 (estimated)
Expected investment payback:	5.3 years
Yearly Average Return: Internal Rate of Return:	21%
Size of each panel:	50 square feet (4′ × 12.5′)
Number of panel:	144
Total Required Area:	7,200 square feet
Panel Tilt:	2 degrees
Panel Orientation:	180 degrees
Total Required Area:	7,200 square feet

Courtesy of Airphase Engineering, CA

ing weather patterns. However, there is a point of diminishing return, where more panels won't add significantly to the pool heating function. Table 4.1 shows statistics for a typical pool heating installation.

Some Useful Suggested Practices

Use of common sense when investing in solar pool heating is very important. The first time buyer should consider the following.

- Buy only from a licensed contractor and check on their experience and reputation.

- Be aware that several factors should be considered when evaluating various system configurations. More solar panels, generally, means your pool will be warmer.

- Use a pool cover, if possible.

- Make sure the system is sized properly. An inadequately sized system is guaranteed dissatisfaction.

- Beware of outrageous claims, such as "90 degree pool temperatures in December with no backup heater." No solar heating system can achieve such a performance.

- The contractor should produce evidence of adequate Worker's Compensation and Liability Insurance.

- Insurance certificates should be directly from the insurance company and not the contractor.

- Check the contractor's referrals before buying.

- Get a written description of the system, including number of solar panels, size of panels, and the make and model number.

- Get a complete operation and maintenance manual and start-up demonstration.

- The price should not be the most important factor. But it should also not be dramatically different from prices of competing bidders for similar equipment.

- Be sure the contractor obtains a building permit if required.

Solar Cooling and Air Conditioning

Most of us associate cooling, refrigeration and air conditioning as a self contained electromechanical devices that are connected to an electrical power source that provide conditioned air for spaces, in which we live as well as refrigerate our food stuff and groceries.

Technically speaking technology that makes the refrigeration possible is based upon basic fundamental concepts of physics called heat transfer. Cold is essentially the absence of heat, likewise darkness is the absence of light.

The branch of physics that deals with the mechanics of heat transfer is called thermodynamics. There are two principal universal laws of thermodynamics. The first law concerns the conservation of energy, which states that energy neither can be created nor destroyed; however, it can be converted from one type to another. The second law of thermodynamics deals with the equalization and transfer of energy from a higher state to a lower one, as shown in Figure 4.4. Simply stated, energy is always transferred from a higher potential or state to a lower one, until two energy sources achieve exact equilibrium. Heat is essentially defined as a form of energy created as a result of transformation of another form of energy, a common example of which is when two solid bodies are rubbed together, which results into friction heat. In general, heat is energy in a transfer state, because it does not stay in any specific position and constantly moves from a warm object to a colder one, until such time, as per the second law of thermodynamics, both bodies reach heat equilibrium.

It should be noted that volume, size, or mass of objects are completely irrelevant in heat transfer process, only state of heat energy levels are factors in the energy balance equation. With the above principle in mind, heat energy flows from a small object, such as hot cup of coffee will transfer heat to ones hand, a much larger mass. The rate of travel of heat is directly proportional to the difference in temperature between two objects.

Heat travels in three forms namely as a radiation, conduction, and convection. As radiation, heat is transferred in waveform similar to radio, microwaves, or light. For example, sun transfers its energy to The Earth by rays or radiation. In conduction, heat energy flows from one media or substance to another by a physical contact. Convection on the other hand is flow of heat between air, gas, liquid and a fluid medium.

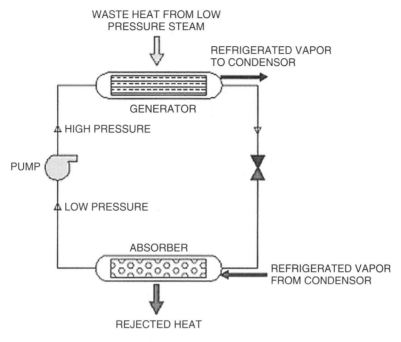

Figure 4.4 Second law of thermodynamics (Courtesy of Vector Delta Design Group, Inc.)

Solar heat collector panels and installation are shown in Figures 4.5 and 4.6. In refrigeration the basic principles are based on the second law of thermodynamics, that is transfer or removal of heat from a higher energy media to a lower one by means of convection.

Figure 4.5 Solar heat collector panel used in hybrid chillers (Courtesy of Solargenix)

Figure 4.6 Solar heat collector panel installation in Arizona Desert (Courtesy of Solargenix)

Temperature

Temperature is a scale for measuring heat intensity with directional flow of energy. Water freezes at zero Centigrade (C) or 32 Fahrenheit (F) scale and boils at 100°C or 212°F. Temperature scales are simply temperature differences between freezing and boiling water temperatures measured at sea level.

As mentioned above, based on the second law of thermodynamics, heat transfer or measurement of temperature is not dependent on the quantity of heat.

Molecular Agitation

Depending on state of heat energy, most substances in general can exist in vapor, liquid, and solid states. As an example depending on the heat energy level, water can exist as solid ice when it refrigerates, liquid at room temperature, or vapor form when heated above boiling temperature of 212°F. In each of the states, water is within or without the two boundary temperatures of 32°F and 212°F.

Steam will condense back to water state if heat energy is removed (cooled) from it. Water will change into a solid state (ice) when sufficient heat energy is removed from it. The processes can be reversed when heat energy is introduced in the media.

The state of change is related to the fact that in various substances, depending upon presence or absence of heat energy, a phenomenon referred to as atomic thermal agitation, causes expansion and contraction of molecules.

Figure 4.7 Hybrid absorption chiller evaporator (Courtesy of Solargenix)

Close contraction of molecules form solids and larger separation transform matter into liquid and gaseous states.

A hybrid absorption chiller evaporator is shown in Figure 4.7.

In border state energy conditions, beyond solid and gaseous state excess lack or surplus of energy state are referred to as super cooled or super heated states.

Principles of Refrigeration

Refrigeration is accomplished by two distinct processes. In one process, referred to as the compression cycle, a medium, such as Freon Gas, is first given heat energy by compression, which turns the gas into liquid. Then in a subsequent cycle, energy is removed from the liquid, in a form of evaporation or gas expansion, which disperses the gas molecules and turns the surrounding chamber into a cold environment.

A circulating media of energy absorbing liquid such as water or air when circulated within the so-called evaporation chamber gives up its heat energy to the expanded gas. The cold water or air is in turn circulated by means of pumps into environments that have higher ambient heat energy levels. The circulated cold air in turn exchanges or passes the cold air into the ambient space through radiator tubes or fins, thus lowering the energy of the environment.

Temperature control is realized by opening and closing of cold media circulating tube valves or air duct control vanes, modulated by a local temperature sensing device, such as a thermostat or a set point control mechanism.

Cooling Technologies

There are two types of refrigeration technologies currently in use, namely an electric vapor-compression (Freon Gas) and heat-driven absorption cooling.

Absorption cooling chillers are operated by steam, hot water, or fossil fuel burners or combinations of all. There are two types of absorption chillers, one uses Lithium-Bromide (LiBr) as an energy conversion medium and water as a refrigerant. In this type of technology the lowest temperature achieved is limited to 40°F.

Another absorption chiller technology uses ammonia as the energy conversion medium and a mix of ammonia and water as the refrigerant. Maximum limit of temperature for this technology is 20°F. Both of the above technologies have been around for about 100 years.

Basic principle of absorption chillers is based on gasification of the LiBr or Ammonia. Gasification takes place when either of the media is exposed to heat. Heat could be derived from fossil fuel gas burners, hot water obtained from geothermal energy (discussed in Chapter 5), passive solar water heaters (discussed earlier in this chapter), or micro-turbine generators, which use land fill gasses to produce electricity and heat energy (discussed later in this chapter). Figure 4.8 shows a gas fired absorption chiller system.

Coefficient of Performance

Energy efficiency of an air conditioning system is defined by a coefficient of performance (COP), which is defined as the ration of cooling energy to the energy supplied to the unit.

Figure 4.8 Gas fired absorption chiller system, Haneda Airport, Japan (Courtesy of Mitsubishi Corporation)

A ton of cooling energy is 12,000 Btu/hr (British thermal units per hour), which as defined in olden days, is the energy required to remove heat from space to ambient air obtained through melting a ton of ice. One ton or 12,000 Btu is equal to 3,413 watts of electrical power.

Based on the above definitions, cooling coefficient of performance of a an air conditioning unit, which requires 1,500 watts of electric power per ton is equal to 12,000 Btu/hr (1.5 kW × 3413) = 2.344. Obviously, a electrical lower energy requirement will increase the COP rating which brings us to a conclusion that lower the amount of energy input the better the efficiency.

Solar Power Cooling and Air Conditioning

A combination use of passive solar and natural gas fired media evaporation has given rise to a generation of hybrid absorption chillers that can produce large tonnage of cooling energy by use of solar or geothermal heated water. A class of absorption, which commonly used LiBr, which have been commercially available for some time, use natural and solar power as the main sources of energy. A 1,000 ton absorption chiller can reduce electrical energy consumption by an average of 1 MW or 1million watts, which will have very significant impact on reducing the electrical power consumption and resulting environmental pollutions as described in earlier chapters.

Desiccant Evaporators

Another solar power cooling technology makes use of a solar-desiccant-evaporator air conditioning technology, which reduces outside air humidity and passes it through an ultra efficient evaporative cooling system. This cooling process, which uses an indirect evaporative process minimizes the air humidity, and this makes use of the technology quite effective in coastal and humid areas, as shown in Figure 4.9. Typical building cooling capacity is shown in Table 4.2.

Direct Solar Power Generation

The following project undertaken by Solargenix Energy makes use of special parabolic reflectors that concentrate the solar energy rays into circular pipes located at the focal center of the parabola. Concentrated reflection of energy elevates temperature of the circulating mineral liquid oil within the pipes, raising the temperature to such levels that allow considerable steam generation via special heat exchangers that drive power turbines. The following abstract reflects a viable electrical power generation in Arizona.

RED ROCK, ARIZ. – APS today broke ground on Arizona's first commercial solar trough power plant and the first such facility constructed in the United States since 1990.

Figure 4.9 Hybrid absorption chiller air-conditioned space (Courtesy of Solargenix)

Located at the company's Saguaro Power Plant in Red Rock, about 30 miles north of Tucson, the APS Saguaro Solar Trough Generating Station will have a one megawatt (MW) generating capacity, enough to provide for the energy needs of approximately 200 average-size homes.

APS has contracted with Solargenix Energy to construct and provide the solar thermal technology for the plant, which is expected to come online in April 2005. Solargenix, formerly Duke Solar, is based out of Raleigh, North Carolina. Solargenix has partnered with Ormat who will provide the engine to convert the solar heat, collected by the Solargenix solar collectors, into electricity.

"The APS Saguaro Solar Trough Power Plant presents a unique opportunity to further expand our renewable energy portfolio," said Peter Johnston, manager of Technology Development for APS. "We are committed to developing clean renewable energy sources today that will fuel tomorrow's economy. We believe solar-trough technology can be part of a renewable solution.

TABLE 4.2. Typical Building Cooling Capacity

Space	Size SF	Cooling Tons
Medium office	50,000	100–150
Hospital	150,000	400–600
Hotel	250,000	400–500
High school	50,000	100–400
Retail store	160,000	170–400

The company's solar-trough technology uses parabolic shaped reflectors (or mirrors) to concentrate the sun's rays to heat a mineral oil between 250 and 570 degrees. The fluid then enters the Ormat engine passing first through a heat exchanger to vaporize a secondary working fluid. The vapor is used to spin a turbine, making electricity. It is then condensed back into a liquid before being vaporized once again.

Historically, solar-trough technology has required tens of megawatts of plant installation to produce steam from water to turn generation turbines. The significant first cost of multi-megawatt power plants had precluded their use in the APS solar portfolio. This solar trough system combines the relatively low cost of parabolic solar trough thermal technology with the commercially available, smaller turbines usually associated with low temperature geothermal generation plants, such as the Ormat unit being used for this project.

In addition to generating electricity for APS customers, the solar trough plant will help APS meet the goals of the Arizona Corporation Commission's Environmental Portfolio Standard, which requires APS to generate 1.1 percent of its energy through renewable sources—60 percent through solar—by 2007. APS owns and operates approximately 4.5 megawatts of photovoltaic solar generation around the state and has partnered on a 3-megawatt biomass plant in Eager, which came online in February, and a 1S-megawatt wind farm to be constructed near St. Johns.

APS, Arizona's largest and longest-serving electricity utility, serves about 902,000 customers in 11 of the state's 1S counties. With headquarters in Phoenix, APS is the largest subsidiary of Pinnacle West Capital Corp. (NYSE: PNW).

Figures 4.10 and 4.11 help illustrate the APS project.

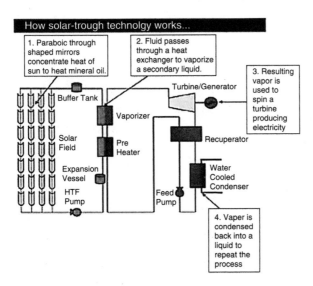

Figure 4.10 APS solar thermal plant diagram by Solargenix

Figure 4.11 Parabolic reflector (Courtesy of Solargenix)

Fuel Cell Technology and Applications

In general, fuel cells are battery like devices, which produce electrical power by means of electrochemical reaction. Unlike batteries, as long as fuel is supplied, the cells produce electricity without degradation or recharging.

At present, fuel cell research and developments have not reached maturity and cannot fully compete with established power generation technologies; however, due to their efficient energy conversion and extremely low emission, the cells represent a viable and promising alternative as a primary or stand-by source of electricity.

Fuel cells have a great potential to promote energy diversity and transition to renewable energy sources. Hydrogen that is the most abundant element on the Earth (and the Universe) can be used as the main source of energy. When Hydrogen is used as an energy source in a fuel cell, the only emission that is created is water, which can be electrolyzed to produce additional Hydrogen.

The above continuous cycle of energy production has real potential in conjunction with solar power technology to replace the traditional energy sources, which cause depletion of precious nonrenewable resources and create pollution.

Short History

Fuel cell was first discovered in 1839 by Sir William Grove, a Welsh judge and a scientist. The discovery became dormant up until the 1960s when practical application of the electrochemical conversion used in U.S. space programs paved the way for today's research and product development.

U.S. space programs in the past chose fuel cells to power the Gemini and Apollo spacecrafts, and still use the technology to provide electricity and water for the space shuttle.

Nowadays, most industrialized nations of the world such as the United States, Canada, Germany, Holland, Japan, and Italy have, extensive nationally sponsored research and development programs, which promises to have significant impact on the world economy and reduction of global greenhouse gas production.

Basic Operation Principles

A basic fuel cell consists of two electrodes that sandwich an electrolytic membrane. Hydrogen fuel when fed into the ANODE (+) of the fuel cell, with the aid of the electrolytic membrane which acts as a catalyst reacts chemically with oxygen or air introduce at the anode (-), as shown in Figure 4.12.

In the above chemical reaction, the Hydrogen atom is split into a Proton and an Electron. The proton passes through the electrolyte membrane. The Electrons on the other hand travel from the anode to the cathode that give rise to electric current. Electrons at the cathode reunited with the hydrogen protons. Hydrogen in turn, reacts chemically with the oxygen, producing water molecules and heat.

The electrochemical process described above makes use of hydrogen as a source of fuel. Some fuel cell systems also include a preprocessing mechanism know as FUEL REFORMER that enables the hydrogen from any form of hydrocarbon based fuel, such as natural gas, methanol, landfill methane gasses, and regular gasoline be separated from the main molecules and used in the electrochemical conversion process.

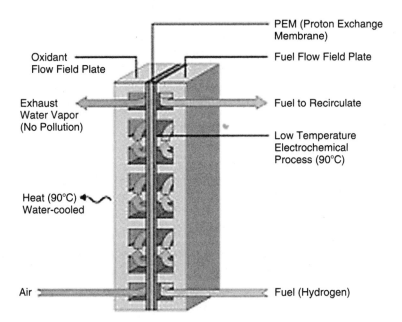

Figure 4.12 Basic construction of fuel cell (Courtesy of Ballard Engineering)

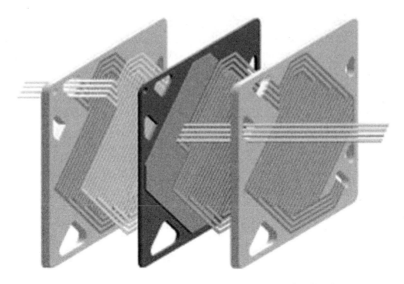

Figure 4.13   Fuel cell membrane components (Courtesy of Ballard Engineering)

Fuel Reformers

As mentioned above, fuel cells use hydrogen as the fuel for electro conversion; however, hydrogen-rich materials such as methanol, ethanol, natural gas, petroleum distillates, liquid propane, and gasified coal can also serve as possible fuel sources.

One method of reformation, known as ENDOTHERMIC STEAM RE-FORMING, combines fuels with steam by vaporizing them together at very high temperature. In this process, hydrogen is separated from the hydrocarbon molecules by use of a special membrane, as shown in Figure 4.13. The main drawback of steam reforming technique is that the process requires energy consumption.

Another type of fuel reformation is known as PARTIAL OXIDATION (POX) that produces carbon dioxide (CO_2) but no particulates, Nitrogen Monoxide (NOX), Sulphur-Monoxide (SOX) smog producing agents or gases. Figure 4.14 shows the operation of a fuel cell.

Phosphoric Acid Fuel Cells

This type of fuel cell uses phosphoric acid compound as the catalytic conversion membrane. This type of fuel cell generates electricity with a conversion efficiency that ranges from 40%. The large amount heat produced by the process (about 400°F) is used for steam production, which through cogeneration is used to produce additional electricity.

To date hundreds of commercially available phosphoric acid fuel cells

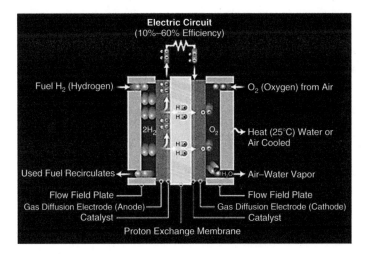

Figure 4.14 Fuel cell operation (Courtesy of Ballard Engineering)

(FAFC) cells have been installed throughout the world which are used by power utility companies, airport terminals, hotels, hospitals, municipal waste dumps, office and buildings. Recently, many automotive manufacturers such as Toyota, Chrysler-Daimler Benz, and many more, use FAFC fuel cells in their hybrid automobiles (using a combination of a fuel cell and an internal combustion engine) and are racing to produce more efficient product system that will ultimately be used in transportation technology as the principle means of power generation.

Proton Exchange Membrane Fuel Cells

Proton exchange membrane fuel cells (PEMFC) operate at low temperature (about 200°F), have relatively high energy density, and are capable of changing output power demand at a quick rate. These particular characteristics make the application of these cells in automobiles, where quick start-up is paramount, very appropriate.

The proton exchange membrane, in this type of fuel cell, is a thin plastic sheet that allows hydrogen ions to pass through it. The membrane is coated on both sides with dispersed platinum alloy particles, which act as a catalyst. Hydrogen extracted by a fuel reformer is fed to the anode side of the fuel cell, where the catalytic membrane separates the electrons and permits passage of protons to the cathode side.

Similar to the FAFC electrochemical process, the hydrogen ions are recombined with the electrons, which subsequently react with the oxygen producing heat and water molecules. A fuel cell assembly stationary power generator is shown in Figure 4.15.

Figure 4.15 Fuel cell assembly stationary power generator (Courtesy of Ballard Engineering)

Molten Carbonate Fuel Cells

The fuel cells in this electro conversion use molten carbonate as a catalyst to separate the Hydrogen electrons from the molecule. The cells operate at very high temperature (1200 degrees F) and are considered to be very efficient.

Molten carbonate fuel cells (MCFC) operate on hydrogen, carbon monoxide, natural gas, propane, landfill gases, marine diesel fuels, and coal gasified products. In Italy and Japan, multi-megawatt MCFC have been successfully installed and tested as a stationary stand-alone power generation system.

Solid Oxide Fuel Cells

This technology uses a uses a hard ceramic solid oxide material as electrolytic conversion catalyst, which operates, at extremely high temperatures (1,800°F). Solid oxide fuel cells(SOFC) are cable of producing several hundred kilowatts of power at efficiency near or exceeding 60%. A special solid oxide fuel cell, known a tubular solid oxide fuel cell, uses tubes of compressed solid oxide discs resembling metal can tops, which are stacked to 100 cm high.

Recently, SOFC technologies have made significant progress in product development and are being manufactured commercially by a number of companies. This fuel cell, due to significant power production capacity and high efficiency, will, in the near future, be used in motor vehicles and as a source for electric power generation.

Alkaline Fuel Cells

Alkaline fuel cells (AFC) use potassium hydroxide in the electrochemical catalytic conversion process and have a conversion efficiency of about 70%. In the last few decades, NASA has used alkaline cells to power space missions.

Up until recently, due to high cost of production, alkaline fuel cells were not available commercially. However, improvements and cost reduction in fuel cell production have created a new opportunity to commercialize the technology.

Direct Methanol Fuel Cells

This type of fuel cell uses a similar proton exchange electro conversion process discussed above uses a polymer membrane as the electrolyte; however, without a reformer mechanism, the anode acts as a catalyst that separates the hydrogen from the liquid methanol.

Direct Methanol fuel cells (DMFC) operate at a relatively low temperature (120°–200°F) and have about 40% efficiency. At more elevated temperatures, these fuel cells operate at higher conversion efficiency.

In the United States, future commercialization of DMFC technology will depend upon genetically modified corn, which could be fermented at low temperatures. Such a breakthrough could indeed make the technology a viable source of electric energy production, which could significantly contribute to reduction of air pollution and minimize expensive import of crude oil.

Regenerative Fuel Cells

This technology, which is still at its early research and development stage, is a closed-loop electro conversion system, which uses solar powered electrolysis to separate hydrogen and oxygen molecules from water. Hydrogen and oxygen are fed into a fuel cell, which in addition to generating electricity produces heat and water.

Benefits of Fuel Cell Technology

It is estimated that fuel cell market within the next decade could exceed $20 billion worldwide. In addition to expanding market for alternative electric energy, a significant percentage of nearly ´ million vehicles produced annually throughout the world, which use internal combustion, will be converted into hybrid technology.

It is also believed that demand for fuel cells by the transportation industry within the next decade will increase annually by an additional $15 billion.

In the United States, passenger vehicles alone consume over 6 million barrels of oil every day, which represents 85% of our oil imports.

If only 25% of vehicles could operate with fuel cells, oil import s could be reduced by 1.8 billion barrels a day or about 650 billion barrels a year, which produces unfavorable balance of trade and considerable amount air pollution. Furthermore, if each vehicle produced in the future was designed to operate on fuel cells, country's electric power generation capacity will increase by 200%.

The U.S. Department of Energy estimates that if only 10% of the nation's vehicles were powered by fuel cells, yearly import of crude oil will be reduced by about 13% or 800,000 barrels. The production of greenhouse gases, such as carbon dioxide, will be reduced by 60 tons and air pollution particulates be reduced by one million tons.

Impact of Fuel Cells on the Global Economy

In view of wide ranging application of technology in markets, such as steel production, electrical power generation, vehicle, and transportation industries, fuel cells could have a significant impact on the global market economy since they could provide employment for tens of thousands of high quality jobs.

It is estimated that each 1000-megawatt of fuel cell energy production will create 5,000 new jobs, and if only 25% of cars in the nation were to use the technology, jobs created would exceed 1,000,000 which will have a significant positive impact on the US gross national product.

Examples of Fuel Cell Demonstrations

Ballard participates in a number of demonstration programs designed to showcase fuel technology around the world, as part of the commercialization process.

California Fuel Cell Partnership

The California Fuel Cell Partnership (CaFCP) is a collaboration of auto manufacturers, fuel suppliers, fuel cell manufacturers, and state governments.

Headquartered in Sacramento, Calif., USA, the CaFC to demonstrate and test fuel cell vehicles under everyday conditions, investigate and demonstrate the viability of site infrastructure technology, promote public awareness of premembrane fuel cell-powered vehicles, and explore the path to commercialization by ideas of potential problems and solutions.

Vancouver Fuel Cell Vehicle Program

The Vancouver Fuel Cell Vehicle Program (VFCVP) is a five-year $9 million joint initiative between Canada, Ford Motor Company, the Government of Canada and Technology Early Action Measures, and the Government of British Columbia.

This project will demonstrate five Ballard-powered fuel cell vehicles in 'real world' conditions on the British Colombia lower mainland and is the first fleet demonstration of fuel cell vehicles in Canada. Demonstrating third generation Ford fuel cell vehicles will provide valuable information on performance and reliability that can be applied toward the evolution of fuel cell vehicles to the commercial marketplace in the transition to a hydrogen economy.

Ballard will have its own fuel cell for the duration of the program. Other vehicles users include the City of Vancouver, the Government of British Columbia, Fuel Cells Canada, and the NRC (National Research Council).

Santa Clara Valley Transportation Authority

The Santa Clara Valley Transportation Authority (VTA) contracted with Gillig Corporation and Ballard Power Systems of Burnaby, Canada, to build three hydrogen-powered, zero-emission cell buses (ZEBs) for use in regular transit service. Air Products & Chemicals, Inc., will supply hydrogen, which is converted to hydrogen gas at VTA's fueling station at Cerone.

European Fuel Cell Bus Project

Ballard heavy-duty fuel cell engines are inside 30 Mercedes buses running in revenue transit service in 10 European ci1 year demonstration program, which includes both the European F Project (nine cities) and the Ecological City Transport System Reykjavik, Iceland. The European Union has led the way of zero-emission fuel cell technology.

Sustainable Transport Energy for Perth

Three Ballard fuel cell-powered buses commenced route Perth, Australia, on September 27, 2004. As of November, the buses were working more than eight hours per day and five days per week. The buses had traveled more than 8,000 kilometers and had operated 400 hours.

Wind Power Energy

Contents of this topic have been based on a wind power tutorial that can be found on the American Wind Energy Association web site. It was prepared in cooperation with the U.S. Department of Energy and the National Renewable Laboratory.

In reality, wind energy is a converted form of solar energy. The sun's radiation heats different parts of the earth at different rates, most notably during the day and night but also when different surfaces (for example, water and land) absorb or reflect at different rates. This causes portions of the atmosphere to warm differently. Hot air rises, reducing the atmospheric pressure at the earth's surface, and cooler air is drawn in to replace it. The result is wind.

Air has mass, and when it is in motion, it contains the energy of that motion, "kinetic energy." Some portion of that energy can converted into other forms, mechanical force or electricity that we can use to perform work.

Basics of Wind Power Turbine Operation

A wind energy system transforms the kinetic energy of the wind into mechanical or electrical energy that can be harnessed for practical use. Mechanical energy is most commonly used for pumping water in rural or remote locations. The "farm windmill" still seen in many rural areas of the United

States is a mechanical wind pump, but it can also be used for many other purposes (grinding grain, sawing, pushing a sailboat, etc.). Wind electric turbines generate electricity for homes, businesses, and state utilities.

There are two basic designs of wind electric turbines, vertical-axis (11 egg-beaters' style) and horizontal-axis (propeller-style) machines. Horizontal-axis wind turbines are most common today, constituting nearly all of the "utility-scale" (100 kilowatts, M, capacity and larger) turbines in the global market.

Turbine system components include the following.

- A blade or a rotor, which converts the wind energy into rotational shaft energy
- An enclosure referred to as nacelle, which contains the drive mechanism consisting of gearbox and electrical generator
- A support structure such as a tower that supports the nacelle
- Electrical equipment and components, such as controls and interconnection equipment

There are also types of turbines that directly drive the generator and do not require a gearbox. The amount of electricity that wind turbines generate depends on turbine's capacity or power rating.

The electricity generated by an utility-scale wind turbine is normally collected and fed into utility power lines, where it is mixed with electricity from other power plants and delivered to utility customers.

Energy Generation Capacity of a Wind Turbine

The ability to generate electricity is measured in watts. Watts are very small units, so the terms kilowatt (kW, 1,000 watts), megawatt (MW, 1 million watts), and gigawatt (pronounced "jig-a-watt," GW, 1 billion watts) are most commonly used to describe the capacity of generating units like wind turbines or other power plants.

Electricity production and consumption are most commonly measured in kilowatt-hours (kWh). A kilowatt-hour means one kilowatt (1,000 watts) of electricity produced or consumed for one hour. One 50-watt tight bulb left on for 20 hours consumes one-kilowatt-hour of electricity (50 watts × 20 hours = 1,000 watt-hours = 1 kilowatt—hour). The output of a wind turbine depends on the turbine's size and the wind's speed through the rotor. Wind turbines being manufactured now have power ratings ranging from 250 watts to 1.8 megawatts (MW).

For example a 10 kW wind turbine, shown in Figure 4.16, can generate about 10,000 kWh annually at a site with wind speeds averaging 12 miles per hour or about enough to power a typical household. A 1.8 MW turbine can produce more than 5.2 million kWh in a year, enough to power more than 500 households. The average U.S. household consumes about 10,000 kWh of electricity each year.

Figure 4.16 Wind turbine installation (Courtesy of American Wind Energy Manufacturers Association [AWEMA])

A practical example of a project is a 250 kW turbine installed at the elementary school in Spirit Lake, Iowa, provides an average of 350,000 kWh of electricity per year, and more than is necessary for the 53,000 square-foot school. Excess electricity is fed into the local utility system, which earned the school $25,000 in the turbine's first five years of operation. The school uses electricity from the utility at times when the wind does not blow. This project has been so successful that the Spirit Lake school district has since installed a second turbine with a capacity of 750 kW.

Wind speed is a crucial element in projecting turbine performance, and a site's wind speed is measured through wind resource assessment prior to a wind system's construction. Generally, an annual average wind speed greater than four meters per second (m/s) (or 9 mph) is required for small wind electric turbines (less wind is required for water-pumping operations). Utility-scale wind power plants require minimum average wind speeds of 6 m/s (13 mph).

The power available in the wind is proportional to the cube of its speed, which means that doubling the wind speed increases the available power by a factor of eight. Thus, a turbine operating at a site with an average wind speed of 12 mph could in theory generate about 33% more electricity than one at an 11 mph site, because the cube of 12 (1,768) is 33% larger than the cube of 11 (1,331). In the real world, the turbine will not produce quite that much more electricity, but it will still generate much more than the 9% difference in wind speed. The important thing to understand is that what seems like a small difference in wind speed can mean a large difference in available energy and in electricity produced, and therefore, a large difference in the cost of the electricity generated. Also, there is little energy to be harvested at very low wind speeds; 6 mph winds contain less than one-eighth the energy of 12 mph winds.

Construction of Wind Turbines

Utility-scale wind turbines for land-based wind farms come in various sizes, with rotor diameters ranging from about 50 meters to about 90 meters, and with towers of roughly the same size. A 90-meter machine, definitely at the large end of the scale, with a 90-meter tower would have a total height from the tower base to the tip of the rotor of approximately 135 meters (442 feet). Offshore turbine designs now under development have rotors that have a 110-meter rotor diameter. It is easier to transport large rotor blades by ship than by land. Small wind turbines intended for residential or small business use are much smaller. Most have rotor diameters of 8 meters or less and would be mounted on towers of 40 meters in height or less.

Most manufacturers of utility-scale turbines offer machines in the 700 kW to 1.8 MW range. Ten 700 kW units would make a 7 MW wind plant; while ten 1.8 MW machines would make an 18 MW facility. In the future, machines of larger size will be available, although they will probably be installed offshore, where larger transportation and construction equipment can be used. Units larger than 4 MW in capacity are now under development.

An average U.S. household uses about 10,000 kilowatt-hours (kWh) of electricity each year. One megawatt of wind energy can generate between 2.4 million and 3 million kWh annually. The towers are mostly tubular and made of steel. The blades are made of fiberglass-reinforced polyester or wood-epoxy. A wind farm is shown in Figure 4.17.

Wind Turbine Energy Economics

The "energy payback time" is a term used to measure the net energy value of a wind turbine or other power plants to determine how long the plant has to operate to generate the amount of electricity that was required for its manufacture and construction.

Several studies have looked at this question, over the years, and have concluded that wind energy has one of the shortest energy payback times of any energy technology. A wind turbine typically takes only a few years (3-8, depending on the average wind speed at its site) to "pay back" the energy needed for its fabrication, installation, operation, and retirement.

Since you can't count on the wind blowing, what does a utility gain by adding 100 megawatts (MW) of wind to its portfolio of generating plants? Does it gain

Figure 4.17 Wind turbine installation (Courtesy of AWEMA)

anything? Or should it also add 100 MW of fueled generation capacity to allow for the times when the wind is calm?

First, it needs to be understood that the bulk of the "value" of any supply resource is in the energy that the resource produces, not the capacity it adds to a utility system. In general, utilities use fairly complicated computer models to determine the value in added capacity that each new generating plant adds to the system. According to some models, the capacity value of a new wind plant is approximately equal to its capacity factor. Thus, adding a 100 MW wind plant with an average capacity factor of 35% to the system is approximately the same as adding 35 MW of conventional fueled generating capacity.

The exact answer depends on, among other factors, the correlation between the time that the wind blows and the time that the utility sees peak demand. Thus wind farms whose output is highest in the spring months or early morning hours will generally have a lower capacity value than wind farms whose output is high on hot summer evenings.

Since wind is a variable energy source, its growing use presents problems for utility system managers. At current levels of use, this issue is still some distance from being a problem on most utility systems.

A conventional utility power plant uses fuel, so it will normally run much of the time unless it is idled by equipment problems or for maintenance. A capacity factor of 40% to 80% is typical for conventional plants.

A wind plant is "fueled" by the wind, which blows steadily at times and not at all at other times. Although modern utility-scale wind turbines typically operate 65% to 80% of the time, they often run at less than full capacity. Therefore, a capacity factor of 25% to 40% is common; although, they may achieve higher capacity factors during windy weeks or months.

It is important to note that while capacity factor is almost entirety a matter of reliability for a fueled power plant, it is not for a wind plant, it is a matter of economical turbine design. With a very large rotor and a very small generator, a wind turbine would run at full capacity whenever the wind blew and would have a 60% to 80% capacity factor, but it would produce very little electricity. The most electricity per dollar of investment is gained by using a larger generator and accepting the fact that the capacity factor will be lower as a result. Wind turbines are fundamentally different from fueled power plants in this respect.

If a wind turbine's capacity factor is 33%, it doesn't that mean it is only running one-third of the time. A wind turbine at a typical location in the Midwestern United States runs about 65% to 80% of the time. Much of the time it will be generating at less than full capacity.

Availability Factor

Availability factor or just "availability" is a measurement of the reliability of a wind turbine or other power plant. It refers to the percentage of time that a plant is ready to generate that is, when it is not out of service or under maintenance or repairs, as shown in Figures 4.18 and 4.19. Modern wind tur-

Figure 4.18 Wind turbine installation (Courtesy of AWEMA)

Figure 4.19 Wind turbine installation (Courtesy of AWEMA)

bines have an availability of more than 98%, higher than most other types of power plant. After two decades of constant engineering refinement, today's wind machines are highly reliable.

Wind Turbine Power Generation Capacity

Utilities must maintain enough power plant capacity to meet expected customer electricity demand at all times, plus an additional reserve margin. All other things being equal, utilities generally prefer plants that can generate as needed (that is, conventional plants) to plants that cannot (such as wind plants).

However, despite the fact that the wind is variable and sometimes does not blow at all, wind plants do increase the overall statistical probability that a utility system will be able to meet demand requirements. A rough rule is that the capacity value of adding a wind plant to a utility system is about the same as the wind plants capacity factor multiplied by its capacity, as shown in the previous section. Thus, a 100-megawatt wind plant with a capacity factor of 35% would be similar in capacity value to a 35 MW conventional generator. For example, in 2001 the Colorado Public Utility Commission found the Capacity of a proposed 162 MW wind plant in eastern Colorado (with a 30% capacity factor) to be approximately 48 MW.

The exact amount of capacity value that a given wind project provides depends on a number of factors, including average wind speeds at the site and the match between wind patterns and utility load (demand) requirements. It also depends on how dispersed geographically wind plants on a utility system are, and how well-connected the utility is with neighboring systems that may also have wind generators. The broader the wind plants are scattered geographically, the greater the chance that some of them will be producing power at any given time.

Wind Turbine Energy Supply Potential for the United States

Wind energy could supply about 20% of the nation's electricity, according to Battelle Pacific Northwest Laboratory, a federal research laboratory. Wind energy resources used for generating electricity can be found in nearly every state.

U.S. wind resources are even greater, however. North Dakota alone is theoretically capable (if there were enough transmission capacity) of producing enough wind-generated power to meet more than one-third of U.S. electricity demand. The theoretical potentials of the windiest states are shown in Table 4.3.

Present projections show that wind power can provide at least up to a fifth of a system's electricity, and the figure could probably be higher. Wind power currently provides nearly 25% of electricity demand in the North German state of Schleswig Holstein. In western Denmark, wind supplies 100% of the electricity that is used during some hours on windy winter nights.

Consistency of Support Policy. Over the past five years, the federal production tax credit has been extended twice, but each time Congress allowed the credit to expire before acting and then only approved short durations. The credit expired again December 31, 2003, and as of March 2004 had still not been renewed. These expiration and extension cycles inflict a high cost on the industry, cause large lay-offs, and hold up investments. Long-term, consistent policy support would help unleash the industry's pent-up potential.

Transmission Line Access. Transmission line operators typically charge generators large penalty fees if they fail to deliver electricity when it is scheduled to be transmitted. The purpose of these penalty fees is to punish generators and deter them from using transmission scheduling as a "gaming" technique to gain advantage against competitors, and the fees are therefore

TABLE 4.3. Top Twenty States

Wind Energy Potential as measured by annual
energy potential in the billions of kWh, factoring in
environmental and land use exclusions for wind
class of 3 and higher.

State	Billions of Kilowatt-hours Per Year
1. North Dakota	1,210
2. Texas	1,190
3. Kansas	1,070
4. South Dakota	1,030
5. Montana	1,020
6. Nebraska	868
7. Wyoming	747
8. Oklahoma	725
9. Minnesota	657
10. Colorado	481
11. New Mexico	435
12. Idaho	73
13. Michigan	65
14. New York	62
15. Illinois	61
16. California	59
17. Wisconsin	58
18. Maine	56
19. Missouri	52
20. Iowa	51

not related to whether the system operator actually loses money as a result
of the generators action. But because the wind is variable, wind plant owners
cannot guarantee delivery of electricity for transmission at a scheduled time.
Wind energy needs a new penalty system that recognizes the different nature
of wind plants and allows them to compete on a fair basis.

New Transmission Lines.   The entire transmission system of the wind-rich High
Plains, which cover the central third of the United States, needs to beexten-
sively redesigned and redeveloped. At present, this system consists mostly of
small distribution lines. Instead, series of new high-voltage transmission lines
are needed to transmit electricity from wind plants to population centers. Such
a redevelopment will be expensive, but it will also benefit consumers and national security, by making the electrical transmission system more reliable
and by reducing shortages and the price volatility of natural gas.

Transmission will be a key issue for the wind industry's future development
over the next two decades.

World Wind Power Production Capacity

As of the end of 2003, there were over 39,000 megawatts of generating capacity operating worldwide, producing some 90 billion kilowatt-hours each year-as much as 9 million average American households use, or as much as a dozen large nuclear power plants could generate. Yet this is but a tiny fraction of the potential of wind.

According to the U.S. Department of Energy, the world's winds could theoretically supply the equivalent of 5,800 quadrillion BTUs (quads) of energy each year-more than 15 times current world energy demand. (A quad is equal to about 172 million barrels of oil or 45 million tons of coal.)

The potential of wind to improve the quality of life in the world's developing countries, where more than two billion people live with no electricity or prospect of utility service in the foreseeable future, is vast.

"Wind Force 12," a study performed by Denmark's BTM Consult for the European Wind Energy Association and Greenpeace, found that by the year 2020, wind could provide 12% of world electricity supplies, meeting the needs of 600 million average European households.

Denmark is revisiting and currently rewriting its wind policy. The degree to which that means the United States should reexamine its own policy revolves around the degree to which our situation is similar to Denmark's. In fact, a brief analysis of some major differences suggests that there are strong reasons for continuing to support wind development in the United States rather than back away from it:

Wind supplies 20% of national electricity demand in Denmark. Although the United States has nearly twice as much installed wind equipment as Denmark, wind generates only 0.4% of our electricity, far below the 10% threshold identified by most analysts as the point at which wind's variability becomes a significant issue for utility system operators.

Denmark is also so small geographically (half the size of Indiana) that high winds can cause many of its wind plants to shut down almost at once. In the United States, wind plants are much more geographically dispersed (from California to New York to Texas) and do not all experience the same wind conditions at the same time.

Rapid development of wind and new small-scale power plants within the past five years have brought Denmark to the point where power produced by so-called nondispatchable resources in the country's west exceeds 100% of demand in the region. At many times, this excess generation leaves the country scrambling to increase electricity export capabilities to handle the surplus. This situation is essentially unimaginable in the United States.

Denmark's approach encourages community involvement, but places particular stress on low-capacity distribution networks (at the "end of the line" on transmission systems). In the United States, our larger wind plants require advance transmission planning, but feed into main transmission lines and do not affect the customer distribution network.

Growing Use of Wind Energy for Utility Systems

Denmark's situation should not cause concern in the United States. Denmark's problem is that wind has been too successful, too quickly in a small country, and it must now take steps to manage that success. It is unfortunate that the United States has not dealt with its energy problems so decisively. At current levels of use, this issue is still some distance from being a problem on most utility systems.

- Up to the point where wind generates about 10% of the electricity that the system is delivering in a given hour of the day, there is not an issue. There is enough flexibility built into the system for reserve backup, varying loads, and so forth that there is effectively little difference between a 10% wind system and a system with 0% wind. Variations introduced by wind are much smaller than routine variations in load (customer demand).

- At the point where wind is generating 10% to 20% of the electricity that the system is delivering in a given hour, wind variation is an issue that needs to be addressed, but that can probably be resolved with wind forecasting (which is fairly accurate in the time frame of interest to utility system operators), system software adjustments, and other changes.

- Once wind is generating more than about 20% of the electricity that the system is delivering in a given hour, the system operator begins to incur significant additional expense because of the need to procure additional equipment that is solely related to the system's increased variability.

These figures assume that the utility system has an "average" amount of resources that are complementary to wind's variability (e.g., hydroelectric dams) and an "average" amount of load that can vary quickly (e.g., electric arc furnace steel mills). Actual utility systems can vary quite widely in their ability to handle as-available output resources like wind farms. However, as wholesale electricity markets grow, fewer, larger utility systems are emerging. Therefore, over time, more and more utility systems will look like an "average" system.

Since wind is a variable energy source, doesn't it cost utilities extra to accommodate on a system that mostly uses fueled power plants with predictable outputs?

However, as the previous answer suggests, the added cost is modest. Three major studies of utility systems with less than 10% of their electricity supplied by wind have found the extra or "ancillary" costs of integrating it to be less than 0.2 cents per kilowatt-hour. Two major studies of systems with wind at 20% or more have found the added cost to be 0.3 to 0.6 cents per kilowatt-hour.

Tidal Energy

Tidal energy works from the power of changing tides. Tidal changes in sea level can be used to generate electricity, by building a dam across a costal bay or estuary with large differences between low and high tides. The high tides allow immense amounts of water to rush into the bay. The gates of the dam then shut when water level is at its maximum height. Holes in the bottom of the dam let water rush past turbines. The flow of water generates enough power to turn the turbines, which creates electricity. The entire process repeats with each high tide.

Tides

Creation of tides is a result of the gravitational force of the Moon and Sun and also the rotation of the Earth.

The gravitational attraction of the moon and sun affect the tides on Earth. The magnitude of this attraction depends on the mass of the object and its distance away. The moon has the greater effect on earth despite having less mass than the sun because it is so much closer. The gravitational force of the moon causes the oceans to bulge along an axis pointing directly at the moon. The rotation of the earth causes the rise and fall of the tides. When the sun and moon are in line their gravitational attraction on the earth combine and cause a "spring" tide. When they are as positioned 90 degrees from each other, the gravitational attractions pulls water in different directions, causing a tide.

The rotational period of the moon is around 4 weeks, while one rotation of the earth takes 24 hours; this results in a tidal cycle of around 12.5 hours. This tidal behavior is easily predictable and this means that, if harnessed, tidal energy could generate power for defined periods of time. These periods of generation could be used to offset generation from other forms, such as fossil or nuclear, which have environmental consequences.

Types of Tidal Energy

Currently there are two developing technologies for harvesting the ocean energy, one from tidal barrage and the other from tidal streams.

Tidal Barrage. A barrage or a dam is built across an estuary or bays that have an adequate tidal range, which is usually in excess of 5 meters. The purpose of the dam or barrages is to let water flow through it into the basin as the tide comes in. The barrages have gates that allow the water to pass through.

The gates are closed when the tide has stops coming in, trapping the water within the basin or estuary and creating a hydrostatic head. As the tide recedes, the barrage, gates that that are channeled through turbines are opened, the hydrostatic head causes the water to come through these gates, driving the turbines and generating power. Power can be generated in both directions through the turbines; however, this usually affects efficiency and the economics of the power plant.

Essentially the turbine technology is similar to hydropower. Construction of barrages in general requires extensive civil engineering design.

Tidal Streams.   Tidal streams are fast flowing volumes of water caused by the motion of the tide. These usually occur in shallow depths of seas where a natural construct forces the water to speed up. The technology involved is similar to wind energy; however, there are some differences.

Water is 800 times denser than air and has a much slower flow-rate; this means that the turbine experiences much larger forces and moments. This results in turbine designs that have much smaller diameters. The turbines used either generate power on both ebbs of the tide or are able to withstand severe structural strain resulted from the currents. The technology is still in developmental stages but has substantial potential as a reliable and predictable renewable energy source.

Tidal stream technology has the advantage over tidal barrages when comparing environmental and ecological issues. The technology is less intrusive than offshore wind turbines or tidal barrages, which create hazards to navigation or shipping.

J.A. Consultants, UK

J.A. Consulting is a tidal power engineering organization that promotes tidal stream energy project concepts. The following photographs, Figures 4.20 and 4.21, are of a tidal turbine model, which is being floated in the Thames during a 2003 test.

Pumping

The turbines in the barrage can also be used to pump extra water into the basin at periods of low demand. This usually coincides with cheap electricity prices, generally at night, when demand is low.

Figure 4.20 Stream energy turbine test (Courtesy of A.J. Consulting, UK)

Figure 4.21 Artist rendering of stream energy turbine (Courtesy of A.J. Consulting, UK)

Establishments that provide tidal power in general buy inexpensive electric energy from grids usually during low demand such as night hours and pump extra water in the basins, and then generate power at times of high demand when prices are high. This practice is commonly used in hydroelectric power providers, and is known as pumped storage.

Economics

The capital required to start construction of a barrage is quite significant and has been the main block in deployment of the technology, which is associated with long payback periods. In general advancement of the technology has always been subsidized by government funding or large organizations getting involved with tidal power. However, once the construction of the barrage is complete, there are few maintenances associated and operational costs. In general the turbines only need replacing once every 30 years.

Key to economic success of tidal barrages is optimum design that could produce the most power with the smallest barrage possible.

Social Implications

The building of a tidal barrage can have many social consequences on the surrounding area. An example is the world's largest tidal barrage, La Rance in France, which took over 5 years to construct.

The barrage can be used as a road or rail link, providing a time saving method of crossing the bay or estuary. The bays could also be used as recreation facilities or tourist attractions.

Environmental Concerns

When constructing tidal barrages it is important to take into consideration environmental and ecological affects on the local area, which may be different for each location.

The change in water level and possible flooding could affect the vegetation around the coast, having an impact on the aquatic and shoreline ecosystems. The quality of the water in the basin or estuary could also be affected, the sediment levels could change, affecting the turbidity of the water and therefore affecting the animals that live in it and depend upon it, such as fish and birds. Fish would undoubtedly be affected unless provision was made for them to pass through the barrages.

Not all of the above changes adversely effect the environment, since they may result in growth of different species of plant and creatures that may flourish in the area where they are not normally found.

Tidal Turbines

This form of generation has many advantages over its other tidal energy rivals. The turbines are submerged in the water and are therefore out of sight. They don't pose a problem for navigation and shipping and require the use of much less material in construction. They are also less harmful to the environment. They function best in areas where the water velocity is 2 m/s to 2.5 m/s. Above this level, the turbine experiences heavy structural loads and not enough generation takes place below this level.

Economics of Tidal Turbines

Tidal stream technology, likewise, is in developmental stages. It holds significant potential to harvest renewable energy. The cost of utilizing tidal streams is in general site specific and depends on the type of technology used.

Once installed, electricity is produced with no fuel costs and with complete predictability. The only operational cost will be turbine maintenance, which will be dependant on the technology used.

There are only a few places where this tide change occurs around the earth. Some power plants are already operating using this idea. One plant in France makes enough energy from tides to power 240,000 homes.

Marine Current Turbine Technologies, UK

Marine current turbines are, in principle, like submerged windmills. They will be installed in the sea at places with high tidal current velocities, to take out energy from the huge volumes of flowing water, as shown in Figure 4.22. These flows have the major advantage of being an energy resource as predictable as the tides that cause them, unlike wind or wave energy, which respond to the more random quirks of the weather system.

Figure 4.22 Artist rendering of marine current turbine (Courtesy of MCT, UK)

The technology under development by Marine Current Turbine (MCT) consists of twin axial flow rotors of 15 m to 20 m in diameter, each now driving a generator via a gearbox much like a hydroelectric turbine or a wind turbine, as shown in Figure 4.23. The twin power units of each system are mounted on wing-like extensions either side of a tubular steel monopile some 3m in diameter, which is set into a hole drilled into the seabed from a jack-up barge.

The technology for placing monopiles at sea is well developed by Seacore Ltd., a specialist offshore engineering company, which is cooperating with MCT in this work. The patented design of the turbine is installed and maintained entirely without the use of costly under water operations.

The artist's impression indicates arrow of turbines and shows one raised for maintenance from a small workboat. The turbine is connected to the shore by a marine cable lying on the seabed, which emerges from the base of the pile.

The submerged turbines, which will generally be rated at from 500 to 1,000 kW each (depending on the local flow pattern and peak velocity), will

Figure 4.23 Artist rendering of combination offshore tidal wind turbine (Courtesy of MCT, UK)

be grouped in arrays or "farms" under the sea, at places with high currents, in much the same way that wind turbines in a wind farm are set out in rows to catch the wind. The main difference is that marine current turbines of a given power rating are smaller, because water is 800 times denser than air, and they can be packed closer together (because tidal streams are normally bidirectional whereas wind tends to be multidirectional). Also the technology has a "low profile" and involves negligible environmental impact.

Environmental impact analyses completed by independent consultants have confirmed that the technology does not offer any serious threat to fish or marine mammals. The rotors turn slowly at 10 rpm to 20 rpm; a ship propeller by comparison typically runs 10 times as fast and moreover our rotors stay in one place, whereas some ships move much faster than sea creatures can swim. There is no significant risk of leakage of noxious substances and the risk of impact from our rotor blades is extremely small bearing in mind that the flow spirals in a helical path through the rotor and that nature has adapted marine creatures so that they do not collide with obstructions (marine mammals generally have sophisticated sonar vision). Another advantage of this technology is that it is modular, so small batches of machines can be installed with only a small period between investment in the technology and the time when revenue starts to flow. This is in contrast to large hydroelectric schemes, tidal barrages, nuclear power stations, or other projects involving major civil engineering, where the lead time between investment and gaining a return can be many

It is expected that turbines will generally be installed in batches of about 10 machines to 20 machines. Many of the potential sites so far investigated are large enough to accommodate many hundreds of turbines. As a site is developed the marginal cost of adding more turbines and of maintaining them will decrease, so considerable economies of scale as the project grows.

Marine Current Technologies, UK

Marine Current Turbines Ltd has currently in process of starting a program of tidal turbine development through research and development (R&D) and demonstration phases, to commercial manufacture. An initial grant of 1 million euros has been received from the European Commission towards R&D costs and this has been followed by a grant towards the cost of the first Phase of work from the UK government, DTI worth 960,000 euros. The German partners also received a grant worth approximately 150,000 euros, from the German government.

The company's plan is to complete the initial R&D phase by 2006 and to start commercial installations at that time. It is planned that some 300 MW of installations will be completed by 2010, and, after that, there is far larger growth potential from a market literally oceanic in size. The main R&D program will be as follows.

Phase 1, 1999-2003. Installation of the first large monopile-mounted experimental 300kW single 11-meter diameter rotor system off Lynmouth, Devon, UK, as shown in Figures 4.24 and 4.25. This uses a dump load in lieu of a grid-connection (to save cost) and will only generally operate with the tide in one direction; phase cost 3.3 million euros.

Figure 4.24 Marine current pile mounted turbine installation (Courtesy of MCT, UK)

Figure 4.25 Marine current pile mounted turbine installation (Courtesy of MCT, UK)

Phase 2, 2003-2005.   Design, manufacture, installation, and testing of the first "full size" twin rotor system to be rated at 750 kW to 1,200 kW (each rotor being slightly larger than for the Phase 1 System - the variation depends on the rated velocity for the site chosen). This will be grid-connected and will function with the flow in both directions. It will in fact be the prototype and test-bed for the commercial technology. This phase is expected to cost approximately 4.5 million euros, including grid connection.

Phase 3, 2004-2005.   Installation of the first small "farm" of tidal turbines interconnected with the Phase 2 system, probably involving 3 to 4 extra units to give an aggregate power for the system of about 4 MW to 5 MW - the actual amount depending on how many units and the rated power for the site.

The project will be partly self-financing through revenue generated from sale of electricity. However, it will still be very much the final phases of the R&D program as much will need to be learned form operating several machines together in an array.

Geothermal Energy

Discussions covered in this section are excerpts from Geothermal Education Office Publications. Geothermal energy is derived from Earth's deep heat, as shown in Figure 4.26, which has tremendous potential for producing electric-

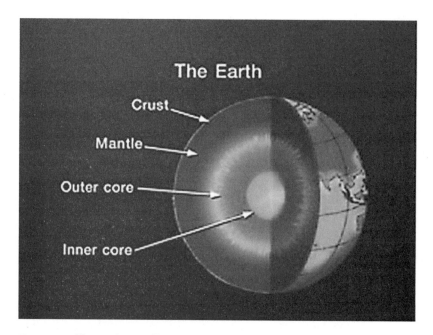

Figure 4.26   The earth core (Courtesy of Geothermal Education Office)

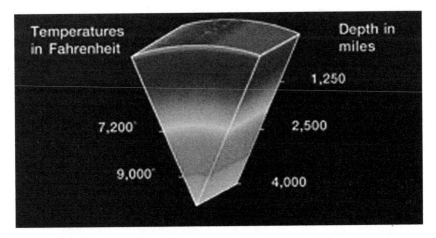

Figure 4.27 Temperature in the earth core (Courtesy of Geothermal Education Office)

ity. The heat is brought near the surface of the earth by the underground circulation of water, by intruding to the Earth's crust of molten magma. Water circulation is achieved by drilling deep wells, as deep as two miles and when in contact with the earths mantle causes the water to be converted into steam or heat up to above 250°F. In general, water when heated above 250 F flows up to ground level by natural pressure. A chart of the temperatures of the Earth is shown in Figure 4.27.

Steam Plants

These classes of plants, an example of which is shown in Figure 4.28, use very hot water and steam, which is heated above 300°F, as found in hot water resources and geysers. The steam is either used directly or is depressurized or "flashed" and purged to eliminate carbon dioxide, nitric oxide, and sulfur, which are usually associated with the process. The clean steam is then used to turn turbines, which drive generators, as shown in Figure 4.29.

Pollution resulted from removal of the above toxic gases and elements is about is about 2 percent of what is generated by traditional, fossil-fuel power plants.

Binary Plants

In this technology, geothermal steam extracted uses lower temperature hot water resources with temperatures that range 100°F to superheated vapor at 300°F. The hot water is passed through heat exchangers, which produce a flow

Figure 4.28 Geothermal plant (Courtesy of Geothermal Education Office)

of secondary fluid, such as isobutene or isopentane, which have a lower boiling point.

The secondary fluid vaporizes and in turns the turbines that generate electricity. The remaining secondary fluids are then recycled through heat exchangers. Upon completion of the process, the geothermal fluid is condensed and returned to the reservoir. Because binary plants use a self-contained cycle, no pollutants are ever emitted or introduced into the atmosphere.

Power plant diagrams are shown in Figures 4.30 and 4.31.

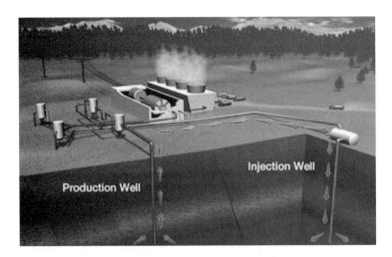

Figure 4.29 Geothermal production (Courtesy of Geothermal Education Office)

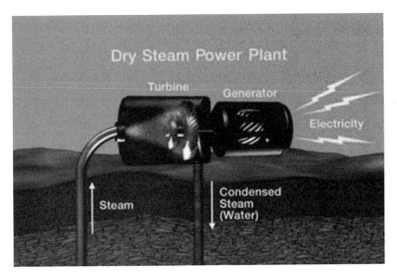

Figure 4.30 Dry type geothermal steam plant (Courtesy of Geothermal Education Office)

Potential

In the United States, the Pacific Northwest has the potential to generate up to 11,000 MW of electricity from geothermal power. A geothermal plant is shown in Figure 4.32. Although estimates of available resources are uncertain, until exploratory work is done, the Northwest Power Planning Council has identified eleven specific areas where it expects there are about 2,000 MW

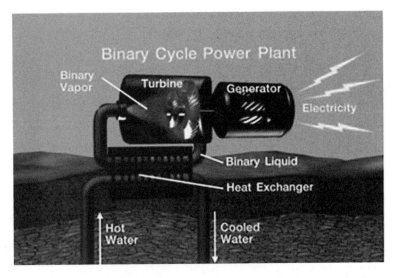

Figure 4.31 Binary geothermal steam plant (Courtesy of Geothermal Education Office)

Figure 4.32 Geothermal power plant (Courtesy of Geothermal Education Office)

to be developed, enough power to serve over 1.3 million homes. A graph is shown in Figure 4.33. Geothermal areas in the Western United States are usually found where there has been a recent volcanic activity, such as the Northwest basins in Oregon, Washington, California, Nevada, and Utah. Low

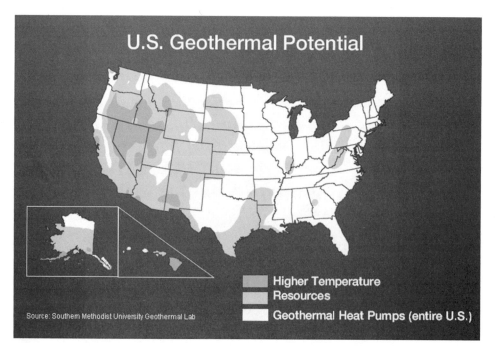

Figure 4.33 U.S. geothermal potential (Courtesy of Southern Methodist University Geothermal Lab)

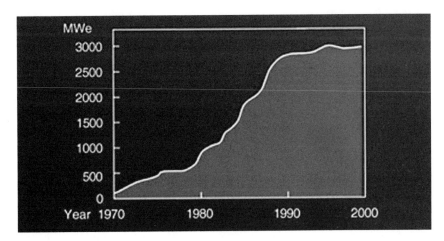

Figure 4.34 Growth in U.S. Geothermal Power, 1970–2000 (Courtesy of Geothermal Education Office)

temperature geothermal heating systems have been in operation for decades in Klamath Falls, Oregon; Boise, Idaho; and the Big Island of Hawaii, which generates 25% of its power from geothermal. Geothermal power production between 1970 and 2000 is shown in Figure 4.34.

Cost of Geothermal Energy and Economics

It is estimated that average cost of geothermal electricity generation per kilowatt-hour is about 4.5 cents to 7 cents. This is comparable to some fossil fuel plants; however, power production does not produce any pollution and, when taking pollution abatement cost, power produced is very competitive. Geothermal plants are built in modular system configurations; each turbine is sized to deliver 25 MW to 50 MW of electric power. When burning fossil fuels such as coal, steam plants generate substantial amounts of noxious gases and precipitants. In general, geothermal steam carries a lesser amount of contaminants.

Geothermal plants are capital-intensive projects, which require no fuel expenditure. Typical projects pay back their capital costs within 15 years. A geothermal plant is shown in Figure 4.35.

Economic Cost Benefits

Geothermal power, similar to other types of renewable energy resources; maintain benefits in the geographic location of installation, which provide local jobs, and contribute royalties and taxes to the county.

Environmental Impact

Although geothermal is one of the less polluting power sources, it must be properly sited to prevent possible environmental impacts. New geothermal

Figure 4.35 Geothermal steam plant (Courtesy of Geothermal Education Office)

systems re-inject water into the earth after its heat is used, in order to preserve the resource and to contain gases and heavy metals sometimes found in geothermal fluids.

Care must be taken in planning geothermal projects to ensure that they don't cool nearby hot springs or cause intermixing with ground water. Geothermal projects can produce some carbon dioxide emissions, but these are fifteen to twenty times lower than the cleanest fossil-fuel power plants, as shown in Figure 4.36.

Benefits of Geothermal Power

- Provides clean and safe energy, using little land space.
- The energy produced is sustainable and renewable.
- Generates continuous, reliable power.
- Power produced is cost competitive.
- Conserves use of fossil fuels.
- Reduces energy imports.
- Benefits local economies.
- Power plants are modular and can be increased in potential incrementally.

Direct Uses

- Balneology—hot springs, baths and bathing
- Agriculture—greenhouse and soil warming

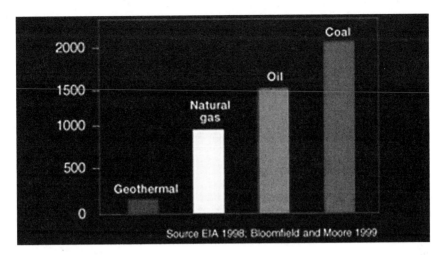

Figure 4.36 CO_2 Emissions Comparison (lbs/MW-hr) (Courtesy of Geothermal Education Office)

- Aquaculture—fish, prawn and alligator farms
- Industrial—product drying and warming
- Direct heating—residential and industrial

World wide geothermal power is used in forty countries and generates about 11,000 MW.

Ocean Thermal Energy

The ocean energy principles use temperature differences in the ocean. The ocean surface and deep water temperature difference is quite significant which allows power plants to be built that use this difference in temperature to make energy. A difference of at least 38 degrees Fahrenheit is needed between the warmer surface water and the colder deep ocean water.

Using this type of energy source is called Ocean Thermal Energy Conversion or OTEC. It is being used in both Japan and in Hawaii in some demonstration projects.

Biomass Energy

For thousands of years, ever since man's existence, human beings have used biomass energy in form of burning wood for heat and cooking food, which generated relatively small amount of carbon dioxide. Since trees and plants for growth remove carbon dioxide from the atmosphere, and are replenished constantly, the net effect of excess gas production on the ecology was kept in balance.

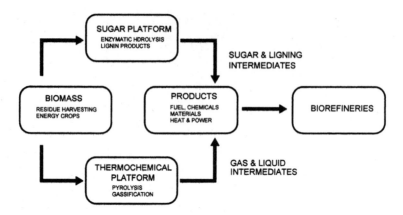

Figure 4.37 Various forms of biomass (Courtesy of DOE/NERL)

With advancement of societies and growing sophistication of lifestyles, use of diverse forms non-renewable forms of biomass such as coal and fossil fuels shifted the balance of carbon dioxide generation and absorption. The net effect of which, as discussed earlier, resulted in greenhouse effects and other air pollution and contaminants, which challenge our very existence.

Fortunately, human intelligence has opened a window of opportunity that allows use of various forms of biomass, as shown in Figure 4.37. Plants; agricultural waste; forestry and lumber residue; organic components of residential, commercial, and industrial waste; and even landfill fumes can be used as bio energy source, which not only reduces the atmospheric pollution but also enables creation of biodegradable products, biofuels, and biopower. These substantially reduce the need use of nonrenewable fossil fuels.

Biofuels

Biofuels are renewable energy sources derived from biomass, such as is shown in Figure 4.38. These are converted into liquid fuels such as ethanol or wood alcohol by a fermentation process. All plant and vegetation material carbohydrates, in form of starch, sugar, and cellulose, like beer and wine, under proper conditions are fermented and converted into ethanol.

Another process of producing methanol is gasification, which involves vaporizing the biomass at very high temperature conditions. Upon vaporization, biomass gases are purged of impurities, by use of special catalytic media.

Ethanol is commonly mixed with gasoline and diesel fuel to reduce vehicular smog emission. Vehicles designed with flexible fuel type engines not only can use methanol as additives but are also capable of using animal fat, vegetable oil, or recycled cooking greases.

Figure 4.38 Biofuels are renewable energy sources that can be converted to liquid fuel (Courtesy of DOE/NERL)

Biomass based alcohols used as pollution-reducing additives are commercially sold as MTBE (methyl tertiary butyl ether) and ETBE (ethyl tertiary ether).

Each year in the United States, we blend 1.5 billion gallons of ethanol with gasoline to reduce air pollution and improve vehicle performance. Most mixed fuels use 10% ethanol and 90% gasoline, which work best in trucks and cars. A mixed gasoline and ethanol fuel is referred to as an E85 grade fuel.

Biopower

Biopower or biomass power is use of direct fired or burning of biomass residue, such as feedstock and forestry residue, to produce steam. The generated steam from the boilers is in turn used to turn steam turbines that convert rotational mechanical energy into electricity. Steam generated is also used to heat buildings and industrial and commercial facilities.

Figure 4.39   A coal-fired plant (Courtesy of DOE/NERL)

Biomass is also used as co-firing agent in coal-fired power plants, shown in Figure 4.39, which quite notably reduces sulfur dioxide emissions.

Gasification System

In this process the biomass is exposed to extremely high temperatures, which cause the hydrocarbon chains to break apart in an oxygen starved environment. Under such conditions, biomass is converted and broken into a mixture of carbon monoxide, hydrogen, and methane.

The gas fuels generated are used to run a jet engine–like gas turbine that is coupled to an electric generator.

Biomass Decay

Biomass when decayed produces methane gas that can be used as an energy source. Decaying organic matter in landfills release considerable amounts of

Figure 4.40   Biomass fuel refinery (Courtesy of DOE/NERL)

methane gas that can be collected by drilling wells. Partially perforated pipes strategically are place in a number of locations throughout the landfill, which are connected to a common header pipe that feeds the collected gas to a chamber, shown in Figure 4.40. The gasses collected are compressed and cleansed by a purging process, which uses water steam to capture corrosive gasses, such hydrogen sulphides. Compressed methane is used either as direct burning fuel or for microturbines and fuel cells to generate electricity and cogenerated heat.

Bioproducts

Interesting uses of biomass are processes that convert them into any product that are presently made from petroleum-based nonrenewable fossil fuel. When converting biomass into biofuels, scientists have developed a technique for releasing sugars, starches, and cellulose that make up the basic structure of plants and vegetation.

Biomasses that have carbon monoxide and hydrogen as their building blocks are used to produce a large variety of products, such as plastics, antifreeze, glues, food sweeteners, food coloring, toothpaste, gelatin, photographic film, synthetic fabrics, textile, and hundreds of products that are completely biodegradable and recyclable.

Chemicals used to produce various renewable materials derived from biomass are referred to as "green chemicals," some of which are shown in Figure 4.41.

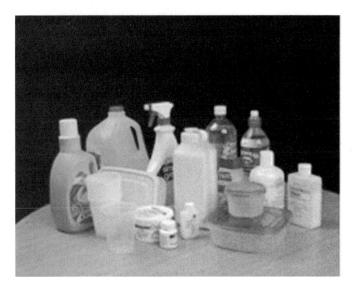

Figure 4.41   Biomass products (Courtesy of DOE/NERL)

Pyrolysis

Under oxygen-starved condition, when biomass is heated at high temperatures, various hydrocarbon components break down and recombine to form an oil referred to as pyrolysis oil. Chemical oil, extracted from the oil called phenol, is principal compound base for foams, adhesives, molded plastics, chipboards and plywood. The liquefaction process diagram is shown in Figure 4.42, and equipment is shown in Figure 4.43.

Some Interesting Facts about Bioenergy

According to the CEC, California produces over 60 million dry tons of biomass each year, only five percent of which is burned to generate electricity. If all of the biomass generated were used, the state could generate 2,000 MW of

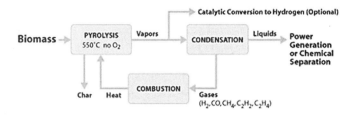

Figure 4.42   Biomass liquefaction via pyrolysis (Courtesy of DOE/NERL)

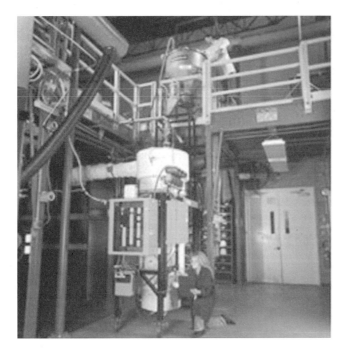

Figure 4.43 Biomass processing lab (Courtesy of DOE/NERL)

electricity, which will be sufficient to supply electricity for about two million homes.

Today biomass energy provides about three to four percent of energy in the United States. Hundreds of U.S. power plants use biomass resources to generate about 56 billion kilowatt-hours of electricity each year.

Combined biopower plants in the U.S. generate a combined capacity of 10.3 GW of power. Which is equal to 1.4% of the nation's total electric generating capacity. With improvement of biopower technology, by year 2020, the power capacity could by increased to about 7% or 55 GW.

It should be noted that biomass fuel, similar to hydroelectric power, is available on continuous basis.

Microturbines

A microturbine, shown in Figure 4.44, is a compact turbine generator that delivers electricity close to the point where it is needed. It operates on a variety of gaseous and liquid fuels and is designed to operate with low BTU landfill gases (LFG). Microturbine technology use became commercialized in 1998.

Microturbines in general serve as primary, emergency backup, or standby power, which add capacity and reduce grid consumption bottlenecks for peak

Figure 4.44 Microturbine installation (Courtesy of Capstone Microturbine)

power shaving purposes. The units deliver energy cost savings, while supplying clean, reliable power with low maintenance needs.

Microturbines are very compact and are packaged in compartments the size of a refrigerator, with power generation capacities of 30 kW to 60 kW of electricity, enough to power a small business.

Maximum thermal efficiencies of Microturbines are achieved when the exhaust is used to recover generated heat, referred to as cogeneration. Generation capacity of the units is literally unlimited when running in parallel, shown in Figure 4.45. Large number of Microturbines connected in parallel can generate up to 1.2 MW of electricity, which can be connected to the grid.

Like a jet engine, microturbines mix fuel with air to create combustion, as shown in Figure 4.46. This combustion turns a magnet generator, compressor, and turbine wheels on a revolutionary single shaft, air-bearing design at high speed with no need for additional lubricants, oils, or coolants. The result is a highly efficient, reliable, clean combustion generator with very low NOx emissions that, unlike diesel generators, can operate around the clock without restrictions. Unlike combined cycle gas turbines, these power systems use no water.

Microturbines are low-emission generators, which are used in application where a combined electricity and heat generation could be used simultaneously. For example, a typical microturbine manufactured by Capstone can provide up to 29 kW of power and 85 kW of heat for combined heat and power applications. The technology makes use of solid-state power electronics that allow synchronized tandem coupling of 2-unit to 20-unit stand-alone with no external hardware except computer cables.

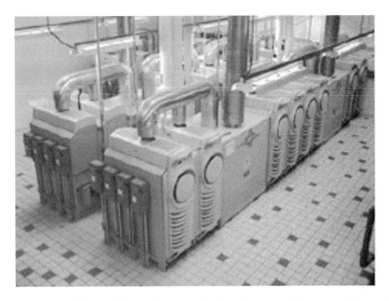

Figure 4.45 Microturbine indoor installation (Courtesy of Capstone Microturbine)

The systems also incorporate circuits that allow automatic grid/stand-alone switching, heat recovery unit, up to100-unit networking, remote monitoring/dispatch, and other functionalities.

Microturbine system major functional components include a **compressor**, combustor, turbine, and permanent magnet generator. The rotating components are mounted on a single shaft, supported by air bearings.

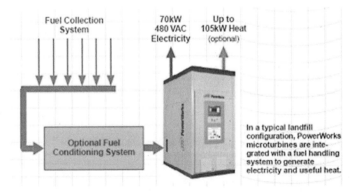

Figure 4.46 Microturbine operational diagram (Courtesy of Capstone Microturbine)

Figure 4.47 Microturbine in landfill installation (Courtesy of Capstone Microturbine)

Land Fill, Wastewater Treatment Plant Biogas

Methane gas is also commonly generated in very large volumes as a byproduct of the biological degradation of organic waste or the result of many industrial processes. Although methane is an excellent waste-gas fuel for microturbines, like the one shown in Figure 4.47, it is also an especially potent greenhouse gas. Land Fill Gasses are created when organic waste in a municipal solid waste landfill decomposes. This gas consists of about 50 percent methane (CH_4), the primary component of natural gas, about 50 percent carbon dioxide (CO_2), and a small amount of nonmethane organic compounds.

Instead of allowing LFG to escape into the air, it can be captured, converted, and used as an energy source, as shown in Figure 4.48. Using LFG helps to reduce odors and other hazards associated with LFG emissions, and helps prevent methane from migrating into the atmosphere and contributing to local smog and global climate change.

Landfill gas is a readily available, local and renewable energy source that offsets the need for nonrenewable resources, such as coal and oil. In fact, LFG is the only renewable energy source that, when used, directly prevents atmospheric pollution. Landfill gas can be converted and used in many ways, generating electricity, heat, or steam; as an alternative vehicle fuel for fleets like school buses, taxis, and mail trucks; or in niche applications like microturbines, fuel cells, and greenhouses.

Of the 6,000 landfills across the United States, there are about 340 energy projects currently in operation. However, EPA estimates that as many as 500

Figure 4.48 LFG can be captured and used as an energy source (Courtesy of Capstone Microturbine)

additional landfills could cost-effectively have their methane turned into an energy source producing electricity to power 1 million homes across the United States. This is equivalent to removing the greenhouse gas emissions that would be generated in a year by 13 million cars.

Hot Water and Hot Air

With a hot water heat exchanger fully integrated into its exhaust system, useful heat is easily extracted from microturbines. This built-in cogeneration ability allows overall system efficiencies to approach 80 percent, depending on the temperature of the inlet water.

Facilities can use this heat in a variety of ways. In suitable climates, the hot water can reduce building heating fuel use by providing space heating. Since the water heat exchanger is rated for potable water use, the system can supply domestic hot water directly.

The hot water can also be used in conjunction with other heat-driven devices such as absorption chillers or desiccant wheels used for dehumidification. In the latter case, the heat provided by the microturbine helps regenerate the desiccant wheel by driving out the captured moisture.

Of course, the 400°F (200°C) exhaust from the microturbine can also be used directly in some applications. Since the gas turbine engine emissions are low, the exhaust is relatively clean. And due to the design of the engine, the exhaust still contains plenty of oxygen and can support follow-up burners to further raise temperature.

Economic Benefits of Using Landfill Gas

Landfill gas projects are a win-win opportunity for all parties involved, whether they are the landfill owners or operators, the local utility, the local government, or the surrounding community. Even before LFG projects produce profits from the sale or use of electricity, they produce a related benefit for communities. Landfill gas projects involve engineers, construction firms, equipment venders, and utilities or end-users of the power produced. Much of this cost is spent locally for drilling, piping, construction, and operational personnel, providing additional economic benefits to the community through increased employment and local sales. Once the LFG system is installed, the captured gas can be sold for use as heat or fuel or be converted and sold on the energy market as renewable "green power." In so doing, the community can turn a financial liability into an asset.

Environmental Benefits of Using Landfill Gas

Converting LFG to energy offsets the need for nonrenewable resources, such as coal and oil and reduces emissions of air pollutants that contribute to local smog and acid rain. In addition LFG can improve the global climate changes discussed earlier.

An Example of Successful Application of Microgenerator Technology

The following application reflects use of Capstone Micro Turbine application in a landfill gas recovery project.

The HOD Landfill, located within the Village of Antioch in Lake County, northeastern Illinois, is a Superfund site consisting of approximately 51 acres of landfill area. On September 28, 1998, the Environmental Protection Agency (EPA) issued a Record of Decision (ROD) for the site requiring that specific landfill closure activities take place. The Remedial Action (in response to the ROD), which was completed in January 2001, included the installation of a landfill gas collection system with 35 dual gas and leachate extraction wells. This system collects approximately 300 cubic feet per minute of landfill gas. In 2001, RMT, Inc., an environmental engineering contractor who undertook project installation, and the Antioch Community School District began exploring the option of using this landfill gas to generate electricity and heat for the local high school. In April 2002, the Antioch Community School District applied for and received a $550,000 grant from the Illinois Department of Commerce and Community Affairs (DECCA) Renewable Energy Resources Program (RERP) to construct a cogeneration system to use the landfill gas to produce electricity and heat at the high school. On December 24, 2002, construction of the system began.

The design and construction of the energy system posed a number of challenges, including resolving local easement issues, meeting local utility re-

Figure 4.49 Antioch Community High School microturbine installation (Courtesy of Capstone Microturbine)

quirements, connecting to the existing school heating system, crossing under a railroad, and meeting the EPA's operational requirements. One-half mile of piping was installed to transfer approximately 200 cubic feet per minute of cleaned and compressed landfill gas to the school grounds, where 12 Capstone MicroTurbines are located in a separate building, shown in Figure 4.49. The 12 microturbines produce 360 kW of electricity and, together with the recovered heat, meet the majority of the energy requirements for the 262,000 square foot school. The system began operating in September 2003.

This use of landfill gas proved beneficial to all parties involved. It provides energy at a low cost for the high school; clean, complete combustion of waste gas; decreased emissions to the environment by reducing the need for traditional electrical generation sources; public relations opportunities for the school and community as being the first school district in the United States

Figure 4.50 Gas compression component installation (Courtesy of Capstone Microturbine)

to get electricity and heat from landfill gas; and educational opportunities in physics, chemistry, economics, and environmental management for Antioch Community High School (ACHS) students, as a result of this state-of-the-art gas-to-energy system being located at the school.

The design of the energy system included tying into the existing gas collection system at the landfill, installing a gas conditioning and compression system, shown in Figures 4.50 and 4.51, and transferring the gas a half-mile to the school grounds for combustion in the micro turbines to generate electricity and heat for the school.

A diagrammatic layout of the landfill gas-to-energy system is shown on Figure 4.52. This work presented many challenges, including resolving easement issues, meeting local utility requirements, connecting to the existing heating system, crossing railroads, cleaning the landfill gas, and meeting the EPA's operational requirements to control landfill gas migration. RMT staff worked with the local government, school officials, and the USEPA, in addition to leading the design efforts and managing the construction activities throughout the project. RMT also provided public relations assistance to ACHS by attending Antioch Village Board meetings to describe the project and to answer any questions from concerned citizens and Village Board members.

Potential options evaluated included using the LFG to the produce electricity, for use in the school's existing boilers, and for use in a combined heat and power system through these evaluations.It was determined that the only economically viable option was to produce electricity and heat for the school.

Figure 4.51 Gas filtration component installation (Courtesy of Capstone Microturbine)

In 2002 ACHS applied for, and received, a $550,000 grant from the Illinois Department of Commerce and Community Affairs to be used for the development of the LFG combined heat and power project shortly after this, RMT and ACHS entered into an agreement to turn the landfill gas into the primary energy source for the high school. The overall cost of this project, including design, permits, and construction was approximately $1.9 million.

RMT was the designer and general contractor on the project. The team was responsible for designing the system, administering contracts, including coordinating access rights, railroad access, obtaining all appropriate permits, creating a health and safety plan, managing construction, and coordinating utility connections.

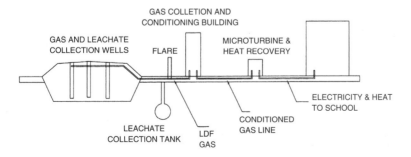

Figure 4.52 Landfill gas configuration diagram (Courtesy of Capstone Microturbine)

Project Design. This project included 12 Capstone micro turbines, to turn landfill gas into the primary energy source for the 262,000-square foot ACHS. This is the first landfill gas project in the U.S. to be owned by and to directly provide heat and power to a school.

The collection system at the HOD Landfill, which includes 35 landfill gas extraction wells, a blower, and a flare, must remain operational to control landfill gas migration. Therefore, the construction of the new cogeneration system required connection to the existing system to allow for excess LFG to be used.

Gas Pipeline to the Microturbines Located at the School High-density polyethylene (HDPE SDR 9) pipe 4 inches in diameter and a half-mile long was installed 4 ft to 12 ft below ground, running from the HOD Landfill to the micro-turbines at the school. The use of horizontal drilling techniques allowed the pipe to cross beneath a stream, a road, public utilities, athletic fields, and a railroad, with minimal disturbance of the ground surface. This was extremely important for the community and the school athletic programs.

Electric Power Generation. Twelve Capstone microturbines are located at the school to provide the electricity and heat from the LFG. Each Capstone microturbine fueled by the landfill gas produces up to 30 kW of three-phase electricity at 480 V, using 12 cubic feet per minute (cfm) to 16 cfm of landfill gas for a total of 360 kW of electricity—enough to power the equivalent of approximately 120 homes. The microturbine system incorporates a combustor, a turbine, and a generator. The rotating components are mounted on a single shaft supported by air bearings that rotate at up to 96,000 RPM. The generator is cooled by airflow into the gas turbine. Built-in relay protection (over/under voltage and over/under frequency) automatically trips off the micro turbines in the event of a utility system outage or a power quality disturbance. Excess electricity not used by ACHS is sold to Commonwealth Edison. A 12-turbine system was selected to provide a system that will remain functional as LFG production from HOD Landfill decreases.

The project's design and construction can be a model for other communities that are interested in the beneficial reuse of nearby landfill gas resources. It is an example of how to deal with the numerous community concerns related to developing an alternative energy system based on landfill gas. To determine, suitable equipment for system design, construction and operation while considering local community needs and requirements, is critical to a successful project.

This project is a prime example of how innovative partnerships and program can take a liability and turn it into a benefit. Solution has created a win-win situation for all involved, including HOD Landfill, ACHS, the Village of Antioch, the State of Illinois, Commonwealth Edison, and the EPA. Each key player is seeing significant benefits of the energy system: Low energy costs for the high school, use of waste heat for internal use in the high school, clean, complete combustion of waste gas, decreased emissions to the environment through reduced need for traditional electrical generation sources, reduction in greenhouse gas emissions, educational opportunities in physics, chemistry, economics, and environmental management as a result of this on-campus, state-of-the art gas-to-energy system.

5

California Energy Commission Rebate Incentive Plans

This section covers partial highlight of CEC rebate Incentive Plan requirements. Complete coverage of the CEC incentive plans can be obtained by visiting the CEC Web site. Intent of this chapter is to familiarize the reader with procedures of applying and procuring California Renewable Energy rebate program requirements. For additional details the readers should refer to California Energy Commission's publication entitled Emerging Renewables Program Handbook (CEC-300-2005-001ED4F).

The Emerging Renewable Program (ERP) was created by California Energy Commision (CEC) to help develop a self-sustaining market for renewable energy systems that supply onsite electricity needs across California. Through this program CEC provides funding to partially offset the cost of purchasing and installing various renewable energy system technologies. The goal of the ERP is to reduce the net cost of renewable energy systems to consumers, and stimulate sales of such systems. Essentially, ERP provides consumers of electricity with a financial incentive to install renewable energy systems on their property. The financial incentives are based on system size, technology, and type of installation. The incentive is only paid when the system installation is complete and operational.

To qualify for the incentive program the consumer and the renewable energy system component must satisfy a number of CEC established requirements.

One of the most important criteria is that the consumer must receive electricity distribution service at the site of installation from an existing electrical service provider, which contributes funds to support the program. In California, electrical and gas service providers that take part in the rebate program are Pacific Gas & Electric Company (PG&E), Southern California Edison Company (SCE), San Diego Gas & Electric Company (SDG&E) and Southern California Water Company (doing business as Bear Valley Electric Service (BVE).

CEC-1038 R1, (1-2005)

R1

RESERVATION APPLICATION FORM
EMERGING RENEWABLES PROGRAM

☐ Modify Existing Record # _____
☐ Affordable Housing Project
☐ New Construction

1. Physical Site of System Installation

Street Address:

City:　　　State:　　　Zip

Submit complete application to:

California Energy Commission
Emerging Renewables Program (MS-45)
1516 Ninth Street
Sacramento, CA 95814-5512

2. Purchaser Name and Mailing Address

Phone: (　)　　　Fax: (　)

6. Equipment (PV modules, turbines, inverters, meters)

	Quantity	Manufacturer, Model (see CEC lists)
Generating Equipment		
Inverters, Meters		

Estimated annual energy production _____ kWh/Year

3. Equipment Seller (Must be registered)

Company:

City:　　　CEC ID (if known):

Phone: (　)　　　Fax: (　)

4. System Installation (Write "Owner" if not hiring contractor)

Company:

City:　　　License No.:

Phone:　　　Fax:

5. Electric Utility (Attach all pages of monthly statement)

☐ PG&E ☐ SCE ☐ SDG&E ☐ BVE　　Service ID:

Billing Period:　　　KWh Used:

Note: If new construction attach building permit. Permit No. _____

7. Rebate and Other Incentives

System Rated Output: _____ watts

Total System Cost: $ _____

Expected Rebate: $ _____

Pay Rebate to:　☐ Purchaser ☐ Seller

Reassign payment?　☐ Yes ☐ No
If yes, submit form 1038 R5 with payment request.

Other Incentives: $ _____
Source/Record No.: _____

8. Declaration

The undersigned parties declare under penalty of perjury that the information in this form and the supporting documentation submitted herewith is true and correct to the best of their knowledge and that the following is true:

1. All system equipment is new and unused and has been purchased within the last 18 months.
2. The generating system is intended primarily to offset Purchaser's electrical needs at the site of installation.
3. The Purchaser's intent is to operate the system at the above site of installation for its useful life or the duration of the lease agreement and
4. The generating system will be interconnected with the distribution system of the electric utility identified above.

The undersigned parties further acknowledge that they are aware of the requirements and conditions of receiving funding under the Emerging Renewables Program (ERP) and agree to comply with all such requirements and conditions as provided in the Energy Commission's ERP Guidebook and Overall Program Guidebook as a condition to receiving funding under the ERP. The undersigned Purchaser authorizes the Energy Commission during the term of the ERP to exchange information on this form with the Purchaser's electric utility to verify compliance with the requirements of the ERP.

Purchaser Signature

Print Name: _____

Signature: _____ Date: _____

Equipment Seller Signature

Print Name: _____

Signature: _____ Date: _____

Necessary Supporting Documentation:
1. All pages of a monthly electric utility bill.
2. Agreements to purchase and install equipment.
3. Payee Data Record (Form STD-204). If payee identified has not previously been paid by the Energy Commission.
4. If not a standard rebate application, attach other required documentation as specified in the ERP Guidebook.

The renewable energy system installed must utilize renewable technologies, such as solar photovoltaic, solar thermal-electric, fuel cells, or small wind turbines. These systems must be interconnected to the utility distribution grid and use components that are tested and certified by CEC. Renewable energy system equipment must be new and have a minimum of a five-year warranty.

To take part in the rebate program, the applicants submit a Reservation Request Form (CEC-1038 R1) and supporting documentation to reserve a fixed amount of reserved CEC rebate funds. Upon reviewing the reservation request forms CEC forwards the applicant a Payment Claim Form (CEC-1038 R2) that specifies the amount of funds reserved and the date which reservation expires.

Upon completion of system installation and operational tests, the applicant submits the Payment Claim Form and supporting documentation to CEC. Upon verification of system eligibility and program criteria requirements, CEC reviews the amount reserved and makes payment in this amount.

Eligibility Requirements

At present the following technologies are eligible for ERP funding.

CEG- 1038 R2 (1-2005)

R2

REBATE PAYMENT CLAIM FORM
EMERGING RENEWABLES PROGRAM

RENEWABLE
ENERGY
PROGRAM

CALIFORNIA ENERGY COMMISSION

Mail complete payment claim to:
California Energy Commission
ERP, Payment Claim
1516 Ninth Street (MS-45)
Sacramento, CA 95814-5512

Record Number _____

Payee Number _____

[CEC use only]   [CEC use only]

Tot.Elig.Cost: $_____   Date CFA: _____

SRO watts: _____   Rebate @ _____ = $_____

1. Confirmation of Reservation Amount

_____ has been granted a reservation of $ _____ for a _____ kW renewable energy generating system. The reservation will expire on _____. The system is being installed at _____ and is expected to produce _____ (kWh per year). The payment will be made to the _____.

The generation system must be completed and the claim submitted with the appropriate documentation by the deadline. Claims must be postmarked by the expiration date or the reservation will expire. This reservation is non-transferable. System must be installed at the installation address and sold to the above.

2. System Equipment (Modules, Wind Turbines, Inverters, kWh Meters)

Number	Manufacturer	Model

Total System Price $ _____
Amount paid by purchaser to date: $ _____
Orientation: *(Circle One)* W, SW, S, SE, E, Other
Tilt: *(Circle one)* None, 1-15, 15-30, >30 Degrees
Tracking system type: _____

3. Modifications

Has any of the information in section 1 or 2 above changed? ☐ Yes ☐ No
If yes note the changes before claiming payment.

_____
_____
_____

The undersigned parties declare under penalty of perjury that the information in this form and the supporting documentation submitted herewith is true and correct to the best of their knowledge. The parties further declare under penalty of perjury that the following statements are true and correct to the best of their knowledge:
(1) The electrical generating system described above and in any attached documents meets the terms and conditions of the Energy Commission's Emerging Renewables Program and has been installed and is operating satisfactorily as of the date stated below.
(2) The electrical generating system described above and in any attached documents is properly interconnected to the utility distribution grid and has or will be issued utility approval to operate the system as interconnected to the distribution grid.
(3) The rated electrical output of the generating system, the physical location of the system, and the equipment identified were installed as stated above.
(4) Except as noted above, there were no changes in the information regarding the seller, installer, purchaser, generating system specifications, installation location, or price from that information provided in the Reservation Request Form originally submitted by the undersigned.
The undersigned parties further acknowledge that they are aware of the requirements and conditions of receiving funding under the Emerging Renewables Program (ERP) and agree to comply with all such requirements and conditions as provided in the Energy Commission's ERP Guidebook and Overall Program Guidebook as a condition to receiving funding under the ERP. As specified in the ERP Guidebook, the undersigned Purchaser authorizes the Energy Commission during the term of the ERP to exchange purchaser information on this form with the Purchaser's electric utility in order to verify compliance with the ERP requirements. If a copy of the utility 'letter of authorization to operate' the system is not submitted with this payment claim form, the undersigned Purchaser understands that he/she is obligated to submit a copy of this letter to the Energy Commission once it is received.

Purchaser	Seller	Is payment assigned to
Print Name: _____	Print Name: _____	*another party?* ☐ Yes ☐ No
Signature: _____	Signature: _____	If yes, attach the payment
Date: _____	Date: _____	assignment form (CEC-1038 R3) with original signatures.

IMPORTANT - Necessary Supporting Documentation
1. Final building permit and final inspection signoff; 2. Final invoice(s) confirming the total amount paid for the system equipment and installation; 3. Five-year warranty (CEC-1038 R3 form); 4. Utility letter of authorization to interconnect the system or the Purchaser's authorization form to access Purchaser's utility data; 5. Utility bill or other proof of electrical service and consumption at the site of installation if not previously provided; 6. Payee Data Record (STD-204)

- Photovoltaic systems which conversion of sunlight to electricity.
- Solar thermal electric technologies that convert sunlight to heat, a medium used to power a generator to produce electricity.
- Fuel cell technologies that convert sewer gases, landfill gases, or other renewable sources of hydrogen or hydrogen rich gas into electricity
- Wind Turbines technologies, which produce electricity, that range in power output of 50 kW or less

Eligibility for renewable energy systems is restricted to private use only and may not be owned by an electrical corporation as defined in the California Public Utilities Code.

Grid Interconnection

Eligible renewable energy systems must be permanently interconnected to and existing electrical distribution grid utility which serves the customer's electrical load, which include PG&E, SCE, SDG&E, and BVE. The system interconnection must comply with applicable electrical codes and utility interconnection requirements.

New Equipment

All system hardware components must be new and must not have been used previously. Equipment purchased or installed more than 18 months prior to applying for a reservation is not eligible.

Renewable Energy System Size

Eligible systems must be sized so that the amount of electricity produced by the system primarily offsets part or all of the customer's electrical needs. Electricity produced by the system may not be more than twice the expected electrical demand load needs of the electricity consumed by the project. This criterion does not apply to systems with less than 10 kW.

System Installation

System installation and integration must be executed under a written contract by a licensed California contractor who holds active A, B, C-10, or C-46 license for photovoltaic systems.

Systems may also be self-installed by the owner; however, in such installations, eligibility for funding without the licensing requirements is subject to a lesser rebate. All installation must be in conformance with the manufacturer's specifications and meet all applicable National Electrical (NEC) and building (UBC) codes and standards.

Warranty Requirements

All systems installations are required to have a minimum five-year warranty to protect the purchaser against system or component breakdown. The warranty is required to cover and provide for no-cost repair or replacement of the system or system components, which also includes labor for five years. The warranty provided must be a combination of support by the manufacturer and installer.

Self-installed systems must also have a minimum five-year warranty to protect the purchaser against breakdown or electrical components; however, the warranty need not cover the labor costs associated with removing or replacing major components.

System Performance Meter

All systems installed require a performance meter so that the customer can determine the amount of energy produced by the system. The above meters

CEC- 1038 R4 (1-2005)

R4	EQUIPMENT SELLER INFORMATION FORM *EMERGING RENEWABLES PROGRAM*

This information must be submitted before a company can become eligible to participate in the ERP. To remain eligible, a company must resubmit this form annually, by March 31. This annual submittal is required even if the information identified in the company's prior R4 submittal has not changed. In addition, a company must submit an updated R4 form any time its reported information has changed. The updated R4 form must be submitted to the Energy Commission within 30 days of the change of any reported information. Registered companies are listed at [www.consumerenergycenter.org/erprebate/database/]

Business name:

Address:

Phone: (   )

Fax : (   )

Email:

Web Site:

Owner or principal Title:

Business license number:

Reseller's license number:

Contractor license number (if applicable):

Select one of the following:

☐ Corporate, LLC, LLP or other that is registered with the California Secretary of State (or appropriate state attached)

☐ Not a corporation, LLC or LLP

The above information applies solely to the business identified above:

Print Name: _____   Title: _____

Signature: _____

Date: _____

Send this completed form by telefax to (916) 653-2543 or by mail to:

ERP Seller Registration
California Energy Commission
1516 9ᵗʰ Street, MS-45
Sacramento, CA 95814-5512

Reminder:
This form must be on file with the Energy Commission for a rebate application with the above company to be considered. It must be resubmitted annually by March 31 for sellers to remain eligible from year to year.

are listed with the CEC, which measures the total energy produced by the system in kilowatt-hours.

The meters are designed to retain the kilowatt-hour production data in the event of a power outage and have a display window to allow the customer view the power output production.

Equipment Distributors

Eligible renewable product (ERP) manufacturers and companies who sell system equipment must provide the CEC with the following information on the Equipment Seller Information Form (CEC-1038 R4).

- Business name, address, phone, fax, and e-mail address
- Owner or principal contact
- Business license number
- Contractor license number (if applicable)
- Proof of good standing on the records of the California Secretary of State, as required for corporate and limited liability entities
- Reseller's license number

Audits and Inspections

During the course of project execution CEC will conduct audits of the applications it receives and verifies that the information provided in the applications are true and correct. The CEC also conducts field inspections to verify that the systems installed are operating properly and within the specified limits of reservation requested.

In the event of payment request that appears to be questionable CEC may stop review of the application containing the questionable information to investigate further or request additional documentation from the contractor, equipment seller, and/or purchaser to verify the accuracy of the questionable information.

Incentives Program

This program offers two types of incentives. The first type of incentive is a rebate, which is based on the generating capacity of a system and is paid in a lump sum. The second type is a performance-based incentive, which is based on the amount of electricity generated by a system and is paid over a three year period. The latter is offered through a pilot program.

Rebates Offered

Rebates offered by CEC vary by system size, technology, and type of installation. The incentive is intended to reduce purchase cost of the eligible system and reduce electrical energy usage from service providers. Table 5.1 lists the rebate levels available by CEC as of January 1, 2005. These rebate levels will be reduced over time.

Additional Incentives

Rebate incentives that may be received from sources other than the ERP system may affect the rebate amount you receive from the CEC. Fifty percent (50%) of incentives received must be subtracted from the rebate amounts listed in rebate table if the incentives are from other utility programs, such as a State of California sponsored incentive program or a Federal Government sponsored incentive program other than tax credits. Applicants will not re-

TABLE 5.1 Rebates Available for Emerging Renewable Systems

Technology	Size	Rebate
Photovoltaic systems	Under 30 kW	$ 2.80 per watt
Solar Thermal Electric	Under 30 kW	$ 3.20 per watt
Fuel Cell using renewable fuel	Under 30 kW	$ 3.20 per watt
Wind energy	First 7.5 kW	$ 1.70 per watt
Additional increments	Up to 30 kW	$ 0.70 per watt

ceive reservation or payment from the CEC if the same system is participating or has participated in the California Public Utilities Commission approved Self Generation Incentive Program, Rebuild San Diego Program, or any other rebate program using ratepayer funds.

At present, approximately $118,125,000 in funding has been allocated to the ERP for 2002 through 2006. Any funding added to the ERP will be allocated to systems less than 30 kW unless otherwise specified. The rebate levels for all technology types are reduced by 20 cents per watt every six months.

It should be noted that the reservation period or expiration date of an approved reservation submitted after January 19, 2005, might not be extended under any circumstances.

Rebate Reservation

To apply for a rebate reservation, applicants must submit the following.

- A completed Reservation Request Form (CEC-1038 R1)
- Copy of agreement(s) to purchase and install a system
- Evidence that site electricity load is supplied by an eligible utility
- Payee data record (Form STD-204) for the rebate recipient

Reservation Request Form

The Reservation Request Form (CEC-1038 R1) identifies information about the proposed system and specifies what information must be submitted with the application. The purchaser of the system must always sign the Reservation Request Form. If the equipment seller is designated as the payee, the seller (retailer or wholesaler) must also sign. It should be noted that eligible equipment sellers must have filed business information with CEC to be eligible to participate in the program.

Evidence of Purchase Agreement

Application forms must accompany evidence of an agreement to purchase and install a system. The document must demonstrate whether the system is owner or contractor installed. Additional information required to complete the application form include the following.

- The quantity, make, and model number (as shown on the CEC lists of eligible equipment) for the photovoltaic modules, wind turbines, or other generating equipment and for the inverters and system performance meters
- The total purchase price of the system before applying the rebate
- Language indicating the purchaser's commitment to buy the system
- Printed names and signatures of the purchaser and equipment seller's authorized representative

Installation contracts must also comply with the Contractors State License Board (CSLB) requirements that must include the following.

- Name, address and contractor's license number of the company performing the system installation
- Site address for the system installation
- Description of the work to be performed
- Total agreed to price to install the system
- Payment terms (payment dates and dollar amounts)
- Printed names and signatures of the purchaser and the company's authorized representative

As mentioned above, qualifying contractors must have a valid A, B, C-10, or C-46 contractor's license.

Owner- or Self-installed System

For owner-installed systems, the applicant must provide the following information.

- An equipment purchase agreement as described above.
- In cases where there is not a signed agreement to purchase equipment, the purchaser may provide invoices or receipts showing that at least 10 percent of the system equipment purchase price has been paid to the seller.

Electric Service Provider Eligibility

For proof of electrical service the purchaser must either contact the utility or request a log of power demand consumption for the most recent 12 months or must submit a recent copy of the utility bill showing the service address of the installation site, the name of the applicant, electric energy usage, and the utility name. The utility bill should not be older than six months from the date of application.

The complete reservation request application must be delivered by mail to:
ERP Reservation Request California
Energy Commission 1516 - 9th StMS-45
Sacramento, CA 95814-5512

Claiming a Rebate Payment

To receive payment of rebate, the owner must comply with all program requirements and make a complete claim for payment before the expiration of reservation.

Payment Claim Form

Upon completion of the required documents, CEC sends a copy of the Payment Claim Form (CEC-1038 R2) to the purchaser and designated payee to confirm the amount of funding reserved on the purchaser's behalf.

Upon review of the form it is returned to the CEC by registered mail. Original signatures are required to process a payment.

Evidence of Final Payment for System Installation

The owners or applicant must upon completion of system installation submit a final system cost documentation, which identifies the final amount paid for the installation of the system. The documentation must include proof of the final amount paid by the applicant to the equipment seller or contractor.

The final amount paid for the system must match the cost information identified in the Payment Claim Form, which must accompany final invoices and a copy of the final agreement. Amount paid by the purchaser to the contractor must be clearly indicated and also must indicate the extent to which the CEC's rebate lowered the cost of the system.

The Energy Commission will conduct spot checks to verify that payments were made as identified in the final invoices or agreements provided by equipment sellers or installers. As part of these spot checks, the Energy Commission will require applicants to submit copies of cancelled checks, credit card statements, or equivalent documentation to substantiate payments made to the equipment seller or installer. When submitting this documentation, applicants are encouraged to redact their personal account numbers or other sensitive information identified in the documentation. Applicants must explain the difference if the final amount paid by the applicant is different from the amount of the purchase or installation shown in any agreement or invoice or in the previously submitted Reservation Request Form (CEC-1038 R1).

Building Permit and Final Inspection

Upon completion of installation, the owner must submit a copy of the building permit and the final inspection signoff for the system installation.

Warranty

A full five-year warranty form (CEC-1038 R3) must be completed and signed by the installer. In the event the applicant is unable to obtain warranty coverage for labor, the application will be treated as an owner installed system and be given a 15 percent lower rebate.

Evidence of Utility Service Eligibility

On new construction, when an electric utility is not available at the time of submitting the reservation request, the applicant must provide a copy of a re-

CEC 1038 R3 (1-2005)

R3
MINIMUM WARRANTY FORM
EMERGING RENEWABLES PROGRAM

System Information

This warranty applies to the following _____ kW renewable energy electric generating system
Description: _____
Located at: _____

What is Covered

This five year warranty is subject to the terms below (check one of the boxes):

☐ All components of the generating system **AND** the system's installation. Said warrantor shall bear
the full cost of diagnosis, repair and replacement of any system or system component, at no cost to the
customer. This warranty also covers the generating equipment against breakdown or degradation in
electrical output of more than ten percent from the originally rated output (PTC rating for modules,
manufacturers rating for wind turbines); or

☐ System's installation only. Said warrantor shall bear the full cost of diagnosis, repair and replacement of
any system or system component, exclusive of the manufacturer's coverage. (Copies of five-year warranty
certificates for the major system components (i.e., solar modules, wind turbines, etc. and inverter- MUST
be provided with this form).

General Terms

This warranty extends to the original purchaser and to any subsequent purchasers or owners at the same
location during the warranty period. For the purpose of this warranty, the terms "purchaser," "subsequent
owner," and "purchase" include a lessee, assignee of a lease, and a lease transaction. This warranty is
effective from _____ (date of completion of the system installation).

Exclusions

This warranty does not apply to:
• Damage, malfunction, or degradation of electrical output caused by failure to properly operate or maintain
the system in accordance with the printed instructions provided with the system.
• Damage, malfunction, or degradation of electrical output caused by any repair or replacement using a part
or service not provided or authorized in writing by the warrantor.
• Damage malfunction, or degradation of electrical output resulting from purchaser or third party abuse,
accident, alteration, improper use, negligence or vandalism, or from earthquake, fire, flood, or other acts of
God.

Obtaining Warranty Service

Contact the following warrantor for service or instructions:

Name: _____   Phone: (   )
Company: _____   Fax: (   )
Address: _____

Signature: _____   Date: _____

cent electric utility bill or a letter from the electric utility to show that electrical service has been provided at the installation site and that utility service was established prior to the expiration date of the reservation. The owner must also provide a separate letter from a qualified architect, electrical engineer, or electrical contractor that identifies the expected electricity consumption at the site and that portion of the demand load requirements is satisfied by the solar power cogeneration.

System Interconnection with Utility Grid

The solar power contractor must demonstrate that the renewable energy system installed has been interconnected to the utility distribution grid and that the utility has approved this interconnection for the system. The owner must demonstrate the above by submitting a letter of authorization to interconnect the system from the utility. For new constructions the utility provider must provide a written confirmation from that a net meter has been set at the site. The owner must also authorize CEC to exchange applicant information with the applicant's utility company to verify compliance with these interconnection and program requirements.

Submitting a Payment Claim

Once a system has been installed and grid-connected and is fully operational, the following documents must be submitted to CEC to claim a rebate payment:

- Rebate Payment Claim Form (CEC-1038 R2)
- Documentation confirming what equipment and labor was purchased and fully paid.
- Building permit and final inspection signoff
- Five-year warranty for the system and labor and material

It should be noted that if the payment request application were incomplete, the CEC would request clarification or provision of all missing or unclear information that must be submitted within 60 days. The request for payment may be denied if all the requested information is not received within the time period.

Assignment of Rebate Payment

The rebate payment may be assigned by the owner to a third party by completing the Reservation Payment Assignment Form (CEC-1038 R5) and submitting it with form (CEC-1038 R2).

CEC- 1038 R5 (07-2004)

R5 **RESERVATION PAYMENT ASSIGNMENT FORM**
EMERGING RENEWABLES PROGRAM

RENEWABLE
ENERGY
PROGRAM
CALIFORNIA ENERGY COMMISSION

Record Number _____
Payee ID Number _____

Reservation Information
Payee Name: _____
Payee Address: _____
                   _____
Payee Contact: _____
Payee Phone #:   _____

Assignment Request

I, _____, the designated payee or authorized representative of the payee, hereby assign the right to receive payment for the above noted reservation under the Emerging Renewables Program to the following individual or entity:

Name: _____
Address: _____
            _____
Phone #:   _____

I request that payment be forwarded to this individual or entity at the address noted. Upon request proof of payment will be forwarded to me.

Acknowledgement

As the designated payee or authorized representative, I understand that I remain responsible for complying with the requirements of the Emerging Renewables Program and will remain liable for any tax consequences associated with the reservation payment, despite the payment's assignment. I further understand that I may revoke this payment assignment at any time prior to the Energy Commission's processing of the payment by providing written notice to the Energy Commission's Technology Market Development Office. Such notice shall be provided to: Emerging Renewables Program, California Energy Commission, 1516 9th Street, MS-45, Sacramento, CA 95814-5512.

Executed on: _____   Signature: _____
                                    Name: _____
                                    Title: _____

This completed form may be submitted with either the Reservation Request Form (CEC-1038 R1) or the Payment Claim Form (CEC-1038 R2) for standard rebates. This form may not be submitted by telefax, as original signatures are needed to process assignment requests.

Changes that Affect the Rebate Amount

Modifications to an approved reservation may be made prior to a payment claim or when the payment claim is submitted. When a modification includes parameters that affect incentive amounts, a new incentive amount will be calculated and the calculation will be based on the program parameters at the time a modification request, when the supporting documentation is deemed complete. Parameters affecting the incentive include the installation type, system size, and technology. If any change results in the installed system differing in its rated electrical output or other parameters from the system originally specified in the Reservation Request Form (CEC-1038 R1), a new rebate payment amount will be calculated.

If any change occurs that would have decreased the original rebate calculation, the amount reserved will also be decreased by the same factor. For example, if the installed system is smaller in output than originally specified in the Reservation Request Form, the new rebate amount will be determined by prorating the amount reserved downward (using the same rebate level that was used to calculate the original rebate amount). Similarly, if the installation type changes from a professional-install to an owner-install the incentive is reduced by 15 percent; this implies that owner installed systems qualify for 15 percent lower incentive.

Reporting System Performance

Renewable energy system performance, which is measured in kWh, could be collected and reported to CEC, if so desired by the owner and electric utility, by a web-based monitoring system administered by a private party. If so chosen, the owner wishing to use this option should make special arrangements with their electric utility and enter into special agreements with their utility provider to ensure that data is recorded on a monthly basis and is reported to the CEC each quarter. In using this option, owners assume full responsibility for all costs associated with their utility's collection and reporting.

Reservation Period

The reservation period is established into two parts. A 12-month preliminary reservation, during which the applicant must purchase and install the proposed system, and a 3-year final reservation period, in which the applicant should provide quarterly invoices to CEC to claim incentive payments for their renewable energy cogeneration. Either of the above options is fixed and could not be extended under any circumstances.

Applicants that could not meet the above deadlines after issuance of reservation will be denied rebate funds. In such an event, the applicants must reapply for a new rebate.

To claim incentive payments, quarterly invoices must be submitted to CEC using special invoice form (CEC-1038 R10). Any addition or deletion of equipment from the system during the reservation period must be reported to CEC.

Special Funding For Affordable Housing Projects

California assembly Bill 58 mandates CEC to establish an additional rebate for systems installed on affordable housing projects. Affordable housing projects are entitled to qualify for an extra 25 percent rebate above the standard rebate level, provided that the total rebated does not exceed 75% of the system cost. Eligibility criteria for qualifying are as follow.

- The affordable housing project must adhere to California health and safety code.
- The property must expressly limit residency to extremely low, very low, lower, or moderate income persons and must be regulated by the California Department of Housing and Community Development.
- Each residential unit (apartments, multifamily homes, etc.) must have individual electric utility meter.
- The housing project must be at least 10% more energy efficient than the current standards specified.

Special Funding For Public and Charter Schools

A special amendment to CEC mandate enacted in February 4, 2004, established Solar Schools Program to provide a higher level of funding for public and charter schools to encourage the installation of photovoltaic generating

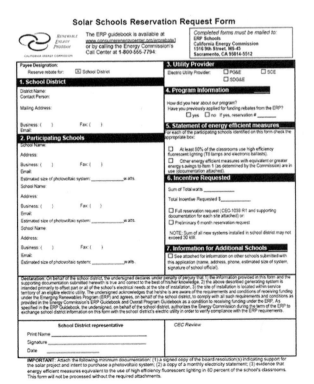

systems at more school sites, see the Solar Schools Reservation Request Form. At present California Department of Finance has allocated a total $2.25 million for this purpose. To qualify for the additional funds the schools must meet the following criteria.

- The public or charter school must provide instruction for any grade between kindergartens through 12th grade.
- The schools must have installed high efficiency fluorescent lighting in at least 80% of classrooms.
- The schools must agree to establish a curriculum tie-in plan to educate students about the benefits of solar energy and energy conservation.

Incentive for Pilot Performance Based Programs

This is an optional program where the incentive payment is based on a photovoltaic power cogeneration and on the systems energy production over a three-year period.

Under this option the incentive is calculated according to the following formula.

$$\text{Incentive Fund} = (\text{PV Array Kw}) \text{ XPTC} \times (8760 \text{ hrs/year}$$
$$\times 25\% \text{ kWh/kW} \times \$0.50/\text{kWh} \times 3 \text{ years}$$

The 25% capacity factor is deliberately set high to ensure sufficient fund reservation. Maximum amount of fund is capped at $400,000 per site. The maximum allowed fund for aggregate system installed under a corporate structure or government program is $1 million.

6

Photo Galleries

Solar Power Systems

Figure 6.1 Roof mounted solar power installation (Courtesy of Solar Electrical Systems)

Figure 6.2 Two hundred kilowatt ground mount solar power installation, Mojave Desert, California (Courtesy of Grant Electric)

Figure 6.3 Ground mount solar power installation (Courtesy of Solar Electrical Systems)

Figure 6.4 Roof mount solar power installation (Courtesy of Solar Electrical Systems)

Figure 6.5 Residential solar power installation in track housing project (Courtesy of Atlantis Energy)

Figure 6.6   Roof mount residential solar power installation (Courtesy of Solar Electrical Systems)

Figure 6.7   Ground mount solar power installation (Courtesy of Solar Electrical Systems)

Figure 6.8 Sunny Boy Inverter system for ground mount solar power installation (Courtesy AES)

Figure 6.9 Canopy and canopy solar power installation (Courtesy of PowerLight Corporation)

Figure 6.10 Commercial roof mount solar power installation (Courtesy of PowerLight Corporation)

Figure 6.11 Roof mount solar power installation (Courtesy of Power-Light Corporation)

Figure 6.12 Entrance canopy solar power installation (Courtesy of Golden Solar Energy)

Figure 6.13 Carport solar power installation (Courtesy of United Solar Ovonic Corporation, Santa Monica, California)

Figure 6.14 Residential solar power installation (Courtesy of Sharp Electronics)

Figure 6.15 Roof mount commercial solar power installation (Courtesy of PowerLight Corporation)

Figure 6.16 Industrial solar power installation (Courtesy of Shell Solar USA)

Figure 6.17 Residential solar power installation (Courtesy of Evergreen Solar)

Figure 6.18 Residential roof mount solar power installation (Courtesy of Evergreen Solar)

Figure 6.19 Residential solar power installation (Courtesy of Sharp Electronics)

Figure 6.20 Four-kilowatt residential solar power installation, Hollywood, California (Courtesy of Grant Electric)

Figure 6.21 Residential solar power installation (Courtesy of Sharp Electronics)

Figure 6.22 Residential solar power installation (Courtesy of Sharp Electronics)

Figure 6.23 Open space solar power installation (Courtesy of California Green Design)

Figure 6.24 Inverter system for ground mount solar power installation (Courtesy of California Green Design)

Figure 6.25 Roof mount solar power instillation (Courtesy of California Green Design)

Figure 6.26 Roof mount solar power instillation (Courtesy of California Green Design)

Figure 6.27 Roof mount solar power support system (Courtesy of California Green Design)

Geothermal Energy Installation

Figure 6.28 Big Island Geothermal Power Generating Station, Hawaii (Courtesy of Department of Geothermal Education)

Figure 6.29 Rokotawa Geothermal Power Generating Station, Japan (Courtesy of Department of Geothermal Education)

Figure 6.30 Geothermal power generating station (Courtesy of Department of Geothermal Education)

Microturbine Power Systems

Figure 6.31 Tandem microturbine installation (Courtesy of Capstone Micro Turbine)

Figure 6.32 City of Burbank Landfill, California (Courtesy of Capstone Micro Turbine)

Figure 6.33 Glacier Ridge landfill, Minnesota (Courtesy of Capstone Micro Turbine)

Solar Cooling Systems

Figure 6.34 Solar cooled office by absorption chiller (Courtesy of Solargenix)

Figure 6.35 Solar cooling installation, industrial application (Courtesy of Solargenix)

Solar Pool Heating Systems

Figure 6.36   (Courtesy of UMA/Heliocol)

Figure 6.37   (Courtesy of UMA/Heliocol)

Figure 6.38   (Courtesy of UMA/Heliocol)

Glossary of Renewable Energy Power Systems

All those technical terms can make renewable energy systems difficult for many people to understand. This glossary aims to cover all of the most commonly used terms, as well as a few of the more specific terms.

A

Alternating Current (AC):   Electrical current that continually reverses direction. The frequency at which it reverses is measured in cycles-per-second, or hertz (Hz). The magnitude of the current itself is measured in amps (A).

Alternator: A device for producing AC electricity. Usually driven by a motor, but can also be driven by other means, including water and wind power.

Ammeter: An electrical or electronic device used to measure current flowing in a circuit.

Amorphous silicone: A noncrystalline form of silicon used to make photovoltaic modules (commonly referred to as solar panels).

Ampere (Amp):   The unit of measurement of electrical current. Its symbol is A.

Ampere-hour, Amp-hour (Ah):   A measurement of electrical charge. One amp-hour of charge would be removed from a battery if a current of one amp flowed out of it for one hour. The amp-hour rating of a battery is the maximum charge that it can hold.

Anode: The positive electrode in a battery, diode, or other electrical device.

Anemometer: A device used to measure wind speed.

Axial flow turbine: A turbine in which the flow of water is in the same direction as the axis of the turbine.

B

Battery: A device, made up of a collection of cells, used for storing electricity, which can be either rechargeable or non-rechargeable. Batteries come in many forms, and include flooded cell, sealed, and dry cell.

Battery charger: A device used to charge a battery by converting (usually) mains voltage AC to a DC voltage suitable for the battery. Chargers often incorporate some form of regulator to prevent overcharging and damage to the battery.

Beta limit: The maximum power (theoretically) that can be captured by a wind turbine from the wind, which equals 59.3% of the wind energy.

Blade: The part of a turbine that water or air reacts against to cause the turbine to spin, which is sometimes incorrectly referred to as the propeller. Most electricity-producing wind turbines will have two or three blades, whereas water-pumping wind turbines will usually have up to twenty or more.

C

Capacitor: An electronic component used for the temporary storage of electricity, as well for removing unwanted noise in circuits. A capacitor will block DC but will pass AC.

Cell: The most basic, self-contained unit that contains the appropriate materials, such as plates and electrolyte, to produce electricity.

Circuit breaker: An electrical device used to interrupt an electrical supply in the event of excess current flow. Can be either magnetically or thermally activated or a combination of both, which can be manually reset.

Conductor: A material used to transfer or conduct electricity, often in the form of wires.

Cathode: The negative electrode in a battery, diode, or other electrical device.

Compact fluorescent lamp: A form of fluorescent lighting that has its tube "folded" into a "U" or other more compact shape, so as to reduce the space required for the tube.

Conduit: A pipe or elongated box used to house and protect electrical cables.

Converter: An electronic device that converts electricity from one DC voltage level to another.

Cross-flow turbine: A turbine where the flow of water is at right angles to the axis of rotation of the turbine.

Current: The rate of flow of electricity, measured in amperes or amps. Analogous to the rate of flow of water measured in liters per second, which is also measured in amperes.

D

Darrius Rotor: A form of vertical-axis wind turbine that uses thin blades.

Direct Current (DC): Electrical current that flows in one direction only, although it may vary in magnitude.

Diode: A semi-conductor device that allows current to flow in one direction, while blocking it in the other.

Dry cell battery: A battery that uses a solid paste for an electrolyte. Common usage refers to small cylindrical 'torch' cells.

E

Earth or Ground: Refers to physically connecting a part of an electrical system to the ground, done as a safety measure, by means of a conductor embedded in suitable soil.

Earth-leakage Circuit Breaker (KLCB): A device used to prevent electrical shock hazards in mains voltage power systems, includes independent power systems, which are also known as residual current devices (RCDs).

Electricity: The movement of electrons (a sub-atomic particle) produced by a voltage through a conductor.

Electrode: An electrically conductive material, forming part of an electrical device, often used to lead current into or out of a liquid or gas. In a battery, the electrodes are also known as plates.

Electrolysis: A chemical reaction caused by the passage of electricity from one electrode to another.

Electrolyte: The connecting medium, often a fluid, which allows electrolysis to occur. All common batteries contain an electrolyte, such as the sulphuric acid used in lead-acid batteries.

Energy: The abstract notion that makes things happens or that has the potential or ability to do work. It can be stored and converted between many different forms, such as heat, light, electricity, and motion. It is never created or destroyed but does become unavailable to us when it ends up as low temperature heat. It is measured in joules (J) or watt-hours (Wh) but more usually mega joules (MJ) or kilowatt-hours (kWh).

Equalizing charge: A flooded lead-acid battery will normally be charged in boost mode until the battery reaches 2.45 volts (V) to 2.5 V per cell, at which time the connected regulator should switch into "float" mode, where the battery will be maintained at 2.3 V to 2.4 V per cell. During an equalizing charge, the cells are overcharged at 2.5 V to 2.6 V per cell to ensure that all cells have an equal (full charge). This is normally achieved by charging from a battery charger, though some regulators will perform this charge when energy use is low, such as when the users are not at home.

F

Float charge: A way of charging a battery by varying the charging current, so that its terminal voltage, the voltage measured directly across its terminals, "floats" at a specific voltage level.

Flooded cell battery: A form of rechargeable battery where the plates are completely immersed in a liquid electrolyte. The starter battery in most cars is of the flooded cell type. Flooded cell batteries are the most commonly used type for independent and remote area power supplies.

Fluorescent light: A form of lighting that uses long thin tubes of glass that contain mercury vapor and various phosphor powders (chemicals based on phosphorus) to produce white light that is generally considered to be the most efficient form of home lighting. See also Compact fluorescent lamp.

Furling: A method of preventing damage to horizontal-axis wind turbines by automatically turning them out of the wind using a spring-loaded tail or other device.

Fuse: An electrical device used to interrupt an electrical supply in the event of excess current flow. Often consists of a wire that melts when excess current flows through it.

G

Gel-cell battery: A form of lead-acid battery where the electrolyte is in the form of a gel or paste. Usually used for mobile installations and when batteries will be subject to high levels of shock or vibration.

Generator: A mechanical device used to produce DC electricity. Coils of wire passing through magnetic fields inside the generator produce power. See also Alternator. Most alternating current generating sets are also referred to as generators.

Gigawatt (GW): A measurement of power equal to a thousand million watts.

Gigawatt-hour (GWh): A measurement of energy. One gigawatt-hour is equal to one gigawatt being used for a period of one hour or one megawatt being used for 1,000 hours.

H

Halogen lamp: A special type of incandescent globe made of quartz glass and a tungsten filament, which also contains a small amount of a Halogen gas (hence the name), enabling it to run at a much higher temperature than a conventional incandescent globe. Efficiency is better than a normal incandescent, but not as good as a fluorescent light.

Head: The vertical distance that water will fall from the inlet of the collection pipe to the water turbine in a hydropower system.

Hertz (Hz): Unit of measurement for frequency. Is equivalent to cycles per second (refer to Alternating Current). Common household mains power is normally 60 Hz.

Horizontal-axis wind turbine: The most common form of wind turbine, consisting of two or three airfoil-style blades attached to a central hub, which drives a generator. The axis or main shaft of the machine is horizontal or parallel to the earth's surface.

I

Incandescent globe: This is the most common form of light globe in the home. It usually consists of a glass globe inside which is a wire filament that glows when electricity is passed through it. They are the least efficient of all electrical lighting systems.

Independent power system: A power generation system that is independent of tile mains grid.

Insolation: The level of intensity of energy from the sun that strikes the earth. Usually given as watts per square meter (W/m^2). A common level in Australia in summer is about 1,000 W/m^2.

Insulation: A material used to prevent the flow of electricity used on electrical wires in order to prevent electric shock. Typical materials used include plastics, such as PVC and polypropylene, ceramics, and minerals, such as mica.

Inverter: An electronic device used to convert DC electricity into AC, usually with an increase in voltage. There are several different basic types of inverters, including sine wave and square-wave inverters.

J

Junction box: An insulating box, usually made from plastics, such as PVC, used to protect the connection point of two or more cables.

K

Kilowatt (kW):   A measurement of power equal to one thousand watts.

Kilowatt-hour (kWh):   A measurement of energy. One kilowatt-hour is equal to one kilowatt being used for a period of one hour.

L

Lead-acid battery: A type of battery that consists of plates made of lead and lead-oxide, surrounded by a sulphuric acid electrolyte. The most common type of battery used in RAPS systems.

Light emitting diode (LED):   A semiconductor device, which produces light of a single or very narrow band of colors. Light emitting diodes are used for indicator lights, as well as for low-level lighting, readily available in red, green, blue, and yellow and amber. The lights have a minimum life of 100,000 hours of use.

Load: The collective appliances and other devices connected to a power source. When used with a shunt regulator, a "dummy" load is often used to absorb any excess power being generated.

M

Megawatt (MW):   A measurement of power equal to one million watts.

Megawatt-hour (MWh):   A measurement of power with respect to time (energy). One megawatt-hour is equal to one megawatt being used for a period of one hour, or one kilowatt being used for 1000 hours.

Meters per second (m/s):   A speed measurement system often used to measure wind speed. One m/s is equal to 2.2 miles per hour or 3.6 kilometers per hour.

Micro-hydro system: A generation system that uses water to produce electricity. Types of water turbine include Pelton, Turgo, cross flow, overshot, and under-shot waterwheels.

Modified square-wave: A type of waveform produced by some inverters. This type of waveform is better than a square wave but not as suitable for some appliances as a sine wave.

Monocrystalline solar cell: A form of solar cell made from a thin slice of a single large crystal of silicon.

N

Nacelle: That part of a wind generator that houses the generator, gearbox, and so forth at the top of the tower.

Nickel-cadmium battery (NICAD): A form of rechargeable battery, having higher storage densities than that of lead-acid batteries, NICADs use a mixture of nickel hydroxide and nickel oxide for the anode and cadmium metal for the cathode. The electrolyte is potassium hydroxide. Very common in small rechargeable appliances, but, rarely found in independent power systems, due to their high initial cost.

Noise: Unwanted electrical signals produced by electric motors and other machines that can cause circuits and appliances to malfunction.

O

Ohm: The unit of measurement of electrical resistance. Symbol used is uppercase Greek letter Omega. A resistance of one ohm will allow one amp of current to pass through it at a voltage drop of one volt.

Ohm's Law: A simple mathematical formula that allows voltage, current, or resistance to be calculated when the other two values are known. The formula is: $V >> I \times R$, where V is the voltage, I is the current, and R is the resistance.

P

Pelton wheel: A water turbine in which specially shaped buckets attached to the periphery of a wheel are struck by a jet of water from a narrow nozzle.

Photovoltaic effect: The effect that causes a voltage to be developed across the junction of two different materials when they are exposed to light.

Pitch: Loosely defined as the angle of the blades of a wind or water turbine with respect to the flow of the wind or water.

Plates: The electrodes in a battery. Usually take the form of flat metal plates. The plates often participate in the chemical reaction of a battery, but sometimes just provide a surface for the migration of electrons through the electrolyte.

Polycrystalline silicon: Silicon used to manufacture photovoltaic panels, which is made up of multiple crystals clumped together to form a solid mass.

Power: The rate of doing work or, more generally, the rate of converting energy from one form to another. See the definition of energy (measured in watts, W). For example, an inverter rated at 800 W can provide that amount of power continuously.

PVC (Poly-vinyl chloride): A plastic used as an insulator on electrical cables, as well as for conduits. Contains highly toxic chemicals and is slowly being replaced with safer alternatives.

Q

Quasi sine wave: A description of the type of waveform produced by some inverters. See modified square-wave.

R

Ram Pump: Water pumping devices that are powered by falling water. They work by using the energy of a large amount of water falling a small height to lift a small amount of water to a much greater height. In this way, water from a spring or stream in a valley can be pumped to a village or irrigation scheme on a hillside. Wherever a fall of water can be sustained, the ram pump can be used as a comparatively cheap, simple, and reliable means of raising water to considerable heights.

Rechargeable battery: A type of battery that uses a reversible chemical reaction to produce electricity, allowing it to be reused many times. Forcing electricity through the battery in the opposite direction to normal discharge reverses the chemical reaction.

Regulator: A device used to limit the current and voltage in a circuit, normally to allow the correct charging of batteries from power sources, such as photovoltaic arrays and wind generators.

RAPS (Remote Area Power Supply):   A power generation system used to provide electricity to remote and rural homes, usually incorporating power generated from renewable sources such as solar panels and wind generators, as well as nonrenewable sources, such as petrol-powered generators.

Renewable energy: Energy that is produced from a renewable source, such as sunlight.

Residual current device (RCD):   See earth-leakage circuit breaker.

Resistance: A material's ability to restrict the flow of electrical current through itself (measured in Ohms).

Resistor: An electronic component used to restrict the flow of current in a circuit, also used specifically to produce heat, such as in a water heater element.

S

Sealed lead-acid battery: A form of lead-acid battery where either immobilizes the electrolyte, being contained in an absorbent fiber separator or gel between the batteries plates. The battery is sealed so that no electrolyte can escape, and thus can be used in any position, even inverted.

Semiconductor: A material that only partially conducts electricity that is neither an insulator, nor a true conductor. Transistors and other electronic devices are made from semiconducting materials and are often called semiconductors.

Shunt: A low-value resistance, connected in series with a conductor that allows measurements of currents flowing in the conductor by measurement of voltage across the shunt, which is often used with larger devices, such as inverters to allow monitoring of the power used.

Sine wave: A sinusoidal-shaped electrical waveform. Mains power is a sine wave, as is the power produced by some inverters. The shape of a sinusoidal wave looks like this: The sine wave is the most ideal form of electricity for running more sensitive appliances, such as radios, TVs, computers, and the like.

Solar cell: A single photovoltaic circuit usually made of silicon that converts light into electricity.

Solar module: A device used to convert light from the sun directly into DC electricity by using the photovoltaic effect. Usually made of multiple silicon solar cells bonded between glass and a backing material.

Solar power: Electricity generated by conversion of sunlight, either directly through the use of photovoltaic panels, or indirectly through solar-thermal processes.

Solar thermal: A form of power generation using concentrated sunlight to heat water or other fluid that is then used to drive a motor or turbine.

Square wave: A type of waveform produced by some inverters. The square wave is the least desirable form of electricity for running most appliances. Simple resistors, such as incandescent globes and heating elements, work well on a square wave.

Storage density: The capacity of a battery compared to its weight (measured in watt-hours per kilogram).

Surge: An unexpected flow of excessive current, usually caused by high voltage that can damage appliances and other electrical equipment. Also, an excessive amount of power drawn by an appliance when it is first switched on.

Switch mode: A form of converting one form of electricity to another by rapidly switching it on and off and feeding it through a transformer to effect a voltage change.

T

Tip-speed ratio: The ratio of blade tip speed to wind speed for a wind turbine.

Transistor: A semiconducting device used to switch or otherwise control the flow of electricity.

Transformer: A device consisting of two or more insulated coils of wire wound around a magnetic material, such as iron, used to convert one AC voltage to another or to electrically isolate the individual circuits.

Turbulence: Airflow that rapidly and violently varies in speed and direction that can cause damage to wind turbines. It is often caused by objects, such as tree or buildings.

V

Vertical-axis wind turbine: A wind turbine with the axis or main shaft mounted vertically, or perpendicular to the earth's surface. This type of turbine does not have to be turned to face the wind—it always does.

Voltage: The electrical pressure that can force an electrical current to flow through a closed circuit (measured in volts, V).

Voltage drop: The voltage lost along a length of wire or conductor due to the resistance of that conductor. This also applies to resistors. The voltage drop is calculated by using Ohm's Law.

Voltmeter: An electrical or electronic device used to measure voltage.

W

Water turbine: A device that converts the motion of the flow of water into rotational motion, which is often used to drive generators or pumps. See micro-hydro system.

Waterwheel: A simple water turbine, often consisting of a series of paddles or boards attached to a central wheel or hub that is connected to a generator to produce electricity or a pump to move water.

Watt (W):   A measurement of power commonly used to define the rate of electricity consumption of an appliance.

Watt-hour (WH):   A measurement of power with respect to time (energy). One watt-hour is equal to one watt being used for a period of one hour.

Wind farm: A group of wind generators that usually feed power into the mains grid.

Wind generator: A mechanical device used to produce electricity from the wind. Typically a form of wind turbine connected to a generator.

Wind turbine: A device that converts the motion of the wind into rotational motion used to drive generators or pumps. Wind generator, wind turbine, windmill, and other terms are commonly used interchangeably to describe complete wind-powered electricity generating machines.

Y

Yaw: The orientation of a horizontal-axis wind turbine.

Z

Zener diode: A diode often used for voltage regulation or protection of other components.

Glossary of Meteorological Terms

Altitude: The angle up from the horizon.

Angle of incidence: The angle between the normal to a surface and the direction of the sun. Therefore, the sun will be perpendicular to the surface if the angle of incidence is zero.

Azimuth: The angle from north measured on the horizon, in the order of N, E, S, and W. Thus, north is zero degrees, and east is 90 degrees.

Horizon: The apparent intersection of the sky with the Earth's surface. For rise and set computations, the observer is assumed to be at sea level, so that the horizon is geometrically 90 degrees from the local vertical direction. Inclination surface tilt is expressed as an angle to the horizontal plane. Horizontal is zero degrees, vertical is 90 degrees.

Local Civil Time (LCT):   It is a locally agreed time scale. The time given out on the radio or television, and the time by which we usually set our clocks. Local Civil Time depends on the time of year and your position on earth. It can be defined as the time at the Greenwich Meridian plus the time zone and the daylight savings corrections.

Orientation: The angle of a structure or surface plane relative to north in the order of N, E, S, and W. Thus, north is zero degrees, and east is 90 degrees.

Shadow angles: Shadow angles refer to the azimuth and altitude of the sun, taken relative to the orientation of a particular surface.

Horizontal Shadow Angle (HSA):   The angle between the orientation of a surface and the solar azimuth.

Vertical Shadow Angle (VSA):   The angle between the HSA and the solar altitude, measured as a normal to the surface plane.

Solar noon: The time when the sun crosses the observer's meridian. The sun has its greatest elevation at solar noon.

Sunrise and sunset: Times when the upper edge of the disk of the sun is on the horizon. It is assumed that the observer is at sea level and that there are no obstructions to the horizon.

Twilight: The intervals of time before sunrise and after sunset when there is natural light provided by the upper atmosphere.

Civil Twilight: Civil Twilight is defined as beginning in the morning and ending in the evening when the center of the sun is geometrically 6 degrees below the horizon.

Renewable Energy Tables and Important Solar Power Facts

1. RECENT ANALYSIS BY DOE, SHOWS THAT BY YEAR 2025, ONE HALF OF THE NEW US ELECTRICITY GENERATION COULD COME FROM THE SUN.

2. THE UNITED STATES GENERATED ONLY 4 GW (1 GW IS 1000 MEGAWATT) OF SOLAR POWER. BY YEAR 2030, IT IS ESTIMATED TO BE 200 GW.

3. A TYPICAL NUCLEAR PLANT GENERATES ABOUT 1 GW OF ELECTRIC POWER, WHICH IS EQUAL TO 5 GW OF SOLAR POWER (DAILY POWER GENERATION IS LIMITED TO AN AVERAGE OF 5-6 HOURS PER DAY).

4. GLOBAL SALES OF SOLAR POWER SYSTEMS HAS BEEN GROWING AT A RATE OF 35% IN THE PAST FEW YEARS.

5. IT IS PROJECTED THAT BY YEAR 2020, THE UNITED STATES WILL BE PRODUCING ABOUT 7.2 GW OF SOLAR POWER.

6. SHIPMENT OF US SOLAR POWER SYSTEMS HAS FALLEN BY 10% ANNUALLY, BUT HAS INCREASED BY 45% THROUGHOUT EUROPE.

7. ANNUAL SALE GROWTH GLOBALLY HAS BEEN 35%.

8. PRESENT COST OF SOLAR POWER MODULES ON THE AVERAGE IS $2.33/WATT. BY 2030 IT SHOULD BE ABOUT $0.38/WATT.

9. WORLD PRODUCTION OF SOLAR POWER IS 1 GW/YEAR

10. GERMANY HAS A $0.50/WATT GRID FEED INCENTIVE THAT WILL BE VAILD FOR THE NEXT 20 YEARS. THE INCENTIVE IS TO BE DECREASED 5% PER YEAR.

TABLE B.1 Projected US Solar Power Statistics

	2004	2050
BASE INSTALLED COST/WATT	$6.50–$9.00	$1.93
ANNUAL POWER PRODUCTION MW	120	31,000
EMPLOYMENT	20,000	350,000
CELL EFFICIENCY (%)	20	22–40
MODULE PERFORMANCE (%)	8–15	20–30
SYSTEM PERFORMANCE (%)	6–12	18–25

11. IN THE PAST FEW YEARS, GERMANY INSTALLED 130 MW OF SOLAR POWER PER YEAR.

12. JAPAN HAS A 50% SUBSIDY FOR SOLAR POWER INSTALLATIONS OF 3 KW 4 KW SYSTEMS AND HAS ABOUT 800 MW OF GRID CONNECTED SOLAR POWER SYSTEMS. SOLAR POWER IN JAPAN HAS BEEN IN EFFECT SINCE 1994.

13. CALIFORNIA, IN 1996, SET ASIDE $540 MILLION FOR RENEWABLE ENERGY, WHICH HAS PROVIDED A $4.50 to $3.00 / WATT BUY BACK AS A REBATE.

14. IN THE YEARS 2015 THROUGH 2024, IT IS ESTIMATED THAT CALIFORNIA COULD PRODUCE AN ESTIMATED $40 BILLION DOLLARS OF SOLAR POWER SALES.

15. IN THE UNITED STATES, 20 STATES HAVE A SOLAR REBATE PROGRAM. NEVADA AND ARIZONA HAVE A SET ASIDE STATE BUDGET FOR SOLAR PROGRAMS.

16. PROJECTED US SOLAR POWER STATISTICS, SHOWN IN TABLE B.1

17. GLOBAL SOLAR POWER INSTALLATIONS, SHOWN IN TABLE B.2

18. TOTAL US PRODUCTION HAS BEEN JUST ABOUT 18% OF GLOBAL PRODUCTION.

19. FOR EACH MW OF SOLAR POWER WE EMPLOY 32 PEOPLE

20. A SOLAR POWER COLLECTOR IN SOUTHWEST OF UNITED STATES, SIZED 100X100 MILES, COULD PRODUCE SUFFICIENT

TABLE B.2 Global Solar Power Installations

JAPAN	800 MW
GERMANY	400 MW
US	340 MW

ELECTRIC POWER TO SATISFY THE COUNTRY'S YEARLY ENERGY NEEDS.

21. FOR EVERY KW OF POWER PRODUCED BY NUCLEAR OR FOSILE FUEL PLANTS, 1/2 GALLON OF WATER IS USED FOR SCRUBBING, CLEANING, AND COOLING. SOLAR POWER PRACTICALLY DOES NOT REQUIRE ANY WATER USAGE.

22. SIGNIFICANT IMPACT OF SOLAR POWER CO-GENERATION.
   - BOOSTS ECONOMIC DEVELOPMENT
   - LOWERS COST OF PEAK POWER
   - PROVIDES GREATER GRID STABILITY
   - LOWERS AIR POLLUTION
   - LOWERS GREENHOUSE GAS EMMISIONS
   - LOWERS WATER CONSUMPTION AND CONTAMINATION

23. A MERE 6.7 MILE PER GALLON EFFICIENCY INCREASE IN CARS DRIVEN IN THE UNITED STATES COULD OFFSET OUR SHARE OF IMPORT OF SAUDI OIL.

24. STATE OF SOLAR POWER TECHNOLOGY AT PRESENT:
   - CRYSTALLINE
   - POLYCRYSTALLINE
   - AMORPHOUS
   - THIN AND THICK FILM TECHNOLOGIES

25. STATE OF SOLAR POWER TECHNOLOGY IN FUTURE:
   - PLASTIC SOLAR CELLS
   - NANO-STRUCTURED MATERIALS
   - DYE SYNTHESIZED CELLS

Solar Installation Warning Signs

ELECTRIC SHOCK HAZARD — DO NOT TOUCH TERMINALS - TERMINALS ON BOTH LINE AND LOAD SIDES MAY BE ENERGIZED IN OPEN POSITION

For Switchgear and Metering System

WARNING – ELECTRICAL SHOCK HAZARD – DOES NOT TOUCH TERMINALS. TERMINALS ON BOTH THE LINE AND LOAD SIDE MAY BE ENERGIZED IN THE OPEN POSITION

Each Piece of Solar Power Equipment

WARNING – ELECTRICAL SHOCK HAZARD – DANGEROUS VOLTAGES AND CURRENTS – NO USER SERVICEABLE PARTS INSIDE – CONTACT QUALIFIED SERVICE PERSONNEL FOR ASSISTANCE

Battery Rooms and Containers

WARNING – ELECTRIC SHOCK HAZARD – DANGEROUS VOLTAGES
AND CURRENTS – EXPLOSIVE GAS – NO SPARKS OF FLAMES – NO
SMOKING – ACID BURNS – WEAR PROTECTIVE CLOTHING WHEN SER-
VICING
TYPICAL SOLAR POWER SYSTEM
SAFETEY WARNING TAGS

TABLE B.3 Tilt Angle Efficiency Multiplier Table

Degrees	Collector Tilt Angle from Horizontal					
	0	15	30	45	60	90
			Fresno			
South	0.90	0.98	1.00	0.96	0.87	0.55
SSE, SSW	0.90	0.97	0.99	0.96	0.87	0.56
SE, SW	0.90	0.95	0.96	0.92	0.84	0.68
ESE, WSW	0.90	0.92	0.91	0.87	0.79	0.57
E, W	0.90	0.88	0.86	0.78	0.70	0.51
			Daggett			
South	0.88.	0.97	1.00	0.97	0.88	0.56
SSE, SSW	0.88	0.96	0.99	0.96	0.87	0.58
SE, SW	0.88	0.94	0.96	0.93	0.85	0.59
ESE, WSW	0.88	0.91	0.91	0.86	0.78	0.57
E, W	0.88	0.87	0.83	0.77	0.69	0.51
			Santa Maria			
South	0.89	0.97	1.00	0.97	0.88	0.57
SSE, SSW	0.89	0.97	0.99	0.96	0.87	0.58
SE, SW	0.89	0.95	0.96	0.93	0.86	0.59
ESE, WSW	0.89	0.92	0.91	0.87	0.79	0.67
E, W	0.89	0.88	0.84	0.78	0.70	0.52
			Los Angeles			
South	0.89	0.97	1.00	0.97	0.88	0.57
SSE, SSW	0.89	0.97	0.99	0.96	0.87	0.58
SE, SW	0.89	0.95	0.96	0.93	0.85	0.69
ESE, WSW	0.89	0.92	0.91	0.87	0.79	0.57
E, W	0.89	0.88	0.85	0.78	0.70	0.51
			San Diego			
South	0.89	0.98	1.00	0.97	0.88	0.57
SSE, SSW	0.89	0.97	0.99	0.96	0.87	0.58
SE, SW	0.89	0.95	0.96	0.92	0.54	0.59
ESE, WSW	0.89	0.92	0.91	0.87	0.79	0.57
E, W	0.89	0.88	0.85	0.78	0.70	0.51

TABLE B.4 Solar Insolation Table in for Major Cities in Killowatt Hours per Square Meter per Day

State	City	High	Low	Avg.	State	City	High	Low	Avg.
AK	Fairbanks	5.87	2.12	3.99	MO	Columbia	5.50	3.97	4.73
AK	Matanuska	5.24	1.74	3.55	MO	S1. Louis	4.87	3.24	4.38
AL	Montgomery	4.69	3.37	4.23	MS	Meridian	4.86	3.64	4.43
AR	Bethel	6.29	2.37	3.81	MT	Glasgow	5.97	4.09	5.15
AR	Little Rock	5.29	3.88	4.69	MT	Great Falls	5.70	3.66	4.93
AZ	Tucson	7.42	6.01	6.57	MT	Summit	5.17	2.36	3.99
AZ	Page	7.30	5.65	6.36	NM	Albuquerque	7.16	6.21	6.77
AZ	Phoenix	7.13	5.78	6.58	NB	Lincoln	5.40	4.38	4.79
CA	Santa Maria	6.52	5.42	5.94	NB	N. Omaha	5.28	4.26	4.90
CA	Riverside	6.35	5.35	5.87	NC	Cape Hatteras	5.81	4.69	5.31
CA	Davis	6.09	3.31	5.10	NC	Greensboro	5.05	4.00	4.71
CA	Fresno	6.19	3.42	5.38	ND	Bismarck	5.48	3.97	5.01
CA	Los Angeles	6.14	5.03	5.62	NJ	Sea Brook	4.76	3.20	4.21
CA	Soda Springs	6.47	4.40	5.60	NV	Las Vegas	7.13	5.84	6.41
CA	La Jolla	5.24	4.29	4.77	NV	Ely	6.48	5.49	5.98
CA	Inyokern	8.70	6.87	7.66	NY	Binghamton	3.93	1.62	3.16
CO	Grandbaby	7.47	5.15	5.69	NY	Ithaca	4.57	2.29	3.79
CO	Grand Lake	5.86	3.56	5.08	NY	Schenectady	3.92	2.53	3.55
CO	Grand Junction	6.34	5.23	5.85	NY	Rochester	4.22	1.58	3.31
CO	Boulder	5.72	4.44	4.87	NY	New York City	4.97	3.03	4.08
DC	Washington	4.69	3.37	4.23	OH	Columbus	5.26	2.66	4.15
FL	Apalachicola	5.98	4.92	5.49	OH	Cleveland	4.79	2.69	3.94
FL	Belie Is.	5.31	4.58	4.99	OK	Stillwater	5.52	4.22	4.99
FL	Miami	6.26	5.05	5.62	OK	Oklahoma City	6.26	4.98	5.59
FL	Gainesville	5.81	4.71	5.27	OR	Astoria	4.76	1.99	3.72
FL	Tampa	6.16	5.26	5.67	OR	Corvallis	5.71	1.90	4.03
GA	Atlanta	5.16	4.09	4.74	OR	Medford	5.84	2.02	4.51
GA	Griffin	5.41	4.26	4.99	PA	Pittsburg	4.19	1.45	3.28
III	Honolulu	6.71	5.59	6.02	PA	State College	4.44	2.79	3.91
IA	Ames	4.80	3.73	4.40	RI	Newport	4.69	3.58	4.23
ill	Boise	5.83	3.33	4.92	SC	Charleston	5.72	4.23	5.06
ill	Twin Falls	5.42	3.42	4.70	SD	Rapid City	5.91	4.56	5.23
IL	Chicago	4.08	1.47	3.14	1N	Nashville	5.20	3.14	4.45
IN	Indianapolis	5.02	2.55	4.21	1N	Oak Ridge	5.06	3.22	4.37
KS	Manhattan	5.08	3.62	4.57	TX	San Antonio	5.88	4.65	5.30
KS	Dodge City	4.14	5.28	5.79	TX	Brownsville	5.49	4.42	4.92
KY	Lexington	5.97	3.60	4.94	TX	EI Paso	7.42	5.87	6.72
LA	Lake Charles	5.73	4.29	4.93	TX	Midland	6.33	5.23	5.83
LA	New Orleans	5.71	3.63	4.92	TX	Fort Worth	6.00	4.80	5.43
LA	Shreveport	4.99	3.87	4.63	UT	Salt Lake City	6.09	3.78	5.26
MA	E. Wareham	4.48	3.06	3.99	UT	Flaming Gorge	6.63	5.48	5.83
MA	Boston	4.27	2.99	3.84	VA	Richmond	4.50	3.37	4.13
MA	Blue Hill	4.38	3.33	4.05	WA	Seattle	4.83	1.60	3.57
MA	Natick	4.62	3.09	4.10	WA	Richland	6.13	2.01	4.44
MA	Lynn	4.60	2.33	3.79	WA	Pullman	6.07	2.90	4.73
MD	Silver Hill	4.71	3.84	4.47	WA	Spokane	5.53	1.16	4.48
ME	Caribou	5.62	2.57	4.19	WA	Prosser	6.21	3.06	5.03
ME	Portland	5.23	3.56	4.51	WI	Madison	4.85	3.28	4.29
MI	Sault Ste. Marie	4.83	2.33	4.20	WV	Charleston	4.12	2.47	3.65
MI	E. Lansing	4.71	2.70	4.00	WY	Lander	6.81	5.50	6.06
MN	St. Cloud	5.43	3.53	4.53					

	LONGITUDE	LATITUDE		LONGITUDE	LATITUDE
ALABAMA			El Cajon	32° 49′ N	116° 58′ W
Alexander City	32° 57′ N	85° 57′ W	El Cerrito AP (S)	32° 49′ N	115° 40′ W
Anniston AP	33° 35′ N	85° 51′ W	Escondido	33° 7′ N	117° 5′ W
Auburn	32° 36′ N	85° 30′ W	Eureka/Arcata AP	40° 59′ N	124° 6′ W
Birmingham AP	33° 34′ N	86° 45′ W	Fairfield-Trafis AFB	38° 16′ N	121° 56′ W
Decatur	34° 37′ N	86° 59′ W	Fresno AP (S)	36° 46′ N	119° 43′ W
Dothan AP	31° 19′ N	85° 27′ W	Hamilton AFB	38° 4′ N	122° 30′ W
Florence AP	34° 48′ N	87° 40′ W	Laguna Beach	33° 33′ N	117° 47′ W
Gadsden	34° 1′ N	86° 0′ W	Livermore	37° 42′ N	121° 57′ W
Huntsville AP	34° 42′ N	86° 35′ W	Lompoc,	34° 43′ N	120° 34′ W
Mobile AP	30° 41′ N	88° 15′ W	Vandenberg AFB		
Mobile Co	30° 40′ N	88° 15′ W	Long Beach AP	33° 49′ N	118° 9′ W
Montgomery AP	32° 23′ N	86° 22′ W	Los Angeles AP (S)	33° 56′ N	118° 24′ W
Selma-Craig AFB	32° 20′ N	87° 59′ W	Los Angeles CO (S)	34° 3′ N	118° 14′ W
Talladega	33° 27′ N	86° 6′ W	Merced-Castle AFB	37° 23′ N	120° 34′ W
Tuscaloosa AP	33° 13′ N	87° 37′ W	Modesto	37° 39′ N	121° 0′ W
ALASKA			Monterey	36° 36′ N	121° 54′ W
Anchorage AP	61° 10′ N	150° 1′ W	Napa	38° 13′ N	122° 17′ W
Barrow (S)	71° 18′ N	156° 47′ W	Needles AP	34° 36′ N	114° 37′ W
Fairbanks AP (S)	64° 49′ N	147° 52′ W	Oakland AP	37° 49′ N	122° 19′ W
Juneau AP	58° 22′ N	134° 35′ W	Oceanside	33° 14′ N	117° 25′ W
Kodiak	57° 45′ N	152° 29′ W	Ontario	34° 3′ N	117° 36′ W
Nome AP	64° 30′ N	165° 26′ W	Oxnard	34° 12′ N	119° 11′ W
ARIZONA			Palmdale AP	34° 38′ N	118° 6′ W
Douglas AP	31° 27′ N	109° 36′ W	Palm Springs	33° 49′ N	116° 32′ W
Flagstaff AP	35° 8′ N	111° 40′ W	Pasadena	34° 9′ N	118° 9′ W
Fort Huachuca AP (S)	31° 35′ N	110° 20′ W	Petaluma	38° 14′ N	122° 38′ W
Kingman AP	35° 12′ N	114° 1′ W	Pomona Co	34° 3′ N	117° 45′ W
Nogales	31° 21′ N	110° 55′ W	Redding AP	40° 31′ N	122° 18′ W
Phoenix AP (S)	33° 26′ N	112° 1′ W	Redlands	34° 3′ N	117° 11′ W
Prescott AP	34° 39′ N	112° 26′ W	Richmond	37° 56′ N	122° 21′ W
Tucson AP (S)	32° 7′ N	110° 56′ W	Riverside-March	33° 54′ N	117° 15′ W
Winslow AP	35° 1′ N	110° 44′ W	AFB (S)		
Yuma AP	32° 39′ N	114° 37′ W	Sacramento AP	38° 31′ N	121° 30′ W
ARKANSAS			Salinas AP	36° 40′ N	121° 36′ W
Blytheville AFB	35° 57′ N	89° 57′ W	San Bernadino,	34° 8′ N	117° 16′ W
Camden	33° 36′ N	92° 49′ W	Norton AFB		
El Dorado AP	33° 13′ N	92° 49′ W	San Diego AP	32° 44′ N	117° 10′ W
Fayetteville AP	36° 0′ N	94° 10′ W	San Fernando	34° 17′ N	118° 28′ W
Fort Smith AP	35° 20′ N	94° 22′ W	San Francisco AP	37° 37′ N	122° 23′ W
Hot Springs	34° 29′ N	93° 6′ W	San Francisco Co	37° 46′ N	122° 26′ W
Jonesboro	35° 50′ N	90° 42′ W	San Jose AP	37° 22′ N	121° 56′ W
Little Rock AP (S)	34° 44′ N	92° 14′ W	San Louis Obispo	35° 20′ N	120° 43′ W
Pine Bluff AP	34° 18′ N	92° 5′ W	Santa Ana AP	33° 45′ N	117° 52′ W
Texarkana AP	33° 27′ N	93° 59′ W	Santa Barbara MAP	34° 26′ N	119° 50′ W
CALIFORNIA			Santa Cruz	36° 59′ N	122° 1′ W
Bakersfield AP	35° 25′ N	119° 3′ W	Santa Maria AP (S)	34° 54′ N	120° 27′ W
Barstow AP	34° 51′ N	116° 47′ W	Santa Monica CIC	34° 1′ N	118° 29′ W
Blythe AP	33° 37′ N	114° 43′ W	Santa Paula	34° 21′ N	119° 5′ W
Burbank AP	34° 12′ N	118° 21′ W	Santa Rosa	38° 31′ N	122° 49′ W
Chico	39° 48′ N	121° 51′ W	Stockton AP	37° 54′ N	121° 15′ W
Concord	37° 58′ N	121° 59′ W	Ukiah	39° 9′ N	123° 12′ W
Covina	34° 5′ N	117° 52′ W	Visalia	36° 20′ N	119° 18′ W
Crescent City AP	41° 46′ N	124° 12′ W	Yreka	41° 43′ N	122° 38′ W
Downey	33° 56′ N	118° 8′ W	Yuba City	39° 8′ N	121° 36′ W

	LONGITUDE	LATITUDE		LONGITUDE	LATITUDE
			Tampa AP (S)	27° 58′ N	82° 32′ W
COLORADO			West Palm Beach AP	26° 41′ N	80° 6′ W
Alamosa AP	37° 27′ N	105° 52′ W	**GEORGIA**		
Boulder	40° 0′ N	105° 16′ W	Albany, Turner AFB	31° 36′ N	84° 5′ W
Colorado Springs AP	38° 49′ N	104° 43′ W	Americus	32° 3′ N	84° 14′ W
Denver AP	39° 45′ N	104° 52′ W	Athens	33° 57′ N	83° 19′ W
Durango	37° 17′ N	107° 53′ W	Atlanta AP (S)	33° 39′ N	84° 26′ W
Fort Collins	40° 45′ N	105° 5′ W	Augusta AP	33° 22′ N	81° 58′ W
Grand Junction AP (S)	39° 7′ N	108° 32′ W	Brunswick	31° 15′ N	81° 29′ W
Greeley	40° 26′ N	104° 38′ W	Columbus,	32° 31′ N	84° 56′ W
Lajunta AP	38° 3′ N	103° 30′ W	Lawson AFB		
Leadville	39° 15′ N	106° 18′ W	Dalton	34° 34′ N	84° 57′ W
Pueblo AP	38° 18′ N	104° 29′ W	Dublin	32° 20′ N	82° 54′ W
Sterling	40° 37′ N	103° 12′ W	Gainsville	34° 11′ N	83° 41′ W
Trinidad	37° 15′ N	104° 20′ W	Griffin	33° 13′ N	84° 16′ W
CONNECTICUT			LaGrange	33° 1′ N	85° 4′ W
Bridgeport AP	41° 11′ N	73° 11′ W	Macon AP	32° 42′ N	83° 39′ W
Hartford, Brainard	41° 44′ N	72° 39′ W	Marietta, Dobbins AFB	33° 55′ N	84° 31′ W
Field			Savannah	32° 8′ N	81° 12′ W
New Haven AP	41° 19′ N	73° 55′ W	Valdosta-Moody AFB	30° 58′ N	83° 12′ W
New London	41° 21′ N	72° 6′ W	Waycross	31° 15′ N	82° 24′ W
Norwalk	41° 7′ N	73° 25′ W	**HAWAII**		
Norwick	41° 32′ N	72° 4′ W	Hilo AP (S)	19° 43′ N	155° 5′ W
Waterbury	41° 35′ N	73° 4′ W	Honolulu AP	21° 20′ N	157° 55′ W
Widsor Locks,	41° 56′ N	72° 41′ W	Kaneohe Bay MCAS	21° 27′ N	157° 46′ W
Bradley Fld			Wahiawa	21° 3′ N	158° 2′ W
DELAWARE			**IDAHO**		
Dover AFB	39° 8′ N	75° 28′ W	Boise AP (S)	43° 34′ N	116° 13′ W
Wilmington AP	39° 40′ N	75° 36′ W	Burley	42° 32′ N	113° 46′ W
DISTRICT OF COLUMBIA			Coeur D'Alene AP	47° 46′ N	116° 49′ W
Andrews AFB	38° 5′ N	76° 5′ W	Idaho Falls AP	43° 31′ N	112° 4′ W
Washington,	38° 51′ N	77° 2′ W	Lewiston AP	46° 23′ N	117° 1′ W
National AP			Moscow	46° 44′ N	116° 58′ W
FLORIDA			Mountain Home AFB	43° 2′ N	115° 54′ W
Belle Glade	26° 39′ N	80° 39′ W	Pocatello AP	42° 55′ N	112° 36′ W
Cape Kennedy AP	28° 29′ N	80° 34′ W	Twin Falls AP (S)	42° 29′ N	114° 29′ W
Daytona Beach AP	29° 11′ N	81° 3′ W	**LLINOIS**		
E Fort Lauderdale	26° 4′ N	80° 9′ W	Aurora	41° 45′ N	88° 20′ W
Fort Myers AP	26° 35′ N	81° 52′ W	Belleville, Scott AFB	38° 33′ N	89° 51′ W
Fort Pierce	27° 28′ N	80° 21′ W	Bloomington	40° 29′ N	88° 57′ W
Gainsville AP (S)	29° 41′ N	82° 16′ W	Carbondale	37° 47′ N	89° 15′ W
Jacksonville AP	30° 30′ N	81° 42′ W	Champaign/Urbana	40° 2′ N	88° 17′ W
Key West AP	24° 33′ N	81° 45′ W	Chicago, Midway AP	41° 47′ N	87° 45′ W
Lakeland Co (S)	28° 2′ N	81° 57′ W	Chicago, O'Hare AP	41° 59′ N	87° 54′ W
Miami AP (S)	25° 48′ N	80° 16′ W	Chicago Co	41° 53′ N	87° 38′ W
Miami Beach Co	25° 47′ N	80° 17′ W	Danville	40° 12′ N	87° 36′ W
Ocala	29° 11′ N	82° 8′ W	Decatur	39° 50′ N	88° 52′ W
Orlando AP	28° 33′ N	81° 23′ W	Dixon	41° 50′ N	89° 29′ W
Panama City,	30° 4′ N	85° 35′ W	Elgin	42° 2′ N	88° 16′ W
Tyndall AFB			Freeport	42° 18′ N	89° 37′ W
Pensacola Co	30° 25′ N	87° 13′ W	Galesburg	40° 56′ N	90° 26′ W
St. Augustine	29° 58′ N	81° 20′ W	Greenville	38° 53′ N	89° 24′ W
St. Petersburg	27° 46′ N	82° 80′ W	Joliet	41° 31′ N	88° 10′ W
Stanford	28° 46′ N	81° 17′ W	Kankakee	41° 5′ N	87° 55′ W
Sarasota	27° 23′ N	82° 33′ W	La Salle/Peru	41° 19′ N	89° 6′ W
Tallahassee AP (S)	30° 23′ N	84° 22′ W			

	LONGITUDE	LATITUDE		LONGITUDE	LATITUDE
ILLINOIS (Continued)			Chanute AP	37° 40' N	95° 29' W
Macomb	40° 28' N	90° 40' W	Dodge City AP (S)	37° 46' N	99° 58' W
Moline AP	41° 27' N	90° 31' W	El Dorado	37° 49' N	96° 50' W
Mt Vernon	38° 19' N	88° 52' W	Emporia	38° 20' N	96° 12' W
Peoria AP	40° 40' N	89° 41' W	Garden City AP	37° 56' N	100° 44' W
Quincy AP	39° 57' N	91° 12' W	Goodland AP	39° 22' N	101° 42' W
Rantoul, Chanute AFB	40° 18' N	88° 8' W	Great Bend	38° 21' N	98° 52' W
Rockford	42° 21' N	89° 3' W	Hutchinson AP	38° 4' N	97° 52' W
Springfield AP	39° 50' N	89° 40' W	Liberal	37° 3' N	100° 58' W
Waukegan	42° 21' N	87° 53' W	Manhattan,	39° 3' N	96° 46' W
INDIANA			Ft Riley (S)		
Anderson	40° 6' N	85° 37' W	Parsons	37° 20' N	95° 31' W
Bedford	38° 51' N	86° 30' W	Russell AP	38° 52' N	98° 49' W
Bloomington	39° 8' N	86° 37' W	Salina	38° 48' N	97° 39' W
Columbus,	39° 16' N	85° 54' W	Topeka AP	39° 4' N	95° 38' W
Bakalar AFB			Wichita AP	37° 39' N	97° 25' W
Crawfordsville	40° 3' N	86° 54' W	**KENTUCKY**		
Evansville AP	38° 3' N	87° 32' W	Ashland	38° 33' N	82° 44' W
Fort Wayne AP	41° 0' N	85° 12' W	Bowling Green AP	35° 58' N	86° 28' W
Goshen AP	41° 32' N	85° 48' W	Corbin AP	36° 57' N	84° 6' W
Hobart	41° 32' N	87° 15' W	Covington AP	39° 3' N	84° 40' W
Huntington	40° 53' N	85° 30' W	Hopkinsville,	36° 40' N	87° 29' W
Indianapolis AP	39° 44' N	86° 17' W	Ft Campbell		
Jeffersonville	38° 17' N	85° 45' W	Lexington AP (S)	38° 2' N	84° 36' W
Kokomo	40° 25' N	86° 3' W	Louisville AP	38° 11' N	85° 44' W
Lafayette	40° 2' N	86° 5' W	Madisonville	37° 19' N	87° 29' W
La Porte	41° 36' N	86° 43' W	Owensboro	37° 45' N	87° 10' W
Marion	40° 29' N	85° 41' W	Paducah AP	37° 4' N	88° 46' W
Muncie	40° 11' N	85° 21' W	**LOUISIANA**		
Peru, Grissom AFB	40° 39' N	86° 9' W	Alexandria AP	31° 24' N	92° 18' W
Richmond AP	39° 46' N	84° 50' W	Baton Rouge AP	30° 32' N	91° 9' W
Shelbyville	39° 31' N	85° 47' W	Bogalusa	30° 47' N	89° 52' W
South Bend AP	41° 42' N	86° 19' W	Houma	29° 31' N	90° 40' W
Terre Haute AP	39° 27' N	87° 18' W	Lafayette AP	30° 12' N	92° 0' W
Valparaiso	41° 31' N	87° 2' W	Lake Charles AP (S)	30° 7' N	93° 13' W
Vincennes	38° 41' N	87° 32' W	Minden	32° 36' N	93° 18' W
IOWA			Monroe AP	32° 31' N	92° 2' W
Ames (S)	42° 2' N	93° 48' W	Natchitoches	31° 46' N	93° 5' W
Burlington AP	40° 47' N	91° 7' W	New Orleans AP	29° 59' N	90° 15' W
Cedar Rapids AP	41° 53' N	91° 42' W	Shreveport AP (S)	32° 28' N	93° 49' W
Clinton	41° 50' N	90° 13' W	**MAINE**		
Council Bluffs	41° 20' N	95° 49' W	Augusta AP	44° 19' N	69° 48' W
Des Moines AP	41° 32' N	93° 39' W	Bangor, Dow AFB	44° 48' N	68° 50' W
Dubuque	42° 24' N	90° 42' W	Caribou AP (S)	46° 52' N	68° 1' W
Fort Dodge	42° 33' N	94° 11' W	Lewiston	44° 2' N	70° 15' W
Iowa City	41° 38' N	91° 33' W	Millinocket AP	45° 39' N	68° 42' W
Keokuk	40° 24' N	91° 24' W	Portland (S)	43° 39' N	70° 19' W
Marshalltown	42° 4' N	92° 56' W	Waterville	44° 32' N	69° 40' W
Mason City AP	43° 9' N	93° 20' W	**MARYLAND**		
Newton	41° 41' N	93° 2' W	Baltimore AP	39° 11' N	76° 40' W
Ottumwa AP	41° 6' N	92° 27' W	Baltimore Co	39° 20' N	76° 25' W
Sioux City AP	42° 24' N	96° 23' W	Cumberland	39° 37' N	78° 46' W
Waterloo	42° 33' N	92° 24' W	Frederick AP	39° 27' N	77° 25' W
KANSAS			Hagerstown	39° 42' N	77° 44' W
Atchison	39° 34' N	95° 7' W	Salisbury (S)	38° 20' N	75° 30' W

	LONGITUDE	LATITUDE		LONGITUDE	LATITUDE
MASSACHUSETTS			**MISSISSIPPI**		
Boston AP	42° 22′ N	71° 2′ W	Biloxi—Keesler AFB	30° 25′ N	88° 55′ W
Clinton	42° 24′ N	71° 41′ W	Clarksdale	34° 12′ N	90° 34′ W
Fall River	41° 43′ N	71° 8′ W	Columbus AFB	33° 39′ N	88° 27′ W
Framingham	42° 17′ N	71° 25′ W	Greenville AFB	33° 29′ N	90° 59′ W
Gloucester	42° 35′ N	70° 41′ W	Greenwood	33° 30′ N	90° 5′ W
Greenfield	42° 3′ N	72° 4′ W	Hattiesburg	31° 16′ N	89° 15′ W
Lawrence	42° 42′ N	71° 10′ W	Jackson AP	32° 19′ N	90° 5′ W
Lowell	42° 39′ N	71° 19′ W	Laurel	31° 40′ N	89° 10′ W
New Bedford	41° 41′ N	70° 58′ W	Mccomb AP	31° 15′ N	90° 28′ W
Pittsfield AP	42° 26′ N	73° 18′ W	Meridian AP	32° 20′ N	88° 45′ W
Springfield,	42° 12′ N	72° 32′ W	Natchez	31° 33′ N	91° 23′ W
Westover AFB			Tupelo	34° 16′ N	88° 46′ W
Taunton	41° 54′ N	71° 4′ W	Vicksburg Co	32° 24′ N	90° 47′ W
Worcester AP	42° 16′ N	71° 52′ W	**MISSOURI**		
MICHIGAN			Cape Girardeau	37° 14′ N	89° 35′ W
Adrian	41° 55′ N	84° 1′ W	Columbia AP (S)	38° 58′ N	92° 22′ W
Alpena AP	45° 4′ N	83° 26′ W	Farmington AP	37° 46′ N	90° 24′ W
Battle Creek AP	42° 19′ N	85° 15′ W	Hannibal	39° 42′ N	91° 21′ W
Benton Harbor AP	42° 8′ N	86° 26′ W	Jefferson City	38° 34′ N	92° 11′ W
Detroit	42° 25′ N	83° 1′ W	Joplin AP	37° 9′ N	94° 30′ W
Escanaba	45° 44′ N	87° 5′ W	Kansas City AP	39° 7′ N	94° 35′ W
Flint AP	42° 58′ N	83° 44′ W	Kirksville AP	40° 6′ N	92° 33′ W
Grand Rapids AP	42° 53′ N	85° 31′ W	Mexico	39° 11′ N	91° 54′ W
Holland	42° 42′ N	86° 6′ W	Moberly	39° 24′ N	92° 26′ W
Jackson AP	42° 16′ N	84° 28′ W	Poplar Bluff	36° 46′ N	90° 25′ W
Kalamazoo	42° 17′ N	85° 36′ W	Rolla	37° 59′ N	91° 43′ W
Lansing AP	42° 47′ N	84° 36′ W	St. Joseph AP	39° 46′ N	94° 55′ W
Marquette Co	46° 34′ N	87° 24′ W	St. Louis AP	38° 45′ N	90° 23′ W
Mt Pleasant	43° 35′ N	84° 46′ W	St. Louis CO	38° 39′ N	90° 38′ W
Muskegon AP	43° 10′ N	86° 14′ W	Sikeston	36° 53′ N	89° 36′ W
Pontiac	42° 40′ N	83° 25′ W	Sedalia—	38° 43′ N	93° 33′ W
Port Huron	42° 59′ N	82° 25′ W	Whiteman AFB		
Saginaw AP	43° 32′ N	84° 5′ W	Sikeston	36° 53′ N	89° 36′ W
Sault Ste. Marie	46° 28′ N	84° 22′ W	Springfield AP	37° 14′ N	93° 23′ W
AP (S)			**MONTANA**		
Traverse City AP	44° 45′ N	85° 35′ W	Billings AP	45° 48′ N	108° 32′ W
Ypsilanti	42° 14′ N	83° 32′ W	Bozeman	45° 47′ N	111° 9′ W
MINNESOTA			Butte AP	45° 57′ N	112° 30′ W
Albert Lea	43° 39′ N	93° 21′ W	Cut Bank AP	48° 37′ N	112° 22′ W
Alexandria AP	45° 52′ N	95° 23′ W	Glasgow AP (S)	48° 25′ N	106° 32′ W
Bemidji AP	47° 31′ N	94° 56′ W	Glendive	47° 8′ N	104° 48′ W
Brainerd	46° 24′ N	94° 8′ W	Great Falls AP (S)	47° 29′ N	111° 22′ W
Duluth AP	46° 50′ N	92° 11′ W	Havre	48° 34′ N	109° 40′ W
Fairbault	44° 18′ N	93° 16′ W	Helena AP	46° 36′ N	112° 0′ W
Fergus Falls	46° 16′ N	96° 4′ W	Kalispell AP	48° 18′ N	114° 16′ W
International Falls AP	48° 34′ N	93° 23′ W	Lewiston AP	47° 4′ N	109° 27′ W
Mankato	44° 9′ N	93° 59′ W	Livingstown AP	45° 42′ N	110° 26′ W
Minneapolis/	44° 53′ N	93° 13′ W	Miles City AP	46° 26′ N	105° 52′ W
St. Paul AP			Missoula AP	46° 55′ N	114° 5′ W
Rochester AP	43° 55′ N	92° 30′ W	**NEBRASKA**		
St. Cloud AP (S)	45° 35′ N	94° 11′ W	Beatrice	40° 16′ N	96° 45′ W
Virginia	47° 30′ N	92° 33′ W	Chadron AP	42° 50′ N	103° 5′ W
Willmar	45° 7′ N	95° 5′ W	Columbus	41° 28′ N	97° 20′ W
Winona	44° 3′ N	91° 38′ W	Fremont	41° 26′ N	96° 29′ W

	LONGITUDE	LATITUDE		LONGITUDE	LATITUDE
NEBRASKA (Continued)			Santa Fe CO	35° 37' N	106° 5' W
Grand Island AP	40° 59' N	98° 19' W	Silver City AP	32° 38' N	108° 10' W
Hastings	40° 36' N	98° 26' W	Socorro AP	34° 3' N	106° 53' W
Kearney	40° 44' N	99° 1' W	Tucumcari AP	35° 11' N	103° 36' W
Lincoln Co (S)	40° 51' N	96° 45' W	**NEW YORK**		
McCook	40° 12' N	100° 38' W	Albany AP (S)	42° 45' N	73° 48' W
Norfolk	41° 59' N	97° 26' W	Albany Co	42° 39' N	73° 45' W
North Platte AP (S)	41° 8' N	100° 41' W	Auburn	42° 54' N	76° 32' W
Omaha AP	41° 18' N	95° 54' W	Batavia	43° 0' N	78° 11' W
Scottsbluff AP	41° 52' N	103° 36' W	Binghamton AP	42° 13' N	75° 59' W
Sidney AP	41° 13' N	103° 6' W	Buffalo AP	42° 56' N	78° 44' W
NEVADA			Cortland	42° 36' N	76° 11' W
Carson City	39° 10' N	119° 46' W	Dunkirk	42° 29' N	79° 16' W
Elko AP	40° 50' N	115° 47' W	Elmira AP	42° 10' N	76° 54' W
Ely AP (S)	39° 17' N	114° 51' W	Geneva (S)	42° 45' N	76° 54' W
Las Vegas AP (S)	36° 5' N	115° 10' W	Glens Falls	43° 20' N	73° 37' W
Lovelock AP	40° 4' N	118° 33' W	Gloversville	43° 2' N	74° 21' W
Reno AP (S)	39° 30' N	119° 47' W	Hornell	42° 21' N	77° 42' W
Reno Co	39° 30' N	119° 47' W	Ithaca (S)	42° 27' N	76° 29' W
Tonopah AP	38° 4' N	117° 5' W	Jamestown	42° 7' N	79° 14' W
Winnemucca AP	40° 54' N	117° 48' W	Kingston	41° 56' N	74° 0' W
NEW HAMPSHIRE			Lockport	43° 9' N	79° 15' W
Berlin	44° 3' N	71° 1' W	Massena AP	44° 56' N	74° 51' W
Claremont	43° 2' N	72° 2' W	Newburgh,	41° 30' N	74° 6' W
Concord AP	43° 12' N	71° 30' W	Stewart AFB		
Keene	42° 55' N	72° 17' W	NYC-Central Park (S)	40° 47' N	73° 58' W
Laconia	43° 3' N	71° 3' W	NYC-Kennedy AP	40° 39' N	73° 47' W
Manchester,	42° 56' N	71° 26' W	NYC-La Guardia AP	40° 46' N	73° 54' W
Grenier AFB			Niagara Falls AP	43° 6' N	79° 57' W
Portsmouth,	43° 4' N	70° 49' W	Olean	42° 14' N	78° 22' W
Pease AFB			Oneonta	42° 31' N	75° 4' W
NEW JERSEY			Oswego Co	43° 28' N	76° 33' W
Atlantic City CO	39° 23' N	74° 26' W	Plattsburg AFB	44° 39' N	73° 28' W
Long Branch	40° 19' N	74° 1' W	Poughkeepsie	41° 38' N	73° 55' W
Newark AP	40° 42' N	74° 10' W	Rochester AP	43° 7' N	77° 40' W
New Brunswick	40° 29' N	74° 26' W	Rome, Griffiss AFB	43° 14' N	75° 25' W
Paterson	40° 54' N	74° 9' W	Schenectady (S)	42° 51' N	73° 57' W
Phillipsburg	40° 41' N	75° 11' W	Suffolk County AFB	40° 51' N	72° 38' W
Trenton Co	40° 13' N	74° 46' W	Syracuse AP	43° 7' N	76° 7' W
Vineland	39° 29' N	75° 0' W	Utica	43° 9' N	75° 23' W
NEW MEXICO			Watertown	43° 59' N	76° 1' W
Alamagordo°			**NORTH CAROLINA**		
Holloman AFB	32° 51' N	106° 6' W	Asheville AP	35° 26' N	82° 32' W
Albuquerque AP (S)	35° 3' N	106° 37' W	Charlotte AP	35° 13' N	80° 56' W
Artesia	32° 46' N	104° 23' W	Durham	35° 52' N	78° 47' W
Carlsbad AP	32° 20' N	104° 16' W	Elizabeth City AP	36° 16' N	76° 11' W
Clovis AP	34° 23' N	103° 19' W	Fayetteville, Pope AFB	35° 10' N	79° 1' W
Farmington AP	36° 44' N	108° 14' W	Goldsboro,	35° 20' N	77° 58' W
Gallup	35° 31' N	108° 47' W	Seymour-Johnson		
Grants	35° 10' N	107° 54' W	Greensboro AP (S)	36° 5' N	79° 57' W
Hobbs AP	32° 45' N	103° 13' W	Greenville	35° 37' N	77° 25' W
Las Cruces	32° 18' N	106° 55' W	Henderson	36° 22' N	78° 25' W
Los Alamos	35° 52' N	106° 19' W	Hickory	35° 45' N	81° 23' W
Raton AP	36° 45' N	104° 30' W	Jacksonville	34° 50' N	77° 37' W
Roswell, Walker AFB	33° 18' N	104° 32' W	Lumberton	34° 37' N	79° 4' W

	LONGITUDE	LATITUDE		LONGITUDE	LATITUDE
New Bern AP	35° 5′ N	77° 3′ W	Norman	35° 15′ N	97° 29′ W
Raleigh/Durham AP (S)	35° 52′ N	78° 47′ W	Oklahoma City AP (S)	35° 24′ N	97° 36′ W
Rocky Mount	35° 58′ N	77° 48′ W	Ponca City	36° 44′ N	97° 6′ W
Wilmington AP	34° 16′ N	77° 55′ W	Seminole	35° 14′ N	96° 40′ W
Winston-Salem AP	36° 8′ N	80° 13′ W	Stillwater (S)	36° 10′ N	97° 5′ W
NORTH DAKOTA			Tulsa AP	36° 12′ N	95° 54′ W
Bismarck AP (S)	46° 46′ N	100° 45′ W	Woodward	36° 36′ N	99° 31′ W
Devils Lake	48° 7′ N	98° 54′ W	**OREGON**		
Dickinson AP	46° 48′ N	102° 48′ W	Albany	44° 38′ N	123° 7′ W
Fargo AP	46° 54′ N	96° 48′ W	Astoria AP (S)	46° 9′ N	123° 53′ W
Grand Forks AP	47° 57′ N	97° 24′ W	Baker AP	44° 50′ N	117° 49′ W
Jamestown AP	46° 55′ N	98° 41′ W	Bend	44° 4′ N	121° 19′ W
Minot AP	48° 25′ N	101° 21′ W	Corvallis (S)	44° 30′ N	123° 17′ W
Williston	48° 9′ N	103° 35′ W	Eugene AP	44° 7′ N	123° 13′ W
OHIO			Grants Pass	42° 26′ N	123° 19′ W
Akron-Canton AP	40° 55′ N	81° 26′ W	Klamath Falls AP	42° 9′ N	121° 44′ W
Ashtabula	41° 51′ N	80° 48′ W	Medford AP (S)	42° 22′ N	122° 52′ W
Athens	39° 20′ N	82° 6′ W	Pendleton AP	45° 41′ N	118° 51′ W
Bowling Green	41° 23′ N	83° 38′ W	Portland AP	45° 36′ N	122° 36′ W
Cambridge	40° 4′ N	81° 35′W	Portland Co	45° 32′ N	122° 40′ W
Chillicothe	39° 21′ N	83° 0′ W	Roseburg AP	43° 14′ N	123° 22′ W
Cincinnati Co	39° 9′ N	84° 31′ W	Salem AP	44° 55′ N	123° 1′ W
Cleveland AP (S)	41° 24′ N	81° 51′ W	The Dalles	45° 36′ N	121° 12′ W
Columbus AP (S)	40° 0′ N	82° 53′ W	**PENNSYLVANIA**		
Dayton AP	39° 54′ N	84° 13′ W	Allentown AP	40° 39′ N	75° 26′ W
Defiance	41° 17′ N	84° 23′ W	Altoona Co	40° 18′ N	78° 19′ W
Findlay AP	41° 1′ N	83° 40′ W	Butler	40° 52′ N	79° 54′ W
Fremont	41° 20′ N	83° 7′ W	Chambersburg	39° 56′ N	77° 38′ W
Hamilton	39° 24′ N	84° 35′ W	Erie AP	42° 5′ N	80° 11′W
Lancaster	39° 44′ N	82° 38′ W	Harrisburg AP	40° 12′ N	76° 46′ W
Lima	40° 42′ N	84° 2′ W	Johnstown	40° 19′ N	78° 50′ W
Mansfield AP	40° 49′ N	82° 31′ W	Lancaster	40° 7′ N	76° 18′W
Marion	40° 36′ N	83° 10′ W	Meadville	41° 38′ N	80° 10′ W
Middletown	39° 31′ N	84° 25′ W	New Castle	41° 1′ N	80° 22′W
Newark	40° 1′ N	82° 28′ W	Philadelphia AP	39° 53′ N	75° 15′ W
Norwalk	41° 16′ N	82° 37′ W	Pittsburgh AP	40° 30′ N	80° 13′ W
Portsmouth	38° 45′ N	82° 55′ W	Pittsburgh Co	40° 27′ N	80° 0′ W
Sandusky Co	41° 27′ N	82° 43′ W	Reading Co	40° 20′ N	75° 38′ W
Springfield	39° 50′ N	83° 50′ W	Scranton/Wilkes-Barre	41° 20′ N	75° 44′ W
Steubenville	40° 23′ N	80° 38′ W	State College (S)	40° 48′ N	77° 52′ W
Toledo AP	41° 36′ N	83° 48′ W	Sunbury	40° 53′ N	76° 46′ W
Warren	41° 20′ N	80° 51′ W	Uniontown	39° 55′ N	79° 43′ W
Wooster	40° 47′ N	81° 55′ W	Warren	41° 51′ N	79° 8′ W
Youngstown AP	41° 16′ N	80° 40′ W	West Chester	39° 58′ N	75° 38′ W
Zanesville AP	39° 57′ N	81° 54′ W	Williamsport AP	41° 15′ N	76° 55′ W
OKLAHOMA			York	39° 55′ N	76° 45′ W
Ada	34° 47′ N	96° 41′ W	**RHODE ISLAND**		
Altus AFB	34° 39′ N	99° 16′ W	Newport (S)	41° 30′ N	71° 20′ W
Ardmore	34° 18′ N	97° 1′ W	Providence AP	41° 44′ N	71° 26′ W
Bartlesville	36° 45′ N	96° 0′ W	**SOUTH CAROLINA**		
Chickasha	35° 3′ N	97° 55′ W	Anderson	34° 30′ N	82° 43′ W
Enid, Vance AFB	36° 21′ N	97° 55′ W	Charleston AFB (S)	32° 54′ N	80° 2′ W
Lawton AP	34° 34′ N	98° 25′ W	Charleston Co	32° 54′ N	79° 58′ W
McAlester	34° 50′ N	95° 55′ W	Columbia AP	33° 57′ N	81° 7′ W
Muskogee AP	35° 40′ N	95° 22′ W	Florence AP	34° 11′ N	79° 43′ W

	LONGITUDE	LATITUDE
SOUTH CAROLINA (Continued)		
Georgetown	33° 23' N	79° 17' W
Greenville AP	34° 54' N	82° 13' W
Greenwood	34° 10' N	82° 7' W
Orangeburg	33° 30' N	80° 52' W
Rock Hill	34° 59' N	80° 58' W
Spartanburg AP	34° 58' N	82° 0' W
Sumter, Shaw AFB	33° 54' N	80° 22' W
SOUTH DAKOTA		
Aberdeen AP	45° 27' N	98° 26' W
Brookings	44° 18' N	96° 48' W
Huron AP	44° 23' N	98° 13' W
Mitchell	43° 41' N	98° 1' W
Pierre AP	44° 23' N	100° 17' W
Rapid City AP (S)	44° 3' N	103° 4' W
Sioux Falls AP	43° 34' N	96° 44' W
Watertown AP	44° 55' N	97° 9' W
Yankton	42° 55' N	97° 23' W
TENNESSEE		
Athens	35° 26' N	84° 35' W
Bristol-Tri City AP	36° 29' N	82° 24' W
Chattanooga AP	35° 2' N	85° 12'W
Clarksville	36° 33' N	87° 22' W
Columbia	35° 38' N	87° 2' W
Dyersburg	36° 1' N	89° 24'W
Greenville	36° 4' N	82° 50'W
Jackson AP	35° 36' N	88° 55' W
Knoxville AP	35° 49' N	83° 59' W
Memphis AP	35° 3' N	90° 0' W
Murfreesboro	34° 55' N	86° 28' W
Nashville AP (S)	36° 7' N	86° 41'W
Tullahoma	35° 23' N	86° 5' W
TEXAS		
Abilene AP	32° 25' N	99° 41' W
Alice AP	27° 44' N	98° 2' W
Amarillo AP	35° 14' N	100° 42' W
Austin AP	30° 18' N	97° 42' W
Bay City	29° 0' N	95° 58' W
Beaumont	29° 57' N	94° 1' W
Beeville	28° 22' N	97° 40' W
Big Spring AP (S)	32° 18' N	101° 27' W
Brownsville AP (S)	25° 54' N	97° 26' W
Brownwood	31° 48' N	98° 57' W
Bryan AP	30° 40' N	96° 33' W
Corpus Christi AP	27° 46' N	97° 30' W
Corsicana	32° 5' N	96° 28' W
Dallas AP	32° 51' N	96° 51' W
Del Rio, Laughlin AFB	29° 22' N	100° 47' W
Denton	33° 12' N	97° 6' W
Eagle Pass	28° 52' N	100° 32' W
El Paso AP (S)	31° 48' N	106° 24' W
Fort Worth AP (S)	32° 50' N	97° 3' W
Galveston AP	29° 18' N	94° 48' W
Greenville	33° 4' N	96° 3' W
Harlingen	26° 14' N	97° 39' W
Houston AP	29° 58' N	95° 21' W

	LONGITUDE	LATITUDE
Houston Co	29° 59' N	95° 22' W
Huntsville	30° 43' N	95° 33' W
Killeen, Robert Gray AAF	31° 5' N	97° 41'W
Lamesa	32° 42' N	101° 56' W
Laredo AFB	27° 32' N	99° 27' W
Longview	32° 28' N	94° 44' W
Lubbock AP	33° 39' N	101° 49' W
Lufkin AP	31° 25' N	94° 48' W
Mcallen	26° 12' N	98° 13' W
Midland AP (S)	31° 57' N	102° 11' W
Mineral Wells AP	32° 47' N	98° 4' W
Palestine Co	31° 47' N	95° 38' W
Pampa	35° 32' N	100° 59' W
Pecos	31° 25' N	103° 30' W
Plainview	34° 11' N	101° 42' W
Port Arthur AP	29° 57' N	94° 1' W
San Angelo° Goodfellow AFB	31° 26' N	100° 24' W
San Antonio AP (S)	29° 32' N	98° 28' W
Sherman, Perrin AFB	33° 43' N	96° 40' W
Snyder	32° 43' N	100° 55' W
Temple	31° 6' N	97° 21' W
Tyler AP	32° 21' N	95° 16' W
Vernon	34° 10' N	99° 18' W
Victoria AP	28° 51' N	96° 55' W
Waco AP	31° 37' N	97° 13' W
Wichita Falls AP	33° 58' N	98° 29' W
UTAH		
Cedar City AP	37° 42' N	113° 6' W
Logan	41° 45' N	111° 49' W
Moab	38° 36' N	109° 36' W
Ogden AP	41° 12' N	112° 1' W
Price	39° 37' N	110° 50' W
Provo	40° 13' N	111° 43' W
Richfield	38° 46' N	112° 5' W
St George Co	37° 2' N	113° 31' W
Salt Lake City AP (S)	40° 46' N	111° 58' W
Vernal AP	40° 27' N	109° 31' W
VERMONT		
Barre	44° 12' N	72° 31' W
Burlington AP (S)	44° 28' N	73° 9' W
Rutland	43° 36' N	72° 58' W
VIRGINIA		
Charlottesville	38° 2' N	78° 31' W
Danville AP	36° 34' N	79° 20' W
Fredericksburg	38° 18' N	77° 28' W
Harrisonburg	38° 27' N	78° 54' W
Lynchburg AP	37° 20' N	79° 12' W
Norfolk AP	36° 54' N	76° 12' W
Petersburg	37° 11' N	77° 31' W
Richmond AP	37° 30' N	77° 20' W
Roanoke AP	37° 19' N	79° 58' W
Staunton	38° 16' N	78° 54' W
Winchester	39° 12' N	78° 10' W

	LONGITUDE	LATITUDE		LONGITUDE	LATITUDE
WASHINGTON			**WISCONSIN**		
Aberdeen	46° 59' N	123° 49' W	Appleton	44° 15' N	88° 23' W
Bellingham AP	48° 48' N	122° 32' W	Ashland	46° 34' N	90° 58' W
Bremerton	47° 34' N	122° 40' W	Beloit	42° 30' N	89° 2' W
Ellensburg AP	47° 2' N	120° 31'W	Eau Claire AP	44° 52' N	91° 29' W
Everett, Paine AFB	47° 55' N	122° 17' W	Fond Du Lac	43° 48' N	88° 27' W
Kennewick	46° 13' N	119° 8' W	Green Bay AP	44° 29' N	88° 8' W
Longview	46° 10' N	122° 56' W	La Crosse AP	43° 52' N	91° 15' W
Moses Lake, Larson AFB	47° 12' N	119° 19' W	Madison AP (S)	43° 8' N	89° 20' W
Olympia AP	46° 58' N	122° 54' W	Manitowoc	44° 6' N	87° 41' W
Port Angeles	48° 7' N	123° 26' W	Marinette	45° 6' N	87° 38' W
Seattle-Boeing Field	47° 32' N	122° 18' W	Milwaukee AP	42° 57' N	87° 54' W
Seattle Co (S)	47° 39' N	122° 18' W	Racine	42° 43' N	87° 51' W
Seattle-Tacoma AP (S)	47° 27' N	122° 18' W	Sheboygan	43° 45' N	87° 43' W
Spokane AP (S)	47° 38' N	117° 31' W	Stevens Point	44° 30' N	89° 34' W
Tacoma, McChord AFB	47° 15' N	122° 30' W	Waukesha	43° 1' N	88° 14' W
Walla Walla AP	46° 6' N	118° 17' W	Wausau AP	44° 55' N	89° 37' W
Wenatchee	47° 25' N	120° 19' W			
Yakima AP	46° 34' N	120° 32' W	**WYOMING**		
WEST VIRGINIA			Casper AP	42° 55' N	106° 28' W
Beckley	37° 47' N	81° 7' W	Cheyenne	41° 9' N	104° 49' W
Bluefield AP	37° 18' N	81° 13' W	Cody AP	44° 33' N	109° 4' W
Charleston AP	38° 22' N	81° 36' W	Evanston	41° 16' N	110° 57' W
Clarksburg	39° 16' N	80° 21' W	Lander AP (S)	42° 49' N	108° 44' W
Elkins AP	38° 53' N	79° 51' W	Laramie AP (S)	41° 19' N	105° 41' W
Huntington Co	38° 25' N	82° 30' W	Newcastle	43° 51' N	104° 13' W
Martinsburg AP	39° 24' N	77° 59' W	Rawlins	41° 48' N	107° 12' W
Morgantown AP	39° 39' N	79° 55' W	Rock Springs AP	41° 36' N	109° 0' W
Parkersburg Co	39° 16' N	81° 34' W	Sheridan AP	44° 46' N	106° 58' W
Wheeling	40° 7' N	80° 42' W	Torrington	42° 5' N	104° 13' W

CANADA LOnGITUDE & LATTITUDES

	LONGITUDE	LATITUDE		LONGITUDE	LATITUDE
ALBERTA			Vancouver AP (S)	49° 11' N	123° 10' W
Calgary AP	51° 6' N	114° 1' W	Victoria Co	48° 25' N	123° 19' W
Edmonton AP	53° 34' N	113° 31' W	**MANITOBA**		
Grande Prairie AP	55° 11' N	118° 53' W	Brandon	49° 52' N	99° 59' W
Jasper	52° 53' N	118° 4' W	Churchill AP (S)	58° 45' N	94° 4' W
Lethbridge AP (S)	49° 38' N	112° 48' W	Dauphin AP	51° 6' N	100° 3' W
McMurray AP	56° 39' N	111° 13' W	Flin Flon	54° 46' N	101° 51' W
Medicine Hat AP	50° 1' N	110° 43' W	Portage La Prairie AP	49° 54' N	98° 16' W
Red Deer AP	52° 11' N	113° 54' W	The Pas AP (S)	53° 58' N	101° 6' W
BRITISH COLUMBIA			Winnipeg AP (S)	49° 54' N	97° 14' W
Dawson Creek	55° 44' N	120° 11' W	**NEW BRUNSWICK**		
Fort Nelson AP (S)	58° 50' N	122° 35' W	Campbellton Co	48° 0' N	66° 40' W
Kamloops Co	50° 43' N	120° 25' W	Chatham AP	47° 1' N	65° 27' W
Nanaimo (S)	49° 11' N	123° 58' W	Edmundston Co	47° 22' N	68° 20' W
New Westminster	49° 13' N	122° 54' W	Fredericton AP (S)	45° 52' N	66° 32' W
Penticton AP	49° 28' N	119° 36' W	Moncton AP (S)	46° 7' N	64° 41' W
Prince George AP (S)	53° 53' N	122° 41' W	Saint John AP	45° 19' N	65° 53' W
Prince Rupert Co	54° 17' N	130° 23' W	**NEWFOUNDLAND**		
Trail	49° 8' N	117° 44' W	Corner Brook	48° 58' N	57° 57' W

	LONGITUDE	LATITUDE		LONGITUDE	LATITUDE
Gander AP	48° 57' N	54° 34' W	Thunder Bay AP	48° 22' N	89° 19' W
Goose Bay AP (S)	53° 19' N	60° 25' W	Timmins AP	48° 34' N	81° 22' W
St John's AP (S)	47° 37' N	52° 45' W	Toronto AP (S)	43° 41' N	79° 38' W
Stephenville AP	48° 32' N	58° 33' W	Windsor AP	42° 16' N	82° 58' W
NORTHWEST TERRITORIES			**PRINCE EDWARD ISLAND**		
Fort Smith AP(S)	60° 1' N	111° 58' W	Charlottetown AP (S)	46° 17' N	63° 8' W
Frobisher AP (S)	63° 45' N	68° 33' W	Summerside AP	46° 26' N	63° 50' W
Inuvik (S)	68° 18' N	133° 29' W	**QUEBEC**		
Resolute AP (S)	74° 43' N	94° 59' W	Bagotville AP	48° 20' N	71° 0' W
Yellowknife AP	62° 28' N	114° 27' W	Chicoutimi	48° 25' N	71° 5' W
NOVA SCOTIA			Drummondville	45° 53' N	72° 29' W
Amherst	45° 49' N	64° 13' W	Granby	45° 23' N	72° 42' W
Halifax AP (S)	44° 39' N	63° 34' W	Hull	45° 26' N	75° 44' W
Kentville (S)	45° 3' N	64° 36' W	Megantic AP	45° 35' N	70° 52' W
New Glasgow	45° 37' N	62° 37' W	Montreal AP (S)	45° 28' N	73° 45' W
Sydney AP	46° 10' N	60° 3' W	Quebec AP	46° 48' N	71° 23' W
Truro Co	45° 22' N	63° 16' W	Rimouski	48° 27' N	68° 32' W
Yarmouth AP	43° 50' N	66° 5' W	St Jean	45° 18' N	73° 16' W
ONTARIO			St Jerome	45° 48' N	74° 1' W
Belleville	44° 9' N	77° 24' W	Sept. Iles AP (S)	50° 13' N	66° 16' W
Chatham	42° 24' N	82° 12' W	Shawinigan	46° 34' N	72° 43' W
Cornwall	45° 1' N	74° 45' W	Sherbrooke Co	45° 24' N	71° 54' W
Hamilton	43° 16' N	79° 54' W	Thetford Mines	46° 4' N	71° 19' W
Kapuskasing AP (S)	49° 25' N	82° 28' W	Trois Rivieres	46° 21' N	72° 35' W
Kenora AP	49° 48' N	94° 22' W	Val D'or AP	48° 3' N	77° 47' W
Kingston	44° 16' N	76° 30' W	Valleyfield	45° 16' N	74° 6' W
Kitchener	43° 26' N	80° 30' W	**SASKATCHEWAN**		
London AP	43° 2' N	81° 9' W	Estevan AP	49° 4' N	103° 0' W
North Bay AP	46° 22' N	79° 25' W	Moose Jaw AP	50° 20' N	105° 33' W
Oshawa	43° 54' N	78° 52' W	North Battleford AP	52° 46' N	108° 15' W
Ottawa AP (S)	45° 19' N	75° 40' W	Prince Albert AP	53° 13' N	105° 41' W
Owen Sound	44° 34' N	80° 55' W	Regina AP	50° 26' N	104° 40' W
Peterborough	44° 17' N	78° 19' W	Saskatoon AP (S)	52° 10' N	106° 41' W
St Catharines	43° 11' N	79° 14' W	Swift Current AP (S)	50° 17' N	107° 41' W
Sarnia	42° 58' N	82° 22' W	Yorkton AP	51° 16' N	102° 28' W
Sault Ste Marie AP	46° 32' N	84° 30' W	**YUKON TERRITORY**		
Sudbury AP	46° 37' N	80° 48' W	Whitehorse AP (S)	60° 43' N	135° 4' W

WORLD LONGITUDE & LATITUDES

	LONGITUDE	LATITUDE		LONGITUDE	LATITUDE
AFGHANISTAN			Brisbane	27° 28' S	153° 2' E
Kabul	34° 35' N	69° 12' E	Darwin	12° 28' S	130° 51' E
ALGERIA			Melbourne	37° 49' S	144° 58' E
Algiers	36° 46' N	30° 3' E	Perth	31° 57' S	115° 51' E
ARGENTINA			Sydney	33° 52' S	151° 12' E
Buenos Aires	34° 35' S	58° 29' W	**AUSTRIA**		
Cordoba	31° 22' S	64° 15' W	Vienna	48° 15' N	16° 22' E
Tucuman	26° 50' S	65° 10' W	**AZORES**		
AUSTRALIA			Lajes (Terceira)	38° 45' N	27° 5' W
Adelaide	34° 56' S	138° 35' E	**BAHAMAS**		
Alice Springs	23° 48' S	133° 53' E	Nassau	25° 5' N	77° 21' W

	LONGITUDE	LATITUDE
BANGLADESH		
Chittagong	22° 21' N	91° 50' E
BELGIUM		
Brussels	50° 48' N	4° 21' E
BERMUDA		
Kindley AFB	33° 22' N	64° 41' W
BOLIVIA		
La Paz	16° 30' S	68° 9' W
BRAZIL		
Belem	1° 27' S	48° 29' W
Belo Horizonte	19° 56' S	43° 57' W
Brasilia	15° 52' S	47° 55' W
Curitiba	25° 25' S	49° 17' W
Fortaleza	3° 46' S	38° 33' W
Porto Alegre	30° 2' S	51° 13' W
Recife	8° 4' S	34° 53' W
Rio De Janeiro	22° 55' S	43° 12' W
Salvador	13° 0' S	38° 30' W
Sao Paulo	23° 33' S	46° 38' W
BELIZE		
Belize	17° 31' N	88° 11' W
BULGARIA		
Sofia	42° 42' N	23° 20' E
BURMA		
Mandalay	21° 59' N	96° 6' E
Rangoon	16° 47' N	96° 9' E
CAMBODIA		
Phnom Penh	11° 33' N	104° 51' E
CHILE		
Punta Arenas	53° 10' S	70° 54' W
Santiago	33° 27' S	70° 42' W
Valparaiso	33° 1' S	71° 38' W
CHINA		
Chongquing	29° 33' N	106° 33' E
Shanghai	31° 12' N	121° 26' E
COLOMBIA		
Baranquilla	10° 59' N	74° 48' W
Bogota	4° 36' N	74° 5' W
Cali	3° 25' N	76° 30' W
Medellin	6° 13' N	75° 36' W
CONGO		
Brazzaville	4° 15' S	15° 15' E
CUBA		
Guantanamo Bay	19° 54' N	75° 9' W
Havana	23° 8' N	82° 21' W
CZECHOSLOVAKIA		
Prague	50° 5' N	14° 25' E
DENMARK		
Copenhagen	55° 41' N	12° 33' E
DOMINICAN REPUBLIC		
Santo Domingo	18° 29' N	69° 54' W
EQUADOR		
Guayaquil	2° 0' S	79° 53' W
Quito	0° 13' S	78° 32' W
EGYPT		
Cairo	29° 52' N	31° 20' E
EL SALVADOR		
San Salvador	13° 42' N	89° 13' W
ETHIOPIA		
Addis Ababa	90° 2' N	38° 45' E
Asmara	15° 17' N	38° 55' E
FINLAND		
Helsinki	60° 10' N	24° 57' E
FRANCE		
Lyon	45° 42' N	4° 47' E
Marseilles	43° 18' N	5° 23' E
Nantes	47° 15' N	1° 34' W
Nice	43° 42' N	7° 16' E
Paris	48° 49' N	2° 29' E
Strasbourg	48° 35' N	7° 46' E
FRENCH GUIANA		
Cayenne	4° 56' N	52° 27' W
GERMANY		
Berlin (West)	52° 27' N	13° 18' E
Hamburg	53° 33' N	9° 58' E
Hannover	52° 24' N	9° 40' E
Mannheim	49° 34' N	8° 28' E
Munich	48° 9' N	11° 34' E
GHANA		
Accra	5° 33' N	0° 12' W
GIBRALTAR		
Gibraltar	36° 9' N	5° 22' W
GREECE		
Athens	37° 58' N	23° 43' E
Thessaloniki	40° 37' N	22° 57' E
GREENLAND		
Narsarssuaq	61° 11' N	45° 25' W
GUATEMALA		
Guatemala City	14° 37' N	90° 31' W
GUYANA		
Georgetown	6° 50' N	58° 12' W
HAITI		
Port Au Prince	18° 33' N	72° 20' W
HONDURAS		
Tegucigalpa	14° 6' N	87° 13' W
HONG KONG		
Hong Kong	22° 18' N	114° 10' E
HUNGARY		
Budapest	47° 31' N	19° 2' E
ICELAND		
Reykjavik	64° 8' N	21° 56' E
INDIA		
Ahmenabad	23° 2' N	72° 35' E
Bangalore	12° 57' N	77° 37' E
Bombay	18° 54' N	72° 49' E
Calcutta	22° 32' N	88° 20' E
Madras	13° 4' N	80° 15' E
Nagpur	21° 9' N	79° 7' E
New Delhi	28° 35' N	77° 12' E

	LONGITUDE	LATITUDE		LONGITUDE	LATITUDE
INDONESIA			Monterrey	25° 40′ N	100° 18′ W
Djakarta	6° 11′ S	106° 50′ E	Vera Cruz	19° 12′ N	96° 8′ W
Kupang	10° 10′ S	123° 34′ E	**MOROCCO**		
Makassar	5° 8′ S	119° 28′ E	Casablanca	33° 35′ N	7° 39′ W
Medan	3° 35′ N	98° 41′ E	**NEPAL**		
Palembang	3° 0′ S	104° 46′ E	Katmandu	27° 42′ N	85° 12′ E
Surabaya	7° 13′ S	112° 43′ E	**NETHERLANDS**		
IRAN			Amsterdam	52° 23′ N	4° 55′ E
Abadan	30° 21′ N	48° 16′ E	**NEW ZEALAND**		
Meshed	36° 17′ N	59° 36′ E	Auckland	36° 51′ S	174° 46′ E
Tehran	35° 41′ N	51° 25′ E	Christchurch	43° 32′ S	172° 37′ E
IRAQ			Wellington	41° 17′ S	174° 46′ E
Baghdad	33° 20′ N	44° 24′ E	**NICARAGUA**		
Mosul	36° 19′ N	43° 9′ E	Managua	12° 10′ N	86° 15′ W
IRELAND			**NIGERIA**		
Dublin	53° 22′ N	6° 21′ W	Lagos	6° 27′ N	3° 24′ E
Shannon	52° 41′ N	8° 55′ W	**NORWAY**		
IRIAN BARAT			Bergen	60° 24′ N	5° 19′ E
Manokwari	0° 52′ S	134° 5′ E	Oslo	59° 56′ N	10° 44′ E
ISRAEL			**PAKISTAN**		
Jerusalem	31° 47′ N	35° 13′ E	Karachi	24° 48′ N	66° 59′ E
Tel Aviv	32° 6′ N	34° 47′ E	Lahore	31° 35′ N	74° 20′ E
ITALY			Peshwar	34° 1′ N	71° 35′ E
Milan	45° 27′ N	9° 17′ E	**PANAMA**		
Naples	40° 53′ N	14° 18′ E	Panama City	8° 58′ N	79° 33′ W
Rome	41° 48′ N	12° 36′ E	**PAPUA NEW GUINEA**		
IVORY COAST			Port Moresby	9° 29′ S	147° 9′ E
Abidjan	5° 19′ N	4° 1′ W	**PARAGUAY**		
JAPAN			Ascuncion	25° 17′ S	57° 30′ W
Fukuoka	33° 35′ N	130° 27′ E	**PERU**		
Sapporo	43° 4′ N	141° 21′ E	Lima	12° 5′ S	77° 3′ W
Tokyo	35° 41′ N	139° 46′ E	**PHILIPPINES**		
JORDAN			Manila	14° 35′ N	120° 59′ E
Amman	31° 57′ N	35° 57′ E	**POLAND**		
KENYA			Krakow	50° 4′ N	19° 57′ E
Nairobi	1° 16′ S	36° 48′ E	Warsaw	52° 13′ N	21° 2′ E
KOREA			**PORTUGAL**		
Pyongyang	39° 2′ N	125° 41′ E	Lisbon	38° 43′ N	9° 8′ W
Seoul	37° 34′ N	126° 58′ E	**PUERTO RICO**		
LEBANON			San Juan	18° 29′ N	66° 7′ W
Beirut	33° 54′ N	35° 28′ E	**RUMANIA**		
LIBERIA			Bucharest	44° 25′ N	26° 6′ E
Monrovia	6° 18′ N	10° 48′ W	**RUSSIA**		
LIBYA			Alma Ata	43° 14′ N	76° 53′ E
Benghazi	32° 6′ N	20° 4′	Archangel	64° 33′ N	40° 32′ E
Tananarive	18° 55′ S	47° 33′ E	Kaliningrad	54° 43′ N	20° 30′ E
MALAYSIA			Krasnoyarsk	56° 1′ N	92° 57′ E
Kuala Lumpur	3° 7′ N	101° 42′ E	Kiev	50° 27′ N	30° 30′ E
Penang	5° 25′ N	100° 19′ E	Kharkov	50° 0′ N	36° 14′ E
MARTINIQUE			Kuibyshev	53° 11′ N	50° 6′ E
Fort De France	14° 37′ N	61° 5′ W	Leningrad	59° 56′ N	30° 16′ E
MEXICO			Minsk	53° 54′ N	27° 33′ E
Guadalajara	20° 41′ N	103° 20′ W	Moscow	55° 46′ N	37° 40′ E
Merida	20° 58′ N	89° 38′ W	Odessa	46° 29′ N	30° 44′ E
Mexico City	19° 24′ N	99° 12′ W	Petropavlovsk	52° 53′ N	158° 42′ E

	LONGITUDE	LATITUDE		LONGITUDE	LATITUDE
Rostov on Don	47° 13' N	39° 43' E	**TAIWAN**		
Sverdlovsk	56° 49' N	60° 38' E	Tainan	22° 57' N	120° 12' E
Tashkent	41° 20' N	69° 18' E	Taipei	25° 2' N	121° 31' E
Tbilisi	41° 43' N	44° 48' E	**TANZANIA**		
Vladivostok	43° 7' N	131° 55' E	Dar es Salaam	6° 50' S	39° 18' E
Volgograd	48° 42' N	44° 31' E	**THAILAND**		
SAUDI ARABIA			Bangkok	13° 44' N	100° 30' E
Dhahran	26° 17' N	50° 9' E	**TRINIDAD**		
Jedda	21° 28' N	39° 10' E	Port of Spain	10° 40' N	61° 31' W
Riyadh	24° 39' N	46° 42' E	**TUNISIA**		
SENEGAL			Tunis	36° 47' N	10° 12' E
Dakar	14° 42' N	17° 29' W	**TURKEY**		
SINGAPORE			Adana	36° 59' N	35° 18' E
Singapore	1° 18' N	103° 50' E	Ankara	39° 57' N	32° 53' E
SOMALIA			Istanbul	40° 58' N	28° 50' E
Mogadiscio	2° 2' N	49° 19' E	Izmir	38° 26' N	27° 10' E
SOUTH AFRICA			**UNITED KINGDOM**		
Cape Town	33° 56' S	18° 29' E	Belfast	54° 36' N	5° 55' W
Johannesburg	26° 11' S	28° 3' E	Birmingham	52° 29' N	1° 56' W
Pretoria	25° 45' S	28° 14' E	Cardiff	51° 28' N	3° 10' W
SOUTH YEMEN			Edinburgh	55° 55' N	3° 11' W
Aden	12° 50' N	45° 2' E	Glasgow	55° 52' N	4° 17' W
SPAIN			London	51° 29' N	0° 0' W
Barcelona	41° 24' N	2° 9' E	**URUGUAY**		
Madrid	40° 25' N	3° 41' W	Montevideo	34° 51' S	56° 13' W
Valencia	39° 28' N	0° 23' W	**VENEZUELA**		
SRI LANKA			Caracas	10° 30' N	66° 56' W
Colombo	6° 54' N	79° 52' E	Maracaibo	10° 39' N	71° 36' W
SUDAN			**VIETNAM**		
Khartoum	15° 37' N	32° 33' E	Da Nang	16° 4' N	108° 13' E
SURINAM			Hanoi	21° 2' N	105° 52' E
Paramaribo	5° 49' N	55° 9' W	Ho Chi Minh City		
SWEDEN			(Saigon)	10° 47' N	106° 42' E
Stockholm	59° 21' N	18° 4' E	**YUGOSLAVIA**		
SWITZERLAND			Belgrade	44° 48' N	20° 28' E
Zurich	47° 23' N	8° 33' E	**ZAIRE**		
SYRIA			Kinshasa (Leopoldville)	4° 20' S	15° 18' E
Damascus	33° 30' N	36° 20' E	Kisangani (Stanleyville)	0° 26' S	15° 14' E

Manufacturer and Consulting Reference

ASE Americas
4 Suburban Park Drive
Billerica, MA 01821-3980
(978) 667-5900
www.asepv.com

AstroPower, Inc.
Solar Park Newark, DE 19716
(302) 366-0400
www.astropower.com

Atlantic Solar Products
PO Box 70060
Baltimore, MD 21237-6060
(410) 686-6221
www.atlanticsolar.com

Atlantis Energy
4610 Northgate Blvd, #150
Sacramento, CA 95834-1122
(916) 920-9500
www.atlantisenergy.com

BP Solar, Inc.
2300 N Warney Way
Fairfield, CA 94533
(707) 428-7800
www.bpsolarex.com

Grant Electric
Solar power integrator
16461 Sherman Way, Suite 175
Van Nuys, CA 91406
(818) 375-1977
GrantElec@aol.com

Kyocera Solar, Inc.
PO Box 14670
Scottsdale, AZ 85267
(602) 948-8003
www.kyocerasolar.com

PowerLight Corporation
2954 San Pablo Ave
Berkeley, CA 94710
(510) 540-0550
www.powerlight.com

Sharp Electronics Corporation
Solar Systems Division
5901 Bolsa Ave
Huntington Beach, CA 92647
(714) 903-4873

Shell Solar
4650 Adohr Lane
Camarillo, CA 93012
(805) 388-6519
www.siemenssolar.com

Solar Electric
Westlake Village, California
UMA/Heliocol
13620, 49th Street
Clearwater, FL 33762

Unite Solar Ovonic
Customer_service@uni-solar.com
(800) 843-3892

Vector Delta Design Group, Inc.
Electrical and solar power design consultants
2325 Bonita Dr.
Glendale, CA 91208
(818) 241-7479
www.vectordelta.com

Solar Power Systems Design and Installation Companies

"Updated listing of this roster can be accessed through www.pvpower.com/pvinteg.html. The author does not endorse the listed companies or assume responsibility for inadvertent errors. Photovoltaic (PV) design and installation companies who wish to be included in the list could register by e-mail under the web site."

21st Century Goods
Business type: PV charge sales
Product types: solar cell phone batteries, radios, flashlights
PO Box 2707
575 N. Bar-Y Rd
Jackson, WY 83001
Phone: (866) 999-8422
Fax: (928) 563-7174
E-mail: info@21st-century-goods.com
URL: http://www.21st-century-goods.com

Alternative Power Systems
Business type: systems design, integration, sales
Product types: systems design, integration, sales
Contact: James Hart
San Diego, CA
Phone: (877) 946-3786 (877-WindSun)
Fax: (760) 434-3407
E-mail: engineering@aapspower.com
URL: http://www.aapspower.com

ABS Alaskan, Inc.
Business type: systems design, integration
Product types: systems design, integration, PV and other small power systems
2130 Van Horn Rd
Fairbanks, AK 99701
Phone: Fairbanks, (907) 451-7145; Anchorage, (907) 562-4949
Toll Free: (800) 478-7145
U.S. Toll Free: (800) 235-0689
Fax: Fairbanks, (907) 451-1949
E-mail: abs@absak.com
URL: www.absak.com

Alternatif Enerji Sistemleri Sanayi Ticaret Ltd. Sti.
Business type: systems design, integration, product sales
Product types: systems design, integration, product sales
Nispetiye Cad. No: 18/A Blok D.6
1.Levent

Istanbul, Turkey
Phone: +90 (212) 283 74 45 pbx
Fax: +90 (212) 264 00 87
E-mail: info@alternatifenerji.com
URL: www.alternatifenerji.com

AES Alternative Energy Systems Inc.
Business type: PV, wind and micro-hydro
  systems design, integration
Product types: systems design,
  integration, charge control/load centers
Contact: J. Fernando Lamadrid B.
9 E 78th St
New York, NY 10021 USA
Phone: (212) 517-9326
Fax: (212) 517-5326
E-mail: aes@altenergysys.com
URL: http://www.altenergysys.com

Abraham Solar Equipment
Business type: PV Systems installation,
  distribution
Product types: system installation,
  distribution
124 Creekside Pl
Pagosa Springs, CO 81147
Phone: (800) 222-7242

Absolute Solar Company
Business type: PV component and systems
  sales
Product type: PV and BOS components
Houston, TX
E-mail: asc_solar@yahoo.com
URL: http://www.solar-panel.net

Advanced Energy Systems, Inc.
Business type: manufacture and distribute
  PV systems and lighting packages
Product types: PV power packages and
  lighting systems and energy-efficient
  lighting
9 Cardinal Dr
Longwood, FL 32779
Phone: (407) 333-3325

Fax: (407) 333-4341
E-mail: magicpwr@magicnet.net
URL: http://www.advancednrg.com

AeroVironment, Inc.
Business type: PV Systems Design
Product types: System Design
222 E Huntington Dr
Monrovia, CA 91016
Phone: (818) 357-9983
Fax: (818) 359-9628
E-mail: avgill@aol.com

Alpha Real, A.G.
Business type: PV systems design,
  installation
Product type: power electronics and
  systems engineering
Feldeggstrasse 89
CH-8008 Zurich, Switzerland
Phone: 01-383-02-08
Fax: 01-383-18-95

Altair Energy, LLC
Business type: PV systems design,
  installation, service
Product type: turnkey PV systems,
  services, warranty and maintenance
  contracts, financing
600 Corporate Cir
Suite M
Golden, CO 80401
Phone: (303) 277-0025 or (800) 836-8951
Fax: (303) 277-0029
E-mail: info@altairenergy.com
URL: http://altairenergy.com

ALTEN srl
Business type: PV systems design,
  engineering, installation, BOS and
  module manufacture
Product types: system design, engineering,
  installation, modules, BOS
Via della Tecnica 57/B4
40068 S. Lazzaro

Bologna, Italy
Phone: ++39 051-6258396, ++39 051-6258624
Fax: ++39 051-6258398
e-mail: alten@tin.it
URL: http://www.bo.cna.it/cermac/alt.htm

Alternative-Energie-Technik GmbH

Business type: PV systems design, engineering, installation, distribution
Product types: system design, engineering, installation, distribution
Industriestraße, 12
D-66280, Sulzbach-Neuweiler GERMANY
Phone: 06897-54337
Fax: 06897-54359
E-mail: info@aet.de
URL: http://www.aet.de

Alternative Energy Engineering

Business type: PV systems design, installation, distribution
Product types: system design, installation, distribution
P.O. Box 339-PV
Redway, CA 95560
Phone/order line: (800) 777-6609
Phone/techline: (707) 923-7216
URL: http://www.alt-energy.com

Alternative Energy Store

Business type: on-line component and system sales
Product types: solar and wind
4 Swan St
Lawrence, MA 01841
Fax/Voice: (877) 242-6718
Phone Orders: (877) 242-6718 or (207) 469-7026
URL: http://www.AltEnergyStore.com

Alternative Mobile Power Systems (A.M.P.S.)

Business Type: mobile systems manufacture and supply

Product types: suitcase solar systems, solar value kits
E-mail: solarguy@mobilepower.com
URL: http://mobilepower.com

Alternative Power, Inc.

Business type: PV systems design, installation, distribution
Product types: system design, installation, distribution
160 Fifth Ave
Suite 711
New York, NY 10010-7003
Phone: (212) 206-0022
Fax: (212) 206-0893
E-mail: dbuckner@altpower.com
URL: http://www.altpower.com

Alternative Solar Products

Business type: PV Systems Design, installation, distribution
Product types: system design, installation, distribution
Contact: Greg Weidhaas
27420 Jefferson Ave
Suite 104 B
Temecula, CA 92590-2668
Phone: (909) 308-2366
Fax: (909) 308-2388

American Photovoltaic Homes and Farms, Inc.

Business type: PV systems integration
Product type: design and construct PV-integrated homes
5951 Riverdale Ave
Riverdale, NY 10471
Phone: (718) 548-0428

APEX

4 rue de l'Industrie
34880 Lavérune
France
Phone: 04 67 07 02 02
Fax: 04 67 69 17 34

e-mail : Apex@hol.fr
URL: http://www.logassist.fr/apex

Applied Power Corporation
Business type: PV systems design
Product type: system design
1210 Homann Dr SE
Lacey, WA 98503
Phone: (360) 438-2110
Fax: (360) 438-2115
E-mail: info@appliedpower.com
URL: http://www.appliedpower.com

Arabian Solar Energy & Technology (ASET)
Business type: PV and DC systems
   design, manufacture, and sales
Product type: PV systems, and DC
   systems
11 Sherif St
Cairo, Egypt
Phone: +20 2 393 6463 or +20 2 395 3996
Fax : +20 2 392 9744
E-mail: aset@asetegypt.com
URL: http://www.asetegypt.com

AriStar Solar Electric
Business type: PV systems sales,
   integration
Product types: systems sales and
   integration
3101 W Melinda Ln
Phoenix, AZ 85027
Phone: (623) 879-8085 or (888) 878-6786
Fax: (623) 879-8096
E-mail: aristar@uswest.net
URL: http://www.azsolar.com

Ascension Technology, Inc.
Business type: PV systems design,
   integration, BOS manufacturer
Product types: systems design and BOS
PO Box 6314
Lincoln, MA 01773
Phone: (781) 890-8844

Fax: (781) 890-2050
URL: http://www.ascensiontech.com

Atlantic Solar Products, Inc.
Business type: PV systems design and
   integration
Product types: systems design and
   integration
PO Box 70060
Baltimore, MD 21237
Phone: (410) 686-2500
Fax: (410) 686-6221
E-mail: mail@atlanticsolar.com
URL: http://www.atlanticsolar.com

Atlantis Energy Systems
Business type: PV system designer,
   manufacturer
Product types: PV systems, modules
9275 Beatty Dr
Sacramento, CA 95820
Phone: (916) 438-2930
E-mail: jomo13@atlantisenergy.com

B.C. Solar
Business type: PV system design,
   installation, training
Product types: systems design,
   installation, training
PO Box 1102
Post Falls, ID 82854
Phone: (208) 667-9608

Backwoods Solar Electric Systems
Business type: PV system design,
   installation, distribution
Product types: systems design,
   installation, distribution
8530-PV Rapid Lightning Creek Rd
Sandpoint, ID 83864
Phone: (208) 263-4290

Big Frog Mountain Corp.
Business type: PV and wind energy
   systems design, sales, integration

Product type: systems design, installation, distribution
Contact: Thomas Tripp
100 Cherokee Blvd
Suite 2109
Chattanooga, TN 37405
Phone: (423) 265-0307
Fax: (423) 265-9030
E-mail: sales@bigfrogmountain.com
URL: http://www.bigfrogmountain.com

Burdick Technologies Unlimited (BTU)

Business Type: PV systems design, installation
Product types: systems design, installation; roofing systems
701 Harlan St, #64
Lakewood, CO 80214
Phone: (303) 274-4358

C-RAN Corporation

Business type: PV systems design, packaging
Product types: systems design (water purification, lighting, security)
666 4th St
Largo, FL 34640
Phone: (813) 585-3850
Fax: (813) 586-1777

CEM Design

Business type: PV systems design
Product types: systems design, architecture
520 Anderson Ave
Rockville, MD 20850
Phone: (301) 294-0682
Fax: (301) 762-3128

CI Solar Supplies Co.

Business type: PV systems
Product type: systems
PO Box 2805
Chino, CA 91710

Phone: (800) 276-5278 (800-2SOLAR8)
E-mail: jclothi@ibm.net
URL: http://www.cisolar.com

California Solar

Business type: PV systems design
Product types: systems design
627 Greenwich Dr
Thousand Oaks, CA 91360
Phone: (805) 379-3113
Fax: (805) 379-3027

CANROM Photovoltaics Inc.

Business type: systems integrator
Product type: systems design, installation
108 Aikman Ave
Hamilton, ON
Canada L8M 1P9
Phone: (905) 526-7634
Fax: (905) 526-9341
URL: http://www.canrom.com

Colorado Solar Electric

Business type: systems integrator
Product type: retail sales
6501 County Rd 313
New Castle, CO 81647
Phone: (970) 618-1839
URL: http://www.cosolar.com

Creative Energy Technologies

Business type: PV systems and products
Product type: systems and efficient appliances
10 Main St
Summit, NY 12175
Phone: (888) 305-0278
Fax: (518) 287-1459
E-mail: info@cetsolar.com
URL: http://www.cetsolar.com

Currin Corporation

Business type: PV systems design, installation
Product types: systems design, installation

PO Box 1191
Midland, MI 48641-1191
Phone: (517) 835-7387
Fax: (517) 835-7395

DCFX Solar Systems P/L
Business type: PV systems design,
   integration
Product types: systems design,
   integration, pyramid power system,
   transportable hybrid package systems
Mt Darragh Rd
PO Box 264
Pambula 2549
N.S.W.
Australia
Phone: +612.64956922
Fax: +612.64956922
E-mail: dcfx@acr.net.au

Dankoff Solar Products, Inc.
Business type: PV systems design,
   installation, distribution
Product types: systems design,
   installation, distribution
2810 Industrial Rd
Santa Fe, NM 87505
Phone: (505) 473-3800
Fax: (505) 473-3830
E-mail: pumps@danksolar.com

Delivered Solutions
Business type: PV product distributor
Product types: PV products
PO Box 891240
Temecula, CA 92589
Phone: (800) 429-7650 (24 hours every
   day)
Phone: (909) 694-3820
Fax: (909) 699-6215

Direct Gain, LLC
Business type: PV systems design,
   installation
Product types: system design, installation

23 Coxing Rd
Cottekill, NY 12419
Phone: (914) 687-2406
Fax: (914) 687-2408
E-mail: RLewand@Worldnet.att.net

Direct Power and Water Corporation
Business type: PV systems design,
   installation
Product types: systems design, installation
3455-A Princeton NE
Albuquerque, NM 87107
Phone: (505) 889-3585
Fax: (505) 889-3548
E mail: dirpowdd@directpower.com
URL:
   http//www.dirpowdd@directpower.com

Diversified Technologies
Business type: PV systems design,
   installation
Product types: systems design, installation
35 Wiggins Ave
Bedford, MA 01730-2345
Phone: (617) 466-9444

ECS Solar Energy Systems
Business type: PV systems packaging
Product types: system packaging modular
   power stations
6120 SW 13th St
Gainesville, FL 32608
Phone: (904) 377-8866
Phone: (904) 338-0056

EMI
Business type: PV systems distribution
Product types: system and products
   distribution
Phone: (888) 677-6527

EV Solar Products, Inc.
Business type: PV systems design,
   installation
Product types: systems design, installation

Contact: Ben Mancini
2655 N Hwy 89
Chino Valley, AZ 86323
Phone: (520) 636-2201
Fax: (520) 636-1664
E-mail: evsolar@primenet.com
URL: http://www.evsolar.com

Eclectic Electric
Business type: PV systems design,
  installation
Product types: systems design,
  installation, training
127 Avenida del Monte
Sandia Park, NM 87047
Phone: (505) 281-9538

EcoEnergies, Inc.
Business type: PV systems design,
  integration, distribution
Product types: PV and other renewables
171 Commercial St
Sunnyvale, CA 94086
Contact: Thomas Alexander
Phone: (408) 731-1228
Fax: (408) 746-3890
URL: http://www.ecoenergies.com

Ecotech (HK) Ltd.
Business type: PV systems and DHW
  design, integration, and distribution
Product types: PV and DHW
Room 608, 6/F.
Yue Fung Industrial Building
35-45 Chai Wan Kok St
Tsuen Wan, N.T., Hong Kong
Phone: (852) 2833 1252
Phone: (852) 2405 2252
Fax: (852) 2405 3252
E-mail: inquiry@ecotech.com.hk
URL: http://www.ecotech.com.hk

**Electronics Trade and Technology
  Development Corp. Ltd.**
Business type: PV distribution and export

Product types: PV distribution and export
3001 Redhill AveBldg
5-103
Costa Mesa, CA 92626
Contact: M.H. Rao, General Manager
Phone: (714) 557-2703
Fax: (714) 545-2723
E-mail: mhrao@pacbell.net

Ehlert Electric and Construction
Business type: PV systems design,
  installation
Product types: pumping systems design,
  installation
HCR 62, Box 70
Cotulla, TX 78014-9708
Phone: (210) 879-2205
Fax: (210) 965-3010

Electro Solar Products, Inc.
Business type: PV systems design,
  installation
Product types: system design,
  manufacture (traffic control, lights,
  pumping)
502 Ives Pl
Pensacola, FL 32514
Phone: (904) 479-2191
Fax: (904) 857-0070

Electron Connection
Business type: PV systems design,
  installation, distribution
Product types: system design, installation,
  distribution
PO Box 203
Hornbrook, CA 96044
Phone/Fax: (916) 475-3401
Phone: (800) 945-7587
E-mail: econnect@snowcrest.net
URL: http://www.snowcrest.net/econnect

Energy Outfitters
Business type: PV systems design,
  integration

Product types: systems design, integration
136 S Redwood Hwy
PO Box 1888
Cave Junction, OR 87523
Phone: (800) 467-6527 (800-GO-SOLAR)
Office phone: (541) 592-6903
Fax: (503) 592-6747
E-mail: nrgoutfit@cdsnet.net

Energy Products and Services, Inc.
Business type: PV systems design,
   integration
Product types: systems design,
   integration, training
321 Little Grove Ln
Fort Myers, FL 33917-3928
Phone: (941) 997-7669
Fax: (941) 997-8828

Enertron Consultants
Business type: PV systems design,
   integration
Product types: systems design, building
   integration
418 Benvenue Ave
Los Altos, CA 94024
Phone: (415) 949-5719
Fax: (415) 948-3442

Enn Cee Enterprises
Business type: PV systems design,
   thermal systems, integration
Product types: solar lanterns, indoor
   lighting, street lighting, garden lighting,
   water heating, dryers
Contact: K.S. Chaugule, Managing
   Director; Vipul K. Chaugule, Director
#542, First Stage, C M H Rd
Indiranagar, Bangalore
Karnataka, India
Phone: +91 (080) 525 9858 (Time
   Zone=GMT+5:30)
Fax: +91 (080) 525 9858

E-mail:
   enncee.chaugule@mantraonline.com;
   chaugule@mantraonline.com

Feather River Solar Electric
Business type: PV systems design,
   integration
Product types: systems design, integration
4291 Nelson St
Taylorsville, CA 95983
Phone: (916) 284-7849

Flack & Kurtz Consulting Engineers
Business type: PV consulting engineers
Product types: systems engineering
Contact: Daniel H. Nall, AIA, PE
475 Fifth Ave
New York, NY 10017
Phone: (212) 951-2691
Fax: (212) 689-7489
E-mail: nall@ny.fk.com

Fortum AES Sweden AB
Box 26
127 21 SkÑrholmen
Phone: 08-449 59 30
Fax 08-740 50 01
URL: http://www.fortumsolenergi.com

Fowler Solar Electric
See New England Solar Electric

Fran-Mar
Business type: PV systems design,
   integration
Product types: systems design, integration
9245 Babcock Rd
Camden, NY 13316
Phone: (315) 245-3916
Fax: (315) 245-3916

Gebrüder Laumans GmbH & Co. KG
Business type: tile company with
   installation license for bmc PV tiles in
   Germany and Benelux

Product types: roof and facade PV tile and slate installation
Stiegstrasse 88
D-41379 Brüggen
GERMANY
Phone: (0 21 57) 14 13 30
Fax: (0 21 57) 14 13 39

Generation Solar Renewable Energy Systems Inc.

Business Type: PV/wind systems design, integration, installation, distribution
Product Types: systems design, integration, installation, distribution
Contact: Richard Heslett
340 George St N
Suite 405
Peterborough ON K9H 7E8 Canada
Phone: (705) 741-1700
email: gensolar@nexicom.net
URL: http://www.generationsolar.com

GenSun, Incorporated

Business type: integrated PV system builder
Product types: unitized, self contained, portable, zero installation
10760 Kendall Rd
PO Box 2000
Lucerne Valley, CA 92356
Phone: (760) 248-2689; (800) 429-3777
Fax: (760) 248-2424
E-mail: solar@gensun.com
URL: http://www.gensun.com

Geosolar Energy Systems, Inc.

Business type: PV systems design, integration
Product types: systems design, integration
3401 N Federal Hwy
Suite 100
Boca Raton, FL 33431 USA
Phone: (407) 393-7127
Fax: (407) 393-7165

Glidden Construction

Business type: PV systems design, integration
Product types: systems design, integration
3727-4 Greggory Way
Santa Barbara, CA 93105
Phone: (805) 966-5555
Fax: (805) 563-1878

Global Resource Options, LLP

Business type: PV systems design, manufacture, sales and consulting
Product type: commercial- and residential-scale PV systems, consulting, design, installation
P.O. Box 51
Strafford, VT 05072
Phone: 802-765-4632
Fax: 802-765-9983
E-mail: global@sover.net
URL: http://www.GlobalResourceOptions.com

GO Solar Company

Business type: PV systems sales and integration
Product types: systems, components, integration
12439 Magnolia Blvd 132
North Hollywood, CA 91607
Phone: (818) 566-6870
Fax: (818) 566-6879
E-mail: solarexpert@solarexpert.com
URL: http://www.solarexpert.com

Great Northern Solar

Business type: PV systems design, integration, distribution
Product types: Systems design, integration, distributor
Rte 1, Box 71
Port Wing, WI 54865
Phone: (715) 774-3374

Great Plains Power
Business type: PV systems design, integration
Product types: systems design, integration
1221 Welch St
Golden, CO 80401
Phone: (303) 239-9963
FAX: (303) 233-0410
E-mail: solar@bewellnet.com
URL:
    http://server2.hypermart.net/solar/public
    _html

Green Dragon Energy
Business type: systems integrator
Product type: PV and wind systems
2 Llwynglas
Bont-Dolgadfan
Llanbrynmair
Powys SY19 7AR
Wales, UK
Phone: + 44 (0) 1650 521 589
Mobile: 0780 386 0003
E-mail: dragonrg@globalnet.co.uk

Heinz Solar
Business type: PV lighting systems
Product types: lighting systems design, integration
16575 Via Corto East
Desert Hot Springs, CA 92240
Phone: (619) 251-6886
Fax: (619) 251-6886

Henzhen Topway Solar Co., Ltd/Shenzhen BMEC
Business type: assembles and manufactures components and packages
Product types: lanterns, lamps, systems, BOS, etc.
RM8-202, Hualian Huayuan, Nanshan Dadao
Nanshan, Shenzhen, P.R. China
Post Code: 518052

Phone: +86 755 6402765; 6647045; 6650787
Fax: +86 755 6402722
E-mail: info@bangtai.com
URL: http://www.bangtai.com

High Resolution Solar
Business Type: PV system design,integration,distribution
Product Types: systems design,integration,distributor
Contact: Jim Mixan
7209 S 39th St
Omaha, NE 68147
Phone: (402) 738-1538
E-mail: jmixansolar@worldnet.att.net

Hitney Solar Products, Inc.
Business type: PV systems design, integration
Product types: systems design, integration
2655 N Hwy 89
Chino Valley, AZ 86323
Phone: (520) 636-1001
Fax: (520) 636-1664

Horizon Industries
Business type: PV systems and product distribution, service
Product types: systems and product distributor, service
2120 LW Mission Rd
Escondido, CA 92029
Phone: (888) 765-2766 (888-SOLAR NOW)
Fax: (619) 480-8322

Hutton Communications
Business type: PV systems design, integration
Product types: systems design, integration
5470 Oakbrook Pkwy, #G
Norcross, GA 30093
Phone: (770) 729-9413
Fax: (770) 729-9567

I.E.I., Intercon Enterprises, Inc.
Business type: North American
   distributor, Helios Technology Srl
Product type: PV modules
Contact: Gilbert Stepanian
12140 Hidden Brook Terr
N Potomac, MD 20878
Phone: (301) 926-6097
Fax: (301) 926-9367
E-mail: gilberts@erols.com

Independent Power and Light
Business type: PV systems design,
   integration, distribution
Product types: systems design,
   integration, distributor
RR 1, Box 3054
Hyde Park, VT 05655
Phone: (802) 888-7194

Innovative Design
Business type: architecture and design
   services
Product types: systems design and
   integration
850 West Morgan St
Raleigh, NC 27603
Phone: (919) 832-6303
Fax: (919) 832-3339
E-mail: innovativedesign@mindspring.com
URL: http://www.innovativedesign.net
Innovative Design, Nevada Office
8275 S Eastern
Suite 220
Las Vegas, NV 89123
Phone: (702) 990-8413
Fax: (702) 938-1017

Integrated Power Corporation
Business type: PV systems design,
   integration
Product types: systems design, integration
7618 Hayward Rd
Frederick, MD 21702
Phone: (301) 663-8279

Fax: (301) 631-5199
E-mail: sales@integrated-power.com

Integrated Solar, Ltd.
Business Type: PV system design,
   integration, distribution, installation,
   service
Product Type: design, integrator,
   distributor, catalog
1331 Conant St
Suite 107
Maumee, OH 43537
Phone: (419) 893-8565
Fax: (419) 893-0006
E-mail: ISL11@ix.netcom.com
URL: http://www.tpusa.com/isolar

Inter-Island Solar Supply
Business type: PV systems design,
   integration, distribution
Product types: systems design,
   integration, distribution
761 Ahua St
Honolulu, HI 96819
Phone: (808) 523-0711
Fax: (808) 536-5586
URL: http://www.solarsupply.com

**ITALCOEL s.r.l., Electronic & Energy
Control Systems**
Business type: system integrator and BOS
   manufacturer
Product types: PV systems, PV inverters,
   design
66, Loc.Crognaleto
I-65010 Villanova (PE) - Italy UE
Phone: ++39.85.4440.1
Fax: ++39.85.4440.240
E-mail: dayafter@iol.it

Jade Mountain
Business type: catalog sales
Product types: PV system components and
   loads
PO Box 4616

Boulder, CO 80306-4616
Phone: (800) 442-1972; (303) 449-6601
Fax: 303-449-8266
E-mail: jade-mtn@indra.com
URL: http://www.jademountain.com

Johnson Electric Ltd.
Business type: PV systems design,
   integration, distribution
Product types: systems design,
   integration, distributor
2210 Industrial Dr
PO Box 673
Montrose, CO 81402
Phone: (970) 249-0840
Fax: (970) 249-1248

Kyocera Solar, Inc.
Business type: manufacturer and
   distributor
Product types: PV modules and systems
7812 E Acoma
Scottsdale, Arizona 85260
Phone: (800) 223-9580; (480) 948-8003
Fax: (480) 483-2986
E-mail: info@kyocerasolar.com
URL: http://www.kyocerasolar.com

L and P Enterprise Solar Systems
Business type: PV systems design,
   integration
Product types: systems design, integration
PO Box 305
Lihue, HI 96766
Phone: (808) 246-9111
Fax: (808) 246-3450

Light Energy Systems
Business type: PV systems design,
   contracting, consulting
Product types: systems design, integration
965 D Detroit Ave
Concord, CA 94518
Phone: (510) 680-4343
E-mail: solar@lightenergysystems.com
URL: http://www.lightenergysystems.com

Lotus Energy Pvt. Ltd.
Business type: PV systems design,
   integration; BOS manufacture; training
Product types: systems design,
   integration; BOS; training
Contact: Jeevan Goff, Managing Director
PO Box 9219
Kathmandu, Nepal
phone: +977 (1) 418 203 (Time
   Zone=GMT+5:45)
fax: +977 (1) 412 924
E-mail: Jeevan@lotusnrg.com.np
URL: http://www.south-
   asia.com/Nepaliug/lotus

MHS Solar
Business type: Product type: PO Box
   31304
Alexandria, VA 22310-9304
Phone: (703) 282-6039
E-mail: sales@mhs-solar.com
URL: http://mhs-solar.com

Maple State Battery
Business type: PV systems and products
   distribution
Product types: systems and products
   distributor
Sutton, VT 05867
Phone: (802) 467-3662

Moonlight Solar
Business type: PV systems design,
   integration
Product types: design, contracting, repair
3451 Cameo Ln
Blacksburg, VA 24060
Phone/Fax: (540) 953-1046
E-mail:
   moonlightsolar@moonlightsolar.com
URL: http://www.moonlightsolar.com

Mytron Systems Ind.
Business type: PV systems
Product type: solar cookers, lantern and
   PV systems

161,Vidyut Nagar B
Ajmer Rd
Jaipur 302021
India
Phone/Fax: 91-141-351434
E-mail: yogeshc@jp1.dot.net.in

Nekolux: Solar, Wind & Water Systems

Business type: PV, wind and microhydro
  systems design and installation
Product types: systems design,
  integration, distributor
Contact: Vladimir Nekola
1433 W. Chicago Ave
Chicago, IL 60622
Phone: 312-738-3776
E-mail: vladimir@nekolux.com
URL: http://www.nekolux.com

New England Solar Electric (formerly Fowler Solar Electric)

Business type: PV systems design,
  integration
Product types: systems design,
  integration, book
401 Huntington Rd
PO Box 435
Worthington, MA 01098
Phone: (800) 914-4131
URL: http://www.newenglandsolar.com

Nextek Power Systems, Inc.

Business type: lighting integration
Product types: DC lighting for commercial
  applications using fluorescent or HID
  lighting
992 S Second St
Ronkonkoma, NY 11779
Phone: (631) 585-1005
Fax (631) 585-8643
E-mail: davem@nextekpower.com
URL: http://www.nextekpower.com
West Coast Office
921 Eleventh St

Suite 501
Sacramento, CA 95814
Phone: (916) 492-2445
Fax (916) 492-2176
E-mail: patrickm@nextekpower.com

Ning Tong High-Tech

Business type: BOS manufacturer
Product Types:solar garden light, solar
  traffic light, batteries, solar tracker,
  solar modules,portable solar systems,
  solar simulator and tester
Room 404
383 Panyu Rd
Shanghai, P.R.China 200052
Phone: 86 21 62803172
Fax: 86 21 62803172
E-mail:songchao38@21cn.com
URL: http://www.ningtong-tech.com

NOOR Web

Business type: PV systems design,
  integration, installation, distribution
Product types: systems design,
  installation, maintenance
Contact: BENNANI Chakib
12, Blvd Moulay Abdallah
40000, Marrakech, Morocco
Phone: +212.4.310427
Fax: +212.4.310499
E-mail: noorweb@cybernet.net.ma

North Coast Power

Business Type: PV systems dealer
Product Type: PV systems dealer
PO Box 151
Cazadero, CA 95421
Phone: (800) 799-1122
Fax: (877) 393-3955
E-mail: mmiller@utilityfree.com
URL: http://www.utilityfree.com

Northern Arizona Wind & Sun

Business type: PV systems integration,
  products distribution

Product types: systems and products
   integrator and distributor
PO Box 125
Tolleson, AZ 85353
Phone: (888) 881-6464; (623) 877-2317
Fax: (623) 872-9215
E-mail: Windsun@Windsun.com
URL: http://www.solar-electric.com,
   http://www.windsun.com
Flagstaff Office:2725 E Lakin Dr, #2
Flagstaff AZ 86004
Phone: (800) 383-0195; (928) 526-8017
Fax: (928) 527-0729

Northern Power Systems

Business type: power systems design,
   integration, installation
Product types: controllers, systems design,
   integration, installation
182 Mad River Park
Waitsfield, VT 05401
Phone: (802) 496-2955, x266
Fax: (802) 879-8600
E-mail: rmack@northernpower.com
URL: http://www.northernpower.com

Northwest Energy Storage

Business type: PV systems design,
   integration, distribution
Product types: systems design,
   integration, distributor
10418 Hwy 95 N
Sandpoint, ID
Phone: (800) 718-8816; (208) 263-6142

Occidental Power

Business type: PV systems design,
   integration, installation
Product types: systems design,
   integration, installation
3629 Taraval St
San Francisco, CA 94116
Phone: (415) 681-8861
Fax: (415) 681-9911
E-mail: solar@oxypower.com
URL: http://www.oxypower.com

Off Line Independent Energy Systems

Business type: PV systems design,
   integration
Product types: systems design, integration
PO Box 231
North Fork, CA 93643
Phone: (209) 877-7080
E-mail: ofln@aol.com

Oman Solar Systems Company, L.L.C.

Division of AJAY Group of Companies
Business Type: systems, design,
   integration, installation, consulting
Product Type: PV systems, wind
   generators, water pumps, solar hot
   water systems
Contact: N.R. Rao
PO Box 1922
RUWI 112
Oman
Phone: 00968 - 592807, 595756, 591692
Fax: 00968 - 591122, 7715490
E-mail: oss.marketing@ajaygroup.com

Phasor Energy Company

Business type: PV systems design,
   integration
Product types: systems design, integration
4202 E Evans Dr
Phoenix, AZ 85032-5469
Phone: (602) 788-7619
Fax: (602) 404-1765

Photocomm,Inc.

See Kyocera Solar

Photovoltaic Services Network, LLC (PSN)

Business type: PV systems design,
   integration, package grid-tied systems
Product types: systems design, integration
215 Union Blvd
Suite 620
Lakewood, CO 80228

Phone: (303) 985-0717; (800) 836-8951
  Fax: (303) 980-1030
E-mail: tschuyler@neosdenver.com

Planetary Systems
Business type: PV systems design,
  integration, distributor
Product types: systems design,
  integration, distributor
PO Box 9876
2400 Shooting Iron Ranch Rd
Jackson, WY 83001
Phone/Fax: (307) 734-8947

Positive Energy, Inc.
Business Type: PV systems design,
  integration
Product types: systems design, integration
3900 Paseo del Sol #201
Santa Fe, NM 87505
Phone: (505) 424-1112
Fax: (505) 424—1113
E-mail: info@positivenergy.com
URL: www.positivenergy.com

PowerPod Corp.
Business type: PV systems design,
  integration
Product types: modular PV systems for
  village electrification
PO Box 321
Placerville, CO 81430
Phone: (970) 728-3159
Fax: (970) 728-3159
E-mail: solar@rmi.com
URL: http://www.powerpod.com

Rainbow Power Company Ltd.
Business type: system design, integration,
  maintenance, repair
Product types: systems integration,
  systems design, maintenance and repair
1 Alternative Way
PO Box 240
Nimbin, NSW, Australia, 2480

Phone: (066) 89 1430
Fax: (066) 89 1109
International Phone: 61 66 89 1088
International Fax: 61 66 89 1109
E-mail: rpcltd@nor.com.au
URL: http://www.rpc.com.au

RGA, Inc.
Business type: PV lighting systems
Product types: lighting systems
454 Southlake Blvd
Richmond, VA 233236
Phone: (804) 794-1592
Fax: (804) 3779-1016

RMS Electric
Business type: PV systems design,
  integration
Product types: systems design, integration
2560 28th St
Boulder, CO 80301
Phone: (303) 444-5909
Fax: (303) 444-1615
E-mail: info@rmse.com
URL: http://www.rmse.com

Real Goods Trading Company
Business type: PV systems design,
  integration, distribution, catalog
Product types: systems design,
  integration, distributor, catalog
966 Mazzoni St
Ukiah, CA 95482
Phone: (800) 762-7325
E-mail: realgood@realgoods.com
URL: http://www.realgoods.com

Remote Power, Inc.
Business type: PV systems design,
  integration
Product types: systems design, integration
12301 N Grant St, #230
Denver, CO 80241-3130
Phone: (800) 284-6978
Fax: (303) 452-9519
E-mail: RPILen@aol.com

Renewable Energy Concepts, Inc.
Business Type: PV system design,
    installation, sales
Product Types: PV panels, wind turbines,
    inverters, batteries
1545 Higuera St
San Luis Obispo, CA 93401
Phone: (805) 545-9700; (800) 549-7053
Fax: (805) 547-0496
E-mail: info@reconcepts.com
URL: http://www.reconcepts.com

Renewable Energy Services, Inc., of Hawaii
Business type: PV systems design,
    integration
Product types: systems design, integration
PO Box 278
Paauilo, HI 96776
Phone: (808) 775-8052
Fax: (808) 7775-0852

Renewable Energy Systems
Business type: system design, integration
Product types: systems integration,
    systems design
Boulder, CO
E-mail: res@xwebco.com
URL: http://www.xwebco.com/res

Roger Preston + Partners
Business type: system design, integration,
    engineering
Product types: systems integration,
    systems design, energy engineering
1050 Crown Point Pkwy
Suite 1100
Atlanta, GA 30338
Phone: (770) 394-7175
Fax: (770) 394-0733
E-mail: rpreston@atl.mindspring.com

Resources & Protection Technology
Business type: PV / BIPV system design,
    integration, distribution
Product types: PV, solar thermal, heat
    pump
4A, Block 2, Dragon Centre
25 Wun Sha St
Tai Hang, Hong Kong
Phone: (852) 8207 0801
Fax: (852) 8207 0802
E-mail: info@rpt.com.hk
URL: http://www.rpt.com.hk

Roseville Solar Electric
Business type: PV systems design,
    integration, distribution, and
    installation
Product type: grid-tie, battery backup,
    residential, commercial
Contact: Kevin Hahner
PO Box 38590
Sacramento, CO 38590
Phone: (916) 772-6977; (916) 240-6977
E-mail: khahner@juno.com

SBT Designs
Business type: system sales and
    installation
Product types: systems sales and
    installation
25840 IH-10 West #1
Boerne, Texas 78006
Phone: (210) 698-7109
Fax: (210) 698-7147
E-mail: sbtdesigns@bigplanet.com
URL: http://www.sbtdesigns.com

S C Solar
Business type: PV and solar thermal
    systems sales, integration
Product types: systems design, sales, and
    distribution
7073 Henry Harris Rd
Lancaster, SC 29720
Phone/Fax: (803) 802-5522
E-mail: dwhigham@scsolar.com
URL: http://www.scsolar.com

SEPCO—Solar Electric Power Co.

Business type: manufacturer of PV
　lighting systems and OEM PV
　systems
Product types: PV lighting and power
　systems
Contact: Steven Robbins
7984 Jack James Dr
Stuart, FL 34997
Phone: (561) 220 6615
Fax: (561) 220 8616
E-mail: sepco@tcol.net

Shenzhen Topway Solar Co., Ltd.

Shenzhen Bangtai Machinery and
　Electronics Ind'l co., Ltd.
Business type: manufacturer and catalog
　distributor
Product types: solar lanterns, garden
　lights, radios, inverters, controllers, 12-
　V lighting
10th Floor, 10L West Ocean Building
　Nanyou Dadao
Shenzhen, P.R. CHINA Post Code:
　518054
Phone: 86-755-6070222; 6070440;
　6070402; 6402765; 6647045
Fax: +86-755-6402722; or +86-755-
　6070222
E-mail: cnsuntopway@sina.com
URL: http://www.solar3000.com;
　http://www.suntopway.com

Siam Solar & Electronics Co., Ltd.

Business type: Solarex distributor
Products: laminator of custom size PV
　modules, sine wave inverters, 12-V dc
　ballasts
Contact: Mr.VIWAT SRI-ON (Managing
　Director)
62/16-25 Krungthep-Nontaburi Rd
Nontaburi 11000 Thailand
Phone: 66-2-5260578
Fax: 66-2-5260579
E-mail: sattaya@loxinfo.co.th

Sierra Solar Systems

Business type: PV systems design,
　integration
Product types: systems design, integration
109 Argall Way
Nevada City, CA 95959
Phone: (800) 517-6527
Fax: (916) 265-6151
E-mail: solarjon@oro.net
URL: http://www.sierrasolar.com

Solar Age Namibia Pty. Ltd.

Business type: PV systems design,
　integration
Product types: systems design,
　integration, village lighting
PO Box 9987
Windhoek, Namibia
Phone: 264-61-215809
Fax: 264-61-215793
E-mail: solarage@iafrica.com.na
URL: http://www.iafrica.com.na/solar

Solar Century

Business type: PV systems design,
　integration
Product types: systems design and
　installation
91-94 Lower Marsh
London SE1 7AB, UK
Phone: +44 (0)207 803 0100
Fax: +44 (0)207 803 0101
URL: http://www.solarcentury.com

Solar Creations

Business type: PV systems design,
　integration
Product types: systems design, integration
2189 SR 511S
Perrysville, OH 44864
Phone: (419) 368-4252

Solar Depot

Business type: PV systems design,
　integration

Product types: systems design, integration
61 Paul Dr
San Rafael, CA 94903
Phone: (415) 499-1333
Fax: (415) 499-0316
URL: http://www.solardepot.com

Solar Design Associates

Business type: PV systems design,
   building integration, architecture
Product types: systems design, building
   integration, architecture
PO Box 242
Harvard, MA 01451
Phone: (978) 456-6855
Fax: (978) 456-3030
E-mail: sda@solardesign.com
URL: http://www.solardesign.com

Solar Dynamics, Inc.

Business type: manufacture portable PV
   system package
Product types: portable PV system
152 Simsbury Rd, Building 9
Avon, CT 06001
Phone: (877) 527-6461 (877-JASMINI);
   (860) 409-2500
Fax: (860) 409-9144
E-mail: info@solar-dynamics.com
URL: http://www.solar-dynamics.com

Solar Electric Engineering, Inc.

Business type: PV systems design,
   integration, distribution
Product types: systems design,
   integration, distributor
116 4th St
Santa Rosa, CA 95401
Phone: (800) 832-1986

Solar Electric Light Fund

Business type: PV systems design,
   integration
Product types: systems design, integration
1734 20th St, NW

Washington, DC 20009
Phone: (202) 234-7265
Fax: (202) 328-9512
URL: http://www.self.org

Solar Electric Light Company (SELCO)

Business type: PV systems design,
   integration
Product types: systems design, integration
35 Wisconsin Cir
Chevy Chase, MD 20815
Phone: (301) 657-1161
Fax: (301) 657-1165
URL: www.selco-intl.com
India: www.selco-india.com
Vietnam: www.selco-vietnam.com
Sri Lanka: www.selco-srilanka.com

Solar Electric Specialties Co.

Business type: PV systems design,
   integration
Product types: systems design, integration
PO Box 537
Willits, CA 95490
Phone: (800) 344-2003
Fax: (707) 459-5132
E-mail: seswillits@aol.com
URL: http://www.solarelectric.com

Solar Electric Inc.

Business type: PV systems design,
   integration, distribution
Product types: systems design,
   integration, distributor
5555 Santa Fe St., #J
San Diego, CA 92109
Phone: (800) 842-5678; (619) 581-0051
Fax: (619) 581-6440
E-mail: solar@cts.com
URL: http://www.solarelectricinc.com

Solar Electric Systems of Kansas City

Business type: PV lighting systems
Product types: lighting systems

13700 W 108th St
Lenexa, KS 66215
Phone: (913) 338-1939
Fax: (913) 469-5522
E-mail: solarelectric@compuserve.com
URL: http://www.solarbeacon.com

Solar Electrical Systems

Business type: PV systems design,
    integration, distribution
Product types: systems design,
    integration, distributor
2746 W Appalachian Ct
Westlake Village, CA 91362
Phone: (805) 373-9433, (310) 202-7882
Fax: (805) 497-7121, (310) 202-1399
E-mail: ses@pacificnet.net

Solar Energy Systems of Jacksonville

Business type: PV systems design,
    integration
Product types: systems design, integration
4533 Sunbeam Rd, #302
Jacksonville, FL 32257
Phone: (904) 731-2549
Fax: (904) 731-1847

Solar Energy Systems Ltd.

Business type: PV Systems Design,
    Integration
Product types: Systems design, integration
Unit 3, 81 Guthrie St
Osborne Park, Western Australia 6017
Phone: +61 (0)8.9204 1521
Fax: +61 (0)8.9204 1519
E-mail: amaslin@sesltd.com.au
URL: http://www.sesltd.com.au

Solar Engineering and Contracting

Business type: PV systems design,
    integration
Product types: systems design, integration
PO Box 690
Lawai, HI 96765
Phone: (808) 332-8890
Fax: (808) 332-8629

The Solar Exchange

Business type: PV systems design,
    integration
Product types: water pumping and home
    systems
PO Box 1338
Taylor, AZ 85939
Phone: (520) 536-2029; (520) 521-0929
E-mail: solarexchange@cybertrails.com
URL:
    http://skybusiness.com/thesolarexchange

Solar Grid

Business type: catalog sales
Product types: PV system components
2965 Staunton Rd
Huntington, WV 25702
Order line: (800) 697-4295
Tech line: (304) 697-1477
Fax: (304) 697-2531
E-mail: sales@solarg.com
URL: http://www.solarg.com

Solar Online Australia

Business type: PV and wind products,
    design, supply, integration
Product types: components, systems,
    design, integration
48 Hilldale Dr
Cameron Park NSW 2285
Australia
Phone: +61 2 4958 6771
E-mail: info@solaronline.com.au
URL: www.solaronline.com.au

Solar Outdoor Lighting, Inc. (SOL)

Business type: PV street lighting systems
Product types: street lighting systems
3131 SE Waaler St
Stuart, FL 34997
Phone: (407) 286-9461
Fax: (407) 286-9616
E-mail: lightsolar@aol.com
URL: http://www.solarlighting.com

Solar Quest, Becker Electric

Business type: PV systems design, integration, distribution
Product types: systems design, integration, distributor
28706 New School Rd
Nevada City, CA 95959
Phone: (800) 959-6354; (916) 292-1725
Fax: (916) 292-1321

Solar Sales Pty. Ltd.

Business type: PV systems design, integration
Product types: systems design, integration
97 Kew St
PO Box 190
Welshpool 6986
Western Australia
Phone: +618.03622111
Fax: +618.94721965
E-mail: solar@ois.com.au
URL: http://www.solarsales.oz.nf

Solar-Tec Systems

Business type: PV systems sales, integration
Product types: systems sales, integration
33971-A Silver Lantern
Dana Point, CA 92629
Phone: (949) 248-9728
Fax: (949) 248-9729
URL: http://solar-tec.com

SolarSense.com

Business type: PV systems integration
Product types: small portable solar power systems and battery chargers
Contact: Lindsay Hardie
7725 Lougheed Hwy
Burnaby, BC, Canada V5A 4V8
Phone: (800) 648-8110; (604) 656-2132
Fax: (604) 420-1591
E-mail: info@solarsense.com
URL: http://www.solarsense.com

Solartronic

Business type: PV systems design, integration, sales
Product types: systems design, integration; product distributor
Morelos Sur No. 90
62070 Col. Chipitlán
Cuernavaca, Mor., Mexico
Phone: 52 (73)18-9714
Fax: 52 (73)18-8609
E-mail: info@solartronic.com
URL: http://www.solartronic.com

Solartrope Supply Corporation

Business type: wholesale supply house
Product types: systems components
Phone: (800) 515-1617

Solar Village Institute, Inc.

Business type: PV systems design, integration
Product types: systems design, integration
PO Box 14
Saxapawhaw, NC 27340
Phone: (910) 376-9530

Solar Utility Company, Inc.

Business type: PV systems design, integration
Product types: systems design, integration
Contact: Steve McKenery
6160 Bristol Pkwy
Culver City, CA 90230
Phone: (310) 410-3934
Fax: (310) 410-4185

SolarWorks!

Business type: PV systems design, integration
Product types: systems design, integration
Contact: Daniel S. Durgin
PO Box 6264
525 Lotus Blossom Ln
Ocean View, HI 96737
Phone: (808) 929-9820

Fax: (808) 929-9831
E-mail: ddurgin@aloha.net
URL: http://solarworks.com
Solar Works, Inc.
Business type: PV systems design,
    integration, distribution
Product types: systems design,
    integration, distributor
64 Main St
Montpelier, VT 05602
Phone: (802) 223-7804
E-mail: LSeddon@solar-works.com
URL: http://www.solar-works.com

Sollatek

Business type: systems design,
    installation, BOS manufacturer
Product types: systems design and
    installation
Unit 4/5, Trident Industrial Estate
Blackthorne Rd
Poyle Slough, SL3 0AX
United Kingdom
Phone: 44 1753 6883000
Fax: 44 1753 685306
E-mail: sollatek@msn.com

Solar World

Business type: PV systems design,
    integration, distribution for Solarex
Product types: systems design,
    integration, distribution
Germany

Soler Energie S.A.

(TOTAL ENERGIE GROUP)
Business type: PV systems design,
    integration
Product types: systems design, integration
BP 4100
98713 Papeete
French Polynesia
Phone: +689 43 02 00
Fax : +689 43 46 00
E-mail: soler@mail.pf
URL: http://www.total-energie.fr

Solo Power

Business type: PV systems design,
    integration
Product types: systems design, integration
1011-B Sawmill Rd, NW
Albuquerque, NM 87104
Phone: (505) 242-8340
Fax: (505) 243-5187

Soltek Solar Energy Ltd.

Business type: PV systems design,
    integration, distribution, catalog
Product type: systems design, integration,
    distributor, catalog
#2-745 Vanalman Ave
Victoria, BC V8Z 3B6 Canada
E-mail: soltek@pinc.com
URL: http://vvv.com/~soltek

SOLutions in Solar Electricity

Business type: PV systems design, sales,
    installation, consulting, training
Product types: system design, installation,
    consulting, training
Contact: Joel Davidson
PO Box 5089
Culver City, CA 90231
Phone: (310) 202-7882
Fax: (310) 202-1399
E-mail: joeldavidson@earthlink.net
URL: http://www.solarsolar.com

Soluz, Inc.

Business type: PV systems design,
    integration
Product types: international systems
    design and distribution
Contact: Steve Cunningham
55 Middlesex St, Suite 221
North Chelmsford, MA 01863-1561
Phone: (508) 251-5290
Fax: (508) 251-5291
E-mail: soluz@igc.apc.org

Southwest Photovoltaic Systems, Inc.
Business type: PV systems design,
    integration
Product types: systems design, integration
212 E Main St
Tomball, TX 77375
Phone: (713) 351-0031
Fax: (713) 351-8356
E-mail: SWPV@aol.com

Sovran Energy, Inc.
Business type: PV systems design,
    integration, distribution
Product types: systems design,
    integration, distributor
13187 Trewhitt Rd
Oyama, BC, Canada V4V 2B17
Phone: (250) 548-3642
Fax: (250) 548-3610
E-mail: sovran@sovran.ca
URL: http://www.sovran.ca/~sovran

Star Power International Limited
Business type: PV systems integration
Product types: systems design, integration
912 Worldwide Industrial Center,
43 Shan Mei St, Fotan, Hong Kong
Phone: (852) 26885555
Fax: (852) 26056466
E-mail: starpwr@hkstar.com

Stellar Sun
Business type: PV systems integration
Product types: systems design, integration
2121 Watt St
Little Rock, Arkansas 72227
Phone: (501) 225-0700
Fax: (501) 225-2920
E-mail: bill@stellarsun.com
URL: http://stellarsun.com

Strong Plant & Supplies FZE
Business Type: PV system design,
    integration, distribution, consulting
    services

Product Types: PV systems, modules,
    charge controllers, powercenters,
    inverters, lighting, and pumping
    products
Contact: Toufic E. Kadri
PO Box 61017
Dubai, United Arab Emirates
Phone: +971 4 835 531
Fax: +971 4 835 914
E-mail: strongtk@emirates.net.ae

**Sudimara Solar/PT Sudimara Energi
    Surya**
Business type: PV systems design,
    integration, distribution
Product types: systems design,
    integration, distributor
JI. Banyumas No. 4
Jakarta 10310 Indonesia
Phone: 3904071-3
Fax: 361639

Sun, Wind and Fire
Business type: PV systems design,
    integration
Product types: systems design, integration
7637 SW 33rd Ave
Portland, OR 97219-1860
Phone: (503) 245-2661
Fax: (503) 245-0414

SunAmp Power Company
Business type: PV systems design,
    integration, distribution
Product types: systems design,
    integration, distributor
7825 E Evans, #400
Scottsdale, AZ 85260
Phone: (800) 677-6527 (800-MR SOLAR)
E-mail: sunamp@sunamp.com
URL: http://www.sunamp.com

Sundance Solar Designs
Business type: PV systems design,
    integration

Product types: systems design, integration
PO Box 321
Placerville, CO 81430
Phone: (970) 728-3159
Fax: (970) 728-3159
E-mail: solar@rmi.com

Sunelco
Business type: PV systems design,
  integration
Product types: systems design, integration
PO Box 1499
100 Skeels St
Hamilton, MT 59840
Phone: (800) 338-6844; (406) 363-6924
Fax: (406) 363-6046
E-mail: sunelco@montana.com
URL: http://www.sunelco.com

Sunergy Systems
Business type: PV equipment and systems
Product types: equipment and systems
PO Box 70
Cremona, AB T0M 0R0 Canada
Phone: (403) 637-3973

Sunmotor International Ltd.
Business type: manufacturer and systems
  installation for PV water pumping
Product types: solar water pumping
  systems
104, 5037 - 50th St
Olds, AB T4H 1R8 Canada
Phone: (403) 556-8755
Fax: (403) 556-7799
URL: http://www.sunpump.com

Sunnyside Solar, Inc.
Business type: PV systems design,
  integration, distribution
Product types: systems design,
  integration, distributor, lighting
RD 4, Box 808
Green River Rd
Brattleboro, VT 05301
Phone: (802) 257-1482

Sunpower Co.
Business type: PV systems design,
  integration, distribution
Product types: systems design,
  integration, distributor, pumping
Contact: Leigh and Pat Westwell
RR3
Tweed, ON K0K 3J0 Canada
Phone: (613) 478-5555
E-mail: sunpower@blvl.igs.net
URL: http://www.mazinaw.on.ca/
  sunpower.html

SunWize Technologies, Inc.
Business type: PV systems design,
  integration, distribution, manufacture of
  portable PV systems
Product types: systems design,
  integration, distributor, portable PV
  systems
1155 Flatbush Rd
Kingston, NY 12401
Contact: Bruce Gould, VP, Sales
Phone: (800) 817-6527; (845) 336-0146
Fax: (845) 336-0457
E-mail: sunwize@besicorp.com
URL: http://www.sunwize.com

Superior Solar Systems, Inc.
Business type: PV systems design,
  integration
Product types: systems design, integration
1302 Bennett Dr
Longwood, FL 32750
Phone: (800) 478-7656 (800-4PVsolar)
Fax: (407) 331-0305

Talmage Solar Engineering, Inc.
Business type: PV systems design,
  integration
Product types: systems design, integration
18 Stone Rd
Kennebunkport, ME 04046
Phone: (888) 967-5945
Fax: (207) 967-5754

E-mail: tse@talmagesolar.com
URL: http://www.talmagesolar.com

Technical Supplies Center Ltd. (TSC)
Business type: BOS distributor and
  system integrator
Product type: PV, wind, batteries, charge
  controllers, inverters
South 60th St, East Awqaff Complex
PO Box 7186, Sana'a
Republic of Yemen
Phone : + 967 1 269 500
Fax : + 967 1 267 067
E-mail: ZABARAH@y.net.ye

Thomas Solarworks
Business type: PV systems design,
  integration
Product types: systems design, integration
PO Box 171
Wilmington, IL 60481
Phone: (815) 476-9208
Fax: (815) 476-2689

Tomato Solar
Business type: PV product manufacture,
  retail sales, exporter
Product types: modules, garden light,
  street light, RV kit, marine kit
GPO Box 6437, Hong Kong
Phone: (852) 2792-8093
Fax : (852) 2792-8040
E-mail: inquiry@tomatosolar.com
URL: http://www.tomatosolar.com

Total Energie
Business type: PV systems design,
  integration
Product types: Systems design, integration
7, chemin du Plateau
69570 Lyon-Dardilly, France
Phone: +33 (0)4 72 52 13 20
Fax : +33 (0)4 78 64 91 00
E-mail: infos@total-energie.fr
URL: http://www.total-energie.fr

Utility Power Group
Business type: PV manufacture, systems
  design, integration
Product types: manufacture, systems
  design, integration
9410-G DeSoto Ave
Chatsworth, CA 91311
Phone: (818) 700-1995
Fax: (818) 700-2518
E-mail: 71263.444@compuserve.com

Vector Delta Design Group, Inc.
Product types: turnkey electrical and solar
  power design and integration
Contact: Dr. Peter Gevorkian
2325 Bonita Dr
Glendale, CA 91208
Phone: (818) 241-7479
Fax: (818) 243-5223
E-mail vectordeltadesign@charter.net
URL: http://www.vectordelta.com

Vermont Solar Engineering
Business type: PV systems design,
  integration, distribution
Product types: systems design,
  integration, distributor
PO Box 697
Burlington, VT 05402
Phone: (800) 286-1252; (802) 863-1202
Fax: (802) 863-7908
E-mail: vtsolar1@together.net
URL: http://www.vtsolar.com

Whole Builders Cooperative
Business type: PV systems design,
  integration
Product types: systems design, integration
2928 Fifth Ave, S
Minneapolis, MN 55408-2412
Phone: (612) 824-6567
Fax: (612) 824-9387

Wind and Sun
Business type: PV systems design,
  integration, distribution

Product types: systems design,
    integration, distributor
The Howe, Watlington
Oxford OX9 5EX UK
Phone: (44) 1491-613859
Fax: (44) 1491-614164

WINSUND

Division of Hugh Jennings Ltd.
Business type: PV and wind systems
    design, installation, distribution
Product types: systems design,
    installation, distribution
Tatham St
Sunderland SR1 2AG
England, UK
Phone: +44 191 514 7050
Fax: +44 191 564 1096
E-mail: info@winsund.com
URL: http://www.winsund.com

Woodland Energy

Business type: portable PV systems
    design, manufacture, and sales
Product type: portable PV systems
PO Box 247
Ashburnham, MA 01430
Phone: (978) 827-3311
E-mail: info@woodland-energy.com
URL: http://www.woodland-energy.com

Zot's Watts

Business type: PV systems design,
    integration, distribution
Product types: systems design,
    integration, distributor
Contact: Zot Szurgot
1701 NE 75th St
Gainesville, FL 32641
Phone: (352) 373-1944
E-mail: roselle@gnv.fdt.net

Index

A
AC. *See* Alternating sinusoidal current
AFC. *See* Alkaline fuel cell
Agriculture
    geothermal effect upon, 137
    global warming's effect upon, 30
Air conditioning, 86, 96
Air quality, global warming's effect upon, 31
Alkaline fuel cell (AFC), 108–109
Alternating sinusoidal current (AC), 3
American Wind Energy Association, 111
Ammonia, as energy conversion medium, 100
Amorphous silicone construction, 5, 7–8
Anode, 105
Appliances, efficiency of, 84
Aquaculture, geothermal effect upon, 137
Area exposure time factor, 9
Atomic thermal agitation, 98–99
Availability factor, 116–117

B
Ballard Power Systems, 111
Balneology, 137
Battelle Pacific Northwest Laboratory, 118
Battery backup, 42
Bear Valley Electric Service (BVE), 155
Binary plants, 131
    structure of, 133
Biofuels, 138–139
Biomass decay, 141
Biomass energy, 138
Biomass liquefaction, 142
Biopower, 140
Bioproducts, 141–142
British thermal unit (Btu), 101

Btu. *See* British thermal unit
Buy-back metering, 15
    programs for, 28–29
BVE. *See* Bear Valley Electric Service

C
CaFCP. *See* California Fuel Cell Partnership
California Energy Commission (CEC), 35, 47,
    59, 142
    ratings by, 80
    rebate funds from, 37, 47, 155–168
        eligibility requirements for, 156–160
California Fuel Cell Partnership (CaFCP), 110
California Public Utilities Code, 157
Capacity factor, 115–118
Carbon dioxide, 87, 106, 110
    in atmosphere, 34
    emissions of, 136–137
CEC. *See* California Energy Commission
Cell conversion, efficiency of, 24
CFCs. *See* Chlorofluorocarbons
Charge regulators, 11
Chillers, hybrid, 97, 101, 102
Chlorofluorocarbons (CFCs), 86
Climate change. *See* Global warming
Clothes washers, 84
Coefficient of Performance (COP), 100–101
Commercial installations, of solar power, 14–15
    design considerations for, 18–20, 61–76
Compression cycle, 99
Concentrators, 8
    qualifications of, 27–28
Condensation, 97
Conduction, as form of heat, 96
Contractors, 95–96

1 line short

About the Author

Peter Gevorkian, Ph.D., PE, is President of Vector Delta Design Group, Inc., an electrical engineering and solar power design consulting firm that works with industrial, commercial, and residential clients. Dr. Gevorkian and company's expertise in renewable energy extends to solar power, fuel cells, and microturbine cogeneration. Dr. Gevorkian is an active member of the Canadian and California Board of Professional Engineers. He has taught computer science and automation control, and has authored several technical papers. He lives in Glendale, California.